Odyssey

Peace & Love Always,

to good memories,

Swifty-S.

Odyssey

A Voyage to Find Heaven

Kenneth M. Piazza, MD, MPH

ISBN-13: 9781542681070
ISBN-10: 1542681073
Library of Congress Control Number: 2017900982
CreateSpace Independent Publishing Platform
North Charleston, South Carolina

For the hearts I've broken…

Contents

Part I
Preparation for Departure

I

Introduction: Our Final Voyage

This is a book about what happens after we die. Curiosity about a trip into the afterlife is not an issue when we're young, but when we find ourselves old and standing at the departure gate, the topic heats up considerably. Our idle thoughts are overtaken by so many questions and so many worrisome details. We can safely assume, however, that those of us worried about what happens after we die must be decent folks—at least decent enough to dispel any fear that our final destinations involve sulfurous lakes of fire or demons in red suits poking us with trident spears. That being said, we can proceed and explore the afterlife in terms of *heaven* and, to a lesser degree, a mysterious realm of *final sanctification* we Catholics call *purgatory*. But, as we are about to see, our theme is much more than a guessing game in individual eschatology.

There have been countless writings about heaven and the afterlife, exploring and speculating about every angle of what lies beyond our final heartbeats. The questions are daunting: Is there consciousness after death? What is the afterlife like? Will I get a new body to replace this broken heap I see in the mirror? Will I have a joyous reunion with my lost loved ones? Will all my unfulfilled wishes on earth be satisfied there? We are going to try to answer these questions using scripture, the Catechism of the Catholic Church, and philosophical musings from Aristotle, Aquinas, and many others, along with a lot of educated speculation.

We must address two glaring facts that stand in the way of our musings about the afterlife, however, and both are sources of existential discomfort *right now*. The first fact is that we must die first to find out what really happens next. We Catholics believe only one creature, the Mother of Jesus, has crossed to the other side without dying, and no one else is so charmed. Even Jesus died before returning to heaven; His death was necessary for our redemption. Fear of death is a most natural thing, but it often drives us into making some very bad choices before we die. The second fact is that how we live our lives now—how we view ourselves in the world, how we view others, how we deal with joys and sorrows, and how we rank the presence of God in our lives—all have an enormous influence on not only how happy we are now but also how *heavenly* heaven might be.

What sets this book apart from the countless others about heaven is the notion that we can do something right now about these two sources of angst. It is well accepted that living well is a sure way to soothe our fears regarding the end of our days here. Yet, changing our lives to ease the pain, learning to love in healthy ways, and understanding the meaning of suffering are daunting tasks. Even more daunting is the challenge to better know our allegedly unknowable God, to develop a real intimacy with the Lord so that we can understand and accept that the evil in the world is our doing and not God's. These daunting tasks have a name. If we are to control our fate, assuage our fear of death, and fully enjoy the voyage—both the passage *and* the destination—we need to make ourselves heavenly now, on earth. This is called *sanctification*, a growth in spirituality that cleanses our souls of the residual muck of earthly values and teaches us the pathways inherent in our heavenly destiny. Sanctification is a road map to heaven and a wonderful guide once we get there, and it is freely available to everyone.

I am suggesting, with some arrogance, that the infinite joy of heaven may be better for some of us than others. This statement is going to rattle a lot of conservative theologians; "seeing" God face to face is, after all, the ultimate fulfillment of our existence. At this wonderful moment, our entire beings are opened to all knowledge, and our souls are permeated with the infinite power of the Divine. Yet my statement has nothing to do with God or the unwavering ecstasy of the Beatific Vision; it has everything to do with the "heavenliness" of our souls at the time we breathe our last. This heavenliness of our souls is beyond simple absolution and repentance of our sins but is rather a state of familiarity in our souls with the ways of heaven. This is, in a word, the de facto definition of sanctification.

We've learned that if we obey the commandments and repent of our sins, we will be transported after we die to a state of eternal bliss called heaven. As we'll see, there is much more to it than that: the privilege of "seeing" God face-to-face requires perfection of the Self. Getting to heaven after we die is easy; enjoying heaven to the fullest may require some serious effort before we die.

To be successful at our earthly quest to become heavenly, we must learn how to communicate with God beyond ordinary prayer—we must learn to speak and petition God at the right time, in the right way, and with the right attitude. Before we can communicate with God thusly, we must find out who we are in a true existential sense, how to express genuine love and tolerance to everyone—good and bad—and how to accept our suffering and tears as Jesus Christ did, without blaming God for bad times.

In its essence, then, this is a book about *holiness*—a prayer book of sorts—but it is not a holy book, and it has certainly not been written by a holy person. It will help, however, with our quest for spiritual growth—growth *before* our last and most important journey. It is this spiritual growth that will make life here as well as in heaven…well, heavenly. It is a book about the most important odyssey of our lives.

> *It is our earthly odyssey, our way to heaven that is heaven.*

—SAINT CATHERINE OF SIENA

—⁓—

Developing an intimacy with God through the process of sanctification—our preparation for a fully joyous afterlife in heaven—involves three areas of personal change. The first is a firm, philosophical grasp on *who we are*, in the fullest existential sense; we need a theory of our existence—who we are and why we are here, manifested in the concept of the *Self*. The second is a psychological exploration of healthy and unhealthy love—perfection of this Self's *ability to love others* on this earth, consistent with the way love—the language of the afterlife—is expressed and shared in heaven. The third area is the development of a *mature acceptance of suffering* as an unfortunate part of our earthly exile; inherent in this goal is a theological defense against our inane persistence to blame God for our pain. In addition to being perfect preparations for a joyous afterlife in heaven, these three areas of change are the foundations of what is crucial for a happy, well-lived life here on earth.

This book, then, is not just about what happens *after* we die; it is also—and perhaps equally important—about what happens *before* we die. Effective sanctification brings heaven to the forefront of our earthly existence. In 1 Corinthians 13:12, the apostle Paul tells us we "see" God and heaven as images in a smoky, dusty mirror; the dirt on this reflection of the Divine is our attraction to worldly values. We see ourselves through the sadness and superficiality of the world; if we clean the mirror with effective sanctification, we begin to see ourselves clearly in the same image as heaven. It is this sparkling new image of ourselves and how we live now that makes earth, as well as heaven, heavenly.

As we'll see, it is ironic that the benefits of our modern times have made us dismal failures in these three critical areas of happiness and well-being. Modern technology allows us to see the lives of others with the click of a mouse or TV remote and to compare ourselves with a very confused and misguided world; this distorted reflection skews how we define ourselves, what we decide is important in this life, and how we define happiness.

We have been horribly misled. We have ignored the existential concept of the Self as an individual with choices and replaced it with a Self whose meaning is only defined by material wealth, social power, and, sadly, the adulation of others. The glowing screens of modern technology and social media feed the cancers of pride and vanity to the point that we have become, as Walker Percy writes, "empty vacuoles" that live life constantly seeking worldly filler. We simply have no idea who we are or what we're doing on this earth.* Yet we press onward to define ourselves, like Fitzgerald's little rowboats untethered against a hidden current of doom, and we fail miserably.† We rely on the deceitful whore of worldliness to give us meaning, but we are ultimately left empty, unsatisfied, and shamed.

---

* Walker Percy, *Lost in the Cosmos.*
† F. Scott Fitzgerald, *The Great Gatsby.*

It is our futile effort to define ourselves with qualifiers outside of the union of the Self with God that causes our existential angst and much of our human misery. We must define ourselves correctly before we try to love others and understand suffering; if we persist at trying to define who we are using worldly values, then our lives, our goals, our love relationships, and our acceptance of suffering are driven by blind fantasy. We wander through life unseeing and unknowing, unable to dodge the snares of our foolish pride, and we live our lives unsatisfied, unfulfilled, and weighted down by a seething and hidden sadness.

We suffer…and, for some strange reason, we blame God for our suffering.

Sanctification through simple but concerted effort derails this train of sadness. Our newfound intimacy with God changes our lives to value what is important in the afterlife. It is such change that puts a taste of heaven onto our parched tongues. Embracing a heavenly existence now may very well make the dynamics of heaven much more suited to our individual needs for fulfillment—exactly what we want from heaven. It is intimacy with God's ways that guarantees us front-row seats to the great eternal show of the afterlife. Heaven is not a place to be stuck in the bleachers.

In the rest of Part I, we are going to discuss how to correctly define the Self, along with exploring the dynamics of healthy and unhealthy love. We are also going to examine suffering—both suffering that is self-made from our misguided ways and suffering that is not our fault. We will defend God from humankind's foolish indictment that our Creator somehow has a divine hand in our misery. It is then, and only then, that we shall be ready to look at heaven and what happens after we die.

But first, we must become amateur philosophers and learn the jargon. If we are to study the Self—our being and essence, the Self's ability to love, the meaning of suffering in this life, and later our speculations about the afterlife—we must be sure of our ability to *know* such things, as well as how far such knowledge can take us.

The netherworld of *epistemology* and its verbiage is our next stop on this odyssey.

II

Epistemology: How Much Can We Really Know?

There are two ways to be fooled. One is to believe what is not true; the second is to refuse to believe what is true.

—Søren Kierkegaard

I would rather live my life as if there is a God and die to find out there isn't, than live my life as if there isn't and die to find out there is.

—Albert Camus

Even if no heaven should exist, I want to be worthy of it at every moment.

—Franz Kafka

Asking questions about what we can know about life here and after death puts us at the edge of a very deep, murky lake. I suppose we could call it "Epistemology Pond." But, unlike Walden, it is a very ugly little lake, full of scary, mysterious theories; it is not for faint-hearted nonswimmers. Epistemology is the study of knowledge: what we can know, how close that knowledge comes to actual truth, and how well we can separate speculation and opinion from reality. As we foolishly jump in, we realize quickly there is no bottom and we are at the mercy of a lot of scary, slimy monsters—put there by ages of debate—swimming about our dangling feet. We have no choice; we must paddle about in this mucky swill if we are to talk about living a well-lived life here as a prelude to an afterlife in heaven.

To remain both safe and sane, we will limit our little swim in Epistemology Pond to a brief float on the surface. If we dare to submerge ourselves in this black, confusing lake, we will intellectually drown. Beneath the surface are literally hundreds of terms, theories, and arguments about what we can and cannot know, and to say that we are going to simplify the polemics is a gross understatement. The topic is insufferably complicated, and to avoid a blistering headache and mind-numbing stupor, we will merely skim the surface. Like a polite guest at a buffet, we shall only take what we need in order to see how well we can answer the questions "Who are we?" and "What happens to us after we die?"

At the very simplest level, there are three ways we can acquire knowledge about what may or may not exist. The first is when the knowledge of something is acquired through our senses or experience; the second is when it is implanted in our minds without sensation or experience; and the third is some combination of the first two. It is this third way—a mysterious combination—that, because of so many differing theories, muddies up our Epistemology Pond and unfortunately is the only way to know the unknown and see the unseen.

The most obvious source of knowledge is *empiricism*, the notion that the only *absolute truth* about reality is what we can perceive through our senses: if we can see it, hear it, smell it, taste it, or touch it, then it is real. The notion of pure empiricism started centuries ago and has acquired many names and twists, but the framework of modern empiricism was constructed by the seventeenth-century English philosopher John Locke. Locke insisted that the mind at birth is blank, like a clean slate—a "tabula rasa"—and that all our knowledge about our existence and the world around us only comes through sensory experience. This is the basis of *agnosticism*: God and heaven cannot exist until proven by the sensory proof of science.

Such pure empiricism was a reaction to the notion of *idealism*, a philosophy started four centuries before Christ by Plato, who said that reality only consisted of ideas in the human mind left there from recollections of past lives (in his *Phaedo*) or perceived from reflections (the shadows on the cave wall in his *Republic*). Aristotle, probably the greatest thinker of all time and Plato's student, unequivocally stated that reality existed whether we were consciously aware of it or not—and the possibility of an afterlife was born.

Saint Augustine brought in God, modified the Platonic notion of idealism, and expanded the ideas of Aristotle to declare that reality beyond experience existed in the mind of God and that God periodically illuminated the mind of man of such things. Centuries later, René Descartes went further and said that some knowledge existed *innately* in the human mind, planted at creation by the Creator's hand. This notion is the basis for Immanuel Kant's work two centuries later, in which he tried to reconcile *rationalism* (knowledge about reality from thought processes) and *empiricism* (knowledge about reality from experience). Kant introduced the idea of a priori knowledge—knowledge about reality that exists within the human mind *before* any sensory experience (as if from God). When empirical knowledge from the senses is combined with a priori knowledge in the blender of human reason, our conscious minds are able to *know* what is real.

This is the third way to know: the mysterious combination of knowledge from experience and knowledge from rational thought using human reason. We can conclude that we can indeed know about ourselves, God, and what happens to us after we die if we use this mysterious combination of gifts. Throughout this book, we will see that experiences in the world, faith in the revelations of scripture and the teachings of the Church, and the guidance of the divine illumination of a priori knowledge can be blended together using our human reason (along with its tool, logic) to produce an answer to our questions about exactly who we are and what happens after we die.

We've greatly simplified some very complex notions about knowledge, yet we are going to further simplify our scheme of knowledge and reality by introducing two familiar philosophical words in a new and unique way. Our new words are relevant to knowing about the dynamics of this life as well as the next. To the distress of many serious philosophers, we are going to take the bold step of referring to everything we can see and touch as *immanent*; what we can't see and touch, we will call *transcendent*.

Transcendence and Immanence–What We Cannot See and What We Can

> *The spirit is willing, but the flesh is weak.*

> —MATTHEW 26:41

To dabble in *ontology*—the study of our existence or being here on earth and there in heaven—we need to kidnap two well-known philosophical terms and use them in a very specific way to suit our needs. The word *transcendent* (an adjective; the noun is *transcendence*; the verb is *transcend*) describes anything that exists above, beyond, or on a different, higher plane than what is the expected norm. Transcendence is anything that exists above or beyond our normal plane of sensory existence. *Transcendent knowledge* gives truth from things beyond sensory or scientific proof.

God, heaven, and the soul are transcendent: we cannot see or touch them.

We must also keep in mind that the verb form—transcend—can be used to describe earthly events that go above or beyond the normal plane we experience. For example, God's creation of the universe from nothing transcends the creation of a symphony by one of the great masters. Someone who unselfishly gives his or her life for others in a disaster transcends normal behavior. Lovers feel they transcend others around them who are not in love. Or narcissistic intelligent people feel they transcend others of only average intellect. For our purposes, however, we will use transcendent in three ways: the *ontological* sense—who we are; the *eschatological* sense—what happens after we die; and the *theological* sense—when we refer to God, heaven, and the soul. Since we have defined transcendent as that which is beyond sensory experience, the term is part of the broader category of the *metaphysical*—literally "beyond the physical world."

To understand the hidden truths about our existence here and in heaven requires transcendent knowledge; we can get such knowledge from transcendent sources such as faith and the personal divine illumination of *grace*, as well as immanent sources like revelation from scripture, the experience of the wonders of the world and man, and the conscious workings of our reason and logic. Understandably, hardcore empiricists and scientists scoff at such notions as legitimate sources of truth.

For all other reality opposite to transcendent, we are going to use the term *immanent** reality (the noun is *immanence*). Our usage is much simpler and may differ from that of many philosophers and theologians. We are going to say that something is immanent if it exists here and now in our earthly reality, as perceived by our senses or proven by empirical, experimental science. Everything we can consciously experience is immanent. Beyond the obvious immanence of material objects and things in the natural world, including people, we'll see that immanence can also include emotions such as love, hate, anger, and sadness; and because we can experience them, immanence can include the workings of the human mind—our conscious thoughts and memories. The soul, however, is completely transcendent.

Yet, as we'll see, some experiences we have (immanent things) may expand beyond the norm to have transcendent qualities. For example, the joy we experience when eating a chocolate bar is immanent joy, but the ecstasy we might encounter during meditative prayer may be described as transcendent joy. The joy of the long-standing love of soul mates transcends the needy attachment of the "crush"—the progenitor of unhealthy, obsessive love. Immanence can also describe things perhaps not seen but provable by science, such as gravity, electricity, atomic particles, and the unseen cosmos. Invisible but real and earth-shaking scientific discoveries are immanent in nature but certainly transcend the obvious. The stars in the sky on a moonless night are certainly immanent to our senses, but the knowledge that certain of these points of light are part of the Andromeda galaxy trillions of miles away transcends our immanent stargazing. The list of potential immanent knowledge is virtually limitless, because there are things that may exist—we *can* know them through experience—but we haven't experienced them yet, such as life from other worlds,

---

* Not to be confused with the adjective *imminent*, which means "about to happen."

undiscovered species, new forms of matter, and even new *dimensions* studied in the mysterious world of theoretical physics.

This brings us to the hidden nature of man's being, the nature of heaven, and what happens after we die. Is part of us really immortal? Does our consciousness live on after death? Is heaven a physical place? Will we have bodies in the afterlife? Will we see and recognize our lost loved ones? If we are both immanent and transcendent, can heaven also be both immanent and transcendent? These questions are key points of age-old philosophical and theological debates that we will hopefully resolve through the rest of this book. The debates have gotten quite contentious in these modern times.

The Great War of Truth: Has Science Vanquished Faith?

We live in a world of knowing too much and being spoiled—we want to *know* for certain what we're doing here and what happens to us after we die. This is not as easy as the modern techno age would have us believe. The real answers to our questions are what we call *absolute* truths—they are the answers to our questions no matter what we believe. The underlying concern is whether we can know with certainty what those truths are. Since we are human, our first and most obvious answer is no—we only know for sure things that we can experience through our senses or prove through the scientific method. We are all empiricists at heart; it is our *nature* and part of our evolved survival mechanism.

Such empiricism from our animal ancestry makes us a skeptical species; if we can't see it, it does not exist. Our inborn evolutionary skepticism is why Jesus performed so many miracles—miracles are events that occur beyond the laws of physics and beyond what our senses expect. Miracles are immanent proofs of transcendence. Jesus used them to prove His divine nature. If we're going to ask questions about the *supernatural*—things beyond nature—we must accept Aristotle's notion that things can exist outside our conscious awareness; we must also accept many other immanent proofs of transcendence, especially the events and teachings of Jesus's ministry. If we reject Aristotle's notion, we must accept that death will really be the end...our entire existence will fade into black nothingness. In other words, to know that we will exist beyond death, we must believe.

The Importance of Believing

We would be in a nasty position indeed if empirical science were the only kind of science possible.

—EDMUND HUSSERL

The modern age has become a double-edged sword. It has given us the time and ease to enjoy creature comforts never imagined a few hundred years ago. We're having so much fun that we ignore the stark truth of our own mortality. Prior to the techno-industrial revolution starting in the seventeen hundreds, survival took precedence over having fun. Back then, we lived about forty years and then died. It was a given. The weaknesses of empirical science kept us clinging to our faith in God to assuage the sadness of daily life. Death was all around us, and we accepted it—children died, loved ones died, animals died, and people over forty died. Our faith unequivocally told us a much better life awaited us after death. Empirical science failed to shake this belief, frankly because science wasn't doing a whole lot of good to keep people alive or make life easier. There were no techno miracles back then, so we had to accept death as a fact of life. Our faith was the only way to cope with the reality of death.

As scientific knowledge grew, however, we started to listen to the promises of modern times. In the last two hundred years or so, empirical science progressed to where we assumed it could know anything, do anything, and give anything…like a benevolent deity. Science was suddenly a god we could see and touch and thus believe with greater certainty. The transcendent and mysterious God and His heaven took a backseat, and any bold confrontation with our limited time on earth and any hope of life afterward began to fade as man saw himself as too creative, too powerful, and too smart to worry about death. Modern man, with his technology, science, and materialism, made himself into a new deity. Could we accept the inevitability of death like the gloomy existentialists, or could it be possible we might really become immortal with the help of science's promises?

Perhaps modern man has gotten too smart for his own good.

In the early twentieth century, German philosophers Edmund Husserl and Martin Heidegger, aware of Kant's *Critique of Pure Reason*, slowed the juggernaut of empirical science with the notion of *phenomenology*: things (or *phenomena*) exist in the world that we can see, but they only become reality after being "digested" or analyzed by the individual human consciousness. It opened up the realm of psychology as a true science and softened the crust of pure empiricism as the only source of truth.

Sadly, though, empirical science pressed onward, culminating in the explosive growth of technology in the twentieth century; this nearly miraculous renaissance reinforced the argument that the only reliable source of truth and knowledge was the god of science—what we could see, prove, and make in the laboratory. Knowledge from faith, reason, and revelation simply did not fit into a modern scientific world. The feeling began to take root that there simply was no need for anything or anyone in the transcendent realm, including, and especially, an all-knowing and all-powerful God and His heaven.

With all the advancements of the neo-deity modernism and its empirical super science, Western societal thought has moved away from man's vulnerability to death, in spite of the existentialists' warnings, and questions about heaven have become less important. Historical images of heaven as a pie-in-the-sky reward for a good life have become archaic and even inane to the sophisticated modern mind. Media images, including movies and cartoons, depict the soul of the deceased as a winged, ethereal form leaving the body and wafting up into the clouds. Heaven, or the desired afterlife, is portrayed as a dull, dimensionless expanse with a fluffy cloud floor, and, for some reason, all the denizens of the movie and cartoon heavens wear white and play harps. Surely, the afterlife must be more interesting than this.

Cynics feed on this silly nonsense and use it to debunk any serious discussion of what happens after we die. What the cynics fail to realize is that portraying heaven is beyond the ability of earthly experience, and one guess is as good as another. The great Renaissance painters like Michelangelo and Raphael wanted to depict the unknowable—the transcendent Creator—but how does one paint what one has never seen, heard, smelled, tasted, or felt? The artists were left to paint the unknowable using notions and images that were knowable. Thus there was the birth of religious icons: cherubic angels were depicted as portly, naked babies with wings, and God Himself was perpetually portrayed as old and gray, with an enormous growth of facial hair.

The ever-present notion that God is an old man certainly springs from the paternalistic attitudes particular to our species dating from the era of Homo erectus. Logic, as well as many cranky feminists, asks us to consider the possibility that God might also be a young woman. Later, we'll see quite convincingly that God is neither man nor woman, neither old nor young, and neither bald nor hirsute.

In fact, God is not even a being, since the notion of "being" carries with it the necessity of "nonbeing"—God has not been created. In the purest existential sense, God simply is: "I am Who I am" (Exodus 3:14).

To the modern cynic, the medieval artistic imagery of God is a reality gap—what *does* God look like? If we don't know what He looks like, how can He exist? This creates a hole in any logical defense for God's existence and an awful conundrum for the philosopher. The sheer beauty of the art forces us to hold on to these images, thus strengthening the empiricists' arguments. It follows, then, that the modernist who only thinks in the scientific mode of empiricism sees such imagery as lacking substance and reality. If empirical science can't prove it, it is not real, says the modern empiricist. If I can't see Him, God is not there.

An archetype of this attitude comes from another cynic named Thomas the Apostle (also called Didymus): "Unless I see...I will not believe" (John 20:24). Christ's response is a sharp rebuke: "Be not unbelieving, but believing." Strangely, *belief and trust* in the Gospel message, along with repentance in the sense of turning away from worldliness, seem to carry more weight than perfect saintliness in the quest for heavenly admittance.

Faith Is Trust, and Trust Is Love—Why God Hides from Us: The Enigma of Deus Absconditus

In light of our seemingly miraculous advances in scientific knowledge, unbelief and skepticism permeate our modern life, not just in matters of theology, but in all areas of trust. The tremendous influx of knowledge about the world from technology may be a cause of this self-serving cynicism. As we rely more on empirical knowledge—believing only what we can perceive through our senses—our ability to trust one another diminishes. Trust and belief in one another are the framework around which love grows, and it's easy to see that stable, lasting love relationships are in trouble in these modern times. Maybe we just know *too much* about each other.

The necessity of trust and belief being a sine qua non for "pure" love may be a simple reason why God hides from us—the notion of Deus absconditus. If we were to "see" God as He really is and "see" what He has in store for us, we would most certainly love Him. Such love, however, would be *conditional*—sadly mimicking much of what we call love on this earth. If we love someone who is rich, handsome, beautiful, powerful, or famous, such love carries the risk of being *contingent* on those traits. The love may very well be pure, but the disturbing possibility silently lurking beneath the veneer of romance is ever present: what happens if the wealth, beauty, power, or celebrity is lost?

God, the Perfect Entity, does not accept conditional love.

As the empiricism of these modern times erodes our ability to believe and trust, our dependence on God and the hope of a transcendent afterlife have sadly diminished far below what our simple agrarian ancestors enjoyed. In the last century or so, the gods of science and technology have taken away our interest in matters of faith. Like Baal, they are leading us down a path of despair into a secular humanism rife with cynicism, agnostic skepticism, and hostility toward the wonders beyond our senses and science.

Yet simple logic and reason tell us that all knowledge cannot come from experience and scientific proof. Is the philosophical notion of a priori knowledge really God placing clues about His existence and divine plan into our human reason? Is this what we call grace? It would certainly seem so. Grace is the lifeblood of faith, and for many philosophers, of human reason also. The more we strengthen our faith and reason through effective prayer, the more receptive we are to the divine gift of grace. As we'll see, grace is the engine that elevates us from immanent reality (the world we can see) to transcendent reality (a world we cannot see), and the fuel of this divinely driven engine is *prayer*. We will use this divine gift—our magical key to a priori truths—along with careful analysis of the Gospels to paint our picture of who we really are and what our life in heaven will be like. Like our agrarian ancestors who prayed and beheld a vision of the afterlife with little doubt, we too will see the invisible and find that grace is indeed truly amazing.

If We Reject Grace

If we stubbornly embrace strict empiricism and become agnostics, our dreams of an afterlife are gone, along with any hope of a cogent theory of man himself. The worship of the here-and-now world and disdain for the mysterious completely detach us from the unknowable wonders that may exist outside our senses. The downside of such unbelief—that is, letting transcendent dreams fade from our daily conscious thought—is that it erases any hope of future consciousness after our last breath. Without such hope, life and its blunt ending into nothingness become, as Camus and others said, *absurd*. Faith in the supernatural and transcendent world unfortunately has been the target of many modern thinkers.

Science and modernism have pushed dozens of philosophers to challenge the mysticism surrounding the notions of God and an afterlife of heaven—sacred ideas held dear by the simple folk of yore, whose faith in the transcendent was, to them, fact. A large contingent of modern philosophers has said that man alone possesses truth and power; there is no place in humanistic thinking for a cosmic superman. Man is his own superman now, and humanistic thinking has begun to erode the mysticism of the transcendent. No doubt it has been the gross misinterpretation of Nietzsche's "God is dead" phrase that has fueled the nascent and arrogant humanistic thinking of the modern age. Religion and its beliefs have been "literalized"—that is, reduced to notions that could be understood in empirical terms. The vast mysticism of belief has been reduced to simplistic, childish imagery.

In the latter half of the nineteenth century, the complicated and bizarre philosophical writings of Friedrich Nietzsche—whom some flippantly call the father of secular humanism—were distorted and misinterpreted in order to support social philosophies contrary to Nietzsche's true beliefs. The most glaring example is anti-Semitism. Nietzsche was in no way anti-Semitic, but, in his later years, his sister purloined his writings and corrupted them to justify her own anti-Semitism. These distorted writings were later embraced by the Nazis to promote their ideals of racial superiority and the horrors that followed. His sister had free access to his writings because she was his caretaker in his last years when he was in the throes of serious mental illness.*

The Return of Spirituality in Modern Philosophy

Modern theologians have fought back, especially against the reductive literalizing of the transcendent to silly notions embraced by the weak. Among his many writings, the Christian existentialist Paul Tillich boldly states that the *questions* about who we are and what happens after we die are best posed by philosophers, but the *answers*

---

* There is little doubt that Nietzsche was floridly psychotic. In 1889, he had a complete breakdown in Turin, where he collapsed while protecting a horse from a vicious beating in the Piazza Carlo Alberto. The origin of his illness is speculative: he may have suffered from bipolar psychosis, a meningioma, or tertiary syphilis acquired in numerous European brothels.

are strictly the business of theology. Science, once the enemy of spiritual mysticism, has unearthed, through the discipline of archeology, immanent proofs of the reality of many biblical tales; such proof has given empirical strength to the answers from modern theologians.

To know the truth about the mysteries of God and His heaven, we must view our reliance on science and empiricism in a proper perspective. We need to have a firm idea about the truth of our existence, because what we believe happens to us after death—bliss, hellfire, or nothingness—strongly influences how we live and love today. No matter what our age, wealth, or status in life, the questions about the end of our life persist; we can look for answers, but only if we invest the time, wisdom, and courage to do just that. The older we get and the closer we get to departure time, the louder the questions about life's end become. The questions are simple: Is this all there is? What really happens after we die?

A Starting Point for Knowing the Unknowable
Real, ultimate truth comes from objectivity, and objectivity comes from a logical presentation of facts as we know them from our sources beyond science—faith, reason, logic, and revelation. In order to know about God and heaven, we'll need both immanent knowledge digested in our conscious minds through reason, and transcendent knowledge gleaned through faith and revelation. But knowing what heaven is and what we want heaven to be may present a problem.

Most of us have notions about life after death, but such ideas are often tainted by earthly impressions and wishes—we want heaven to be Earth 2.0. In later chapters, we'll discuss an early picture of what heaven might be like and how the immanent wish fulfillment of near-death experiences and private apparitions may be leading us astray. We may be seeing things that look transcendent but in reality are quite immanent...we may be seeing what we want or need to see. Our bias is firmly placed: our lives are filled with man-made religious icons and human constructs depicting the afterlife as exactly what we *want* it to be. The resulting images are often a bit too theatrical to be credible—think of the lofty visions of white lights, tunnels, out-of-body experiences, overwhelming peace and calm, and dead relatives, down to the simplistic images of Jesus in the clouds, harps, angel wings, and fluffy white stuff.

So we are going to start with the very simple premise from the Catechism of the Catholic Church (1024) that says, "Heaven is the ultimate end and fulfillment of the deepest human longings, the state of supreme, definitive happiness." As we'll see, man is a creature imbued with longings. Walker Percy writes, "Man is a peculiar species, born longing for someone or something; he lives his life constantly longing and dies longing." Heaven, by our simple definition, is going to relieve our longings in some magnificent but mysterious way. We will work from our simple definition to formulate ideas and images of who we are and what the afterlife might be like. With the help of many learned scholars and selected passages from scripture, we may see ourselves and heaven from a very different perspective—different from what we've been taught. New ideas bring new hope, and new hope may be just what we need to make our lives better here and now.

Non semper ea sunt quae videntur...*

---

* Things are not always what they appear to be...

III

The Self: The Traveler in Our Odyssey

*Man has not the faintest idea of who he is or what he
is doing.*

—WALKER PERCY, *LOST IN THE COSMOS*

*The self only becomes itself when it becomes itself
transparently before God.*

—SØREN KIERKEGAARD

What Is the Self?

What exactly do we mean by the "Self"? Since we will be using our
terms *transcendent* and *immanent* quite a bit in describing the com-
plexities of the Self, we should recall the special way that we use
them. We must remember: *immanent* refers to things we can see and
experience with our senses, or ordinary things in this earthly life;
transcendent indicates things we cannot see or experience with our
senses, things above or beyond ordinary earthly life, or anything
metaphysical, supernatural, or heavenly. We can say there are parts of
ourselves that we can know by the senses and parts we cannot know

by the senses. We can call these parts the immanent self and the transcendent self; together they make up our complete Self—who we are on this earth. It is reasonable to say the *immanent self* is made up of our body, including our brain (we can see it), and our conscious mind (we can experience it). Our conscious mind is not a thing as much as it is a result of a process that uses the brain and nervous system to produce streams of thought from sensory data and from memory. We assume that we evolved this complex system to ensure survival and well-being. Animals possess consciousness, but they do not possess a conscious mind, the source of our rational thought.

The notion of an unseen *transcendent self* has been argued for centuries. Does it exist? Where is it? Is it really separate from the body? Does it exist after death? Does it distinguish us from other living things? Since we are believers, the answers seem easy—yes, the transcendent self exists, and no, we don't know where it is, because it is transcendent (beyond the senses). It is indeed separate from the body because it is immortal, whereas the body is not. And yes, it is the sine qua non of being human: if we were able to transplant a human brain into our nearest relative—the chimpanzee—we would not have a human, only a very smart ape. If only it were that simple.

But *what* is the transcendent self? Is it some sort of unseen life force that exists and operates in the living body but not the dead? As a physician, I have stood at the bedside of dying patients who did not want to be resuscitated. In their final moments, they appeared to be sleeping, calm, and at peace, breathing slowly. Then, their breathing stopped. Their hearts ceased to beat a few moments later, but they still appeared to be sleeping, calm, and at peace. Except for the absence of respiration, they *looked* exactly the same as before. I did not see any spiritual wisp rise out of a patient and go somewhere else, but there must have been some unseen force that *animated*—gave life to—each person I watched over, a force that was there before death and gone after. The Latin word for it is *anima;* the English translation is *soul.* I didn't see anything, because the human soul is transcendent, literally "beyond the senses."

Before we deal with *where* the soul is, we have other, more basic questions to consider. This is where things get complicated. In this "philosophy of the mind" realm, we'll see that there are a great many theories, starting centuries ago, about the "mind-body" problem—that is, exactly what the relationship dynamics are of the mind, spirit, soul, consciousness, and body. What are they? Is the mind the same as the soul? From where do they arise? What does each do? How do they interact? And most importantly, what happens to each after death? Here is where we need to make a choice—there are dozens of theories about these questions put forth by many great scholars. We need to formulate one simple and plausible scenario about the soul that answers our questions and, more importantly, makes logical sense. To succeed at our quest, we will turn to some of the best thinkers in the field of ontology in order to "see" the unseen transcendent soul: Socrates, Plato, Aristotle, Saint Augustine, Saint Thomas Aquinas, Descartes, Immanuel Kant, and numerous more modern *dualists.* (Dualists believe that the soul and body are separate entities and that the soul leaves the body at death.) As we'll see, our ideas about the soul and body are logical and make sense, and they generally coincide with most religious beliefs of both Eastern and Western cultures.

Ideas about the invisible soul and its relationship with the visible body seem to have arisen with the ancient Greeks. Socrates was the first to say that the soul and body were separate entities and, furthermore, that the soul left the body at death. In *The Republic,* his student Plato agreed, but he insisted the soul was tripartite—a three-part entity that explained human behavior and social standing; such ideas did not fit well with later Christian doctrine. Plato's student, Aristotle, used the term *soul* in a different sense—his "soul" was the mind and was not separate from the body, and thus not immortal.

Socrates and Plato, then, were the first dualists, who agreed that the soul left the body at death, but then they added the strange idea that after death, the soul was reincarnated into another new individual body. This occurred over and over again until the soul was somehow purified and cleansed in successive bodily lives. Except for the reincarnation part, this idea of purification of the soul from the residuals of sin is eerily similar to the Catholic concept of the final purification of purgatory. Christians, including Catholics, reject any notion of reincarnation: "It is appointed for men to die once" (Catechism 1013). The notion of some kind of corrective migration of the soul, however, is a mainstay in many cultures and religions, particularly Hinduism. The obvious need for some souls to undergo a final purification to be worthy of heaven leaves us wondering what really happens after we die.

Is life here on earth really a purgatory? Are we in hell with a hidden exit? Are we reborn over and over until we get it right? Do we get as many chances as we need to become worthy of heaven? Our sources neither affirm nor deny such notions; scripture tells us only that there is justification after death (Matthew 12:32), and the Catechism describes a "final sanctification" (1030) in purgatory. Neither source tells us where or how such cleansing occurs.

The Soul, Mind, and Consciousness

If the soul is invisible, what about the human mind—the source of our conscious thoughts? Many early dualists agreed that the soul leaves the body at death but that the mind and soul are the same transcendent entity—both will travel to the afterlife after death. In reality, however, they must be separate and different entities. The soul, by its nature, is all good, created in the image and likeness of God, and since it is all good, the soul animates the mind to choose thoughts and actions that are good. But, in addition to the morally good input from the divinely created soul, the mind also has input from the brain and senses about the immanent world around us, and it can choose good or bad, influenced by our moral strength or our worldly appetites. Thus, the soul and the mind are separate and different entities, but only the soul is transcendent—we are aware of our thoughts from the mind, so the earthly mind is immanent and thus will end at death along with its source, the brain. In heaven, then—in order to be conscious of the joys therein—we will have a *new mind* that will only have the glorified, divinely united soul to animate it—there will be no bad thoughts from worldly, sensory input in heaven.

What about conscious thought and its natural results, conscious decisions and actions? Rather than considering conscious thought as a *thing*, we should see it as a result, an *output* from the mind. As we said, the earthly mind receives input from the soul—only good input—as well as input from the immanent world through the brain and senses: input that can be good, neutral, or bad. We can visualize these three—the soul, the mind, and conscious thought—by comparing their function to something familiar to all of us: a computer system. We can think of the mind as a computer processor capable of organizing, analyzing, and outputting, but only after something is put into it. For the "mind computer," the input is not from the Internet or a keyboard, but from the soul as well as sensory information from the outside world—both immediate input and input from memory. Conscious thought is simply what we see on the viewing screen.

Our obvious question is, which parts of this marvelous and complex "computer system" follow us into the afterlife? Our faith reassures us that the human soul is immortal and travels to the next life.

It seems illogical that a "good Internet"—the soul—would exist in heaven without a computer or viewing monitor. Thus, there is credence to our idea of a new mind in heaven. Again, there is one caveat to remember: after death, there will be no input from the immanent world; life on earth and all its temptations for evil, pain, suffering, and worries cease to exist. After we die, our "computer" minds will only receive good input from the soul as well as the overwhelming good of heaven and the Beatific Vision. This correlates with the stories of near-death survivors who tell of feeling remarkable serenity, peace, and calm as well as an overwhelming feeling of being loved immediately after death. The reassuring aspect of this is that conscious thought will indeed exist in the afterlife. In a strange, new sense, we will be fully "awake" during our final odyssey beginning at our death. *Death will not be as final as we fear.*

Hardcore scientists, though, are a cranky bunch and, as such, dismiss all this type of talk as a giant fairy tale. If something cannot be proven by scientific experiment, it cannot be true. They deny that faith and reason can have any valid contribution to proving that something is true. It's their job to say this. Many scientists, however, are believers, but their faith is something they keep to themselves—no scientist in his or her right mind would discuss heaven at a scientific meeting. To science, death is the end of the road for the human mind, human consciousness, and any unseen animating force referred to as a soul. Scientists deal with the immanent; the transcendent simply cannot be proven in the laboratory.

In a 1971 article in *The New Republic*, Charles Krauthammer tells of an incident that occurred at Harvard University in which neurobiologist and Nobel laureate Sir John Eccles was speaking about the brain and conscious thought.* Eccles tried to convey the awe he felt

---

* From Walker Percy, *Lost in the Cosmos.*

when he studied the complex wonders of the human mind and conscious thought. At the end of his lecture, he said that science could not explain the workings of the human mind, and such wonder could only come from something transcendent. The esteemed scientists hissed at Eccles like snarky schoolchildren. Scientists do not like God talk.

There is one more facet of the Self to consider that is uniquely human: *free will*. Free will arises in the mind and manifests itself in conscious thought and actions; it allows us to make choices about potential thoughts, attitudes, or actions. Animals do not have free will. They will always obey a very predictable set of laws: the laws of nature that keep the animal and plant kingdoms in perfect balance. When a predatory animal needs to eat, it does not have to make a moral choice about killing its prey. According to the laws of nature, the animal obeys and kills to survive. This is immanent law governing immanent behavior.

Even though man is at the top of the evolutionary phylogenetic tree, above all other species, he is still heavily influenced by the immanent laws of nature, especially the instincts to survive and reproduce. But man has the *choice* to override the immanent natural laws. This can be a bad thing, allowing behaviors destructive to his natural well-being (self-destructive personal behaviors, destruction to the environment, interference with nature, etc.), or a good thing, where moral law controls and hopefully defuses the animal instincts in all of us. Man is the only species that is also governed by moral laws—as believers, we know that the basis of all moral law is divine, set forth in religious traditions and scripture.

Humankind has not managed its freedom of choice well at all. History has taught us that man is capable of horrendous cruelty to his own species, and the origin of that capability may be funneled into the concept of original sin—that man has an evil side. We must keep an open mind to the possibility that the serpent-and-apple story in Genesis may be a universal allegory to man's nature: all humans truly have the freedom of choice in matters of thought and action but are too weak without the power of God to always choose good over evil. Many theologians, starting with the sometimes-controversial Teilhard de Chardin, suggest that man was created with a *privation* or lack of divine influence in his soul, and this allowed the free will of man to make bad choices. The farther from divine influence we allow ourselves to stray, the more frequent and terrible our bad choices become.

God, however, assures us that we have an unlimited supply of divine influence in the presence of His Son. In Saint John's Gospel story of the wedding at Cana, the groom is mortified when the wine runs out. Mary, the Mother of Jesus, whispers in her Son's ear, "They have no wine." Jesus has the servants fill large pots with water, and by His mere presence, the water is changed to wine.* There are many deeper meanings to this story, but the one pertinent here is that the soul of man can transform back into its divinely perfect state by the work of Christ, aided by the urgings of Mary.

God's influence on the will of man does not lessen it—the Self has the free choice to accept and rely on the help of grace or to ignore it. The bad choices are made in the mind and consciousness, arising from temptations from the urges of the natural law or from outside worldly sources of sin. At the moment of death, we are freed from the temptation to make bad choices; our fate has been locked in place. There is no further need for the will—there are no choices to be made in heaven, only a constant influx of joy and wish fulfillment. Our wills are fused with God's will as part of the very purpose of heaven and God's plan to get us there and be in a perfect union with Him.

------

* Water is a liturgical symbol for humanity, and wine symbolizes the Divine.

On earth, there is a special relationship between the soul and the conscious mind with its decision-making free will. While the soul animates the mind and thus the will, the choices made by the will also affect the soul each time a choice for a good or evil action is made. Good choices, such as acts of moral obedience, kindness, tolerance, forgiveness, generosity, selfless love, and especially prayer, affect and feed back onto the soul in a positive way—conditioning the soul, so to speak, making it more Godlike. This gradual process throughout life is what we have called sanctification—like the Cana miracle, water gradually becomes wine. Likewise, bad choices, including outright disregard for the moral law—sin—affect the soul in a bad way. Sin has been traditionally seen as a bad choice that leaves some sort of mark on the soul that can be erased through contrition, confession, and absolution. The nuns in Catholic grade school used to say our souls were made "pure white" again after the stains of sin have been "washed away" by confession and absolution. But there is something missing in this image, and that is the notion of *repentance*.

Repentance is a conversion of the heart that begins at baptism. It literally means "going back and changing our intentions and attitudes toward our bad choices." Repentance does not require abstinence from repeated sin, only the commitment and resolve to try. We are all doomed by original sin, and our weakened natures are susceptible to sinning over and over; only divine help in the form of grace can give us the strength to overcome our vulnerability to bad choices. Our part is to begin a lifelong commitment to focusing on the Transcendent will and to letting go of immanent worldliness. The essence of true repentance is a personal struggle—"a fight," as described by Saint Paul*—to overcome the world and its lies. True repentance enhances the sanctification process and makes the soul

---

* 2 Timothy 4:7.

"healthier," even in the presence of future slipups, which, because we're human, will plague us until we are freed by death.

Forming a Healthy Self

It would seem that when we ask questions about what happens after death, we should only be concerned with the transcendent Self—the soul—since it is only our souls that make the voyage into the afterlife. Yet our main premise tells us this is incorrect. We must consider the immanent Self—the mind, the body, and the senses along with their product, conscious awareness—because it is the immanent Self that is the tool of sanctification. The soul cannot interact with the immanent world without the physical body; it is the earthly body and earthly mind that interact with the good and evil choices presented by the world. The soul is sanctified when the body, by its free will, makes choices that are good. The soul cannot sanctify itself without the body interacting with the world and making good choices. It is the immanent Self that makes the transcendent Self heavenly.

Traveling into the realm of the afterlife, a soul whose earthly life has been partnered with an earthly body and mind wasted by obsession with earthly treasures and by pursuit of that which is unattainable will be less able to identify with the values of heaven. Because such a soul has never entered into the growing process of knowing God and heavenly values on earth, the afterlife may very well be a lukewarm experience. In this sense, then, there may very well be different levels of heavenly joy for every traveler into the afterlife. Granted, the light of God in heaven shines with the same degree of brilliance for all to take in, but the ability of each individual to comprehend and enjoy heaven may depend on the degree of sanctification attained on earth.

There is another equally important reason to develop a healthy Self in addition to making heaven heavenly, and that is because a healthy Self makes our earthly lives heavenly as well. Sanctification is the inner glow that engenders happiness and satisfaction in the healthy Self. This statement leads to the daring conclusion that true happiness on earth determines our comfort level with heaven. As we said, all kinds of red flags jump up at us with this idea, but we must look at our evolutionary beginnings.

Before the appearance of a supernatural soul in our total essence, we followed the natural path to seek pleasure and avoid pain. This is the deceitful promise of worldliness—that the immanent treasures of this life can give us happiness without suffering. The presence of our supernatural soul, however—made in the image and likeness of God—exposes this lie and repeatedly tries to tell us that we are in a place of suffering and that accepting this suffering with the stoic humility of God Himself, in the earthly Person of Jesus Christ, is a sine qua non for having a healthy, heaven-bound Self. As we'll see, accepting suffering is a tough sell to modern man. Walker Percy writes, "Art Immelmann is right. Man is not made for suffering, night sweats, and morning terrors."*

Developing a healthy Self, then, is clearly a lifelong work in progress. Our efforts should center about three general areas of change. First, we must *redefine ourselves* as creatures of God with the specific purpose of following the divine plan to get us into a joyous afterlife called heaven. Second, we must *accept suffering* as a natural part

---

* From Walker Percy, *Love in the Ruins*. Art Immelmann is a snake-oil salesman who promises unlimited satisfaction of all earthly desires and removal of all suffering with the use of a magical machine. He is a demagogue preaching to an unhappy society, knowing his immanent promises are lies and that those falling for his deceit are to meet certain destruction. His last name is no coincidence; he is Percy's metaphor for Satan himself.

of this exile in which we exist and, where appropriate, realize our individual choices may have contributed to our misery. Third, most important and by far the most difficult, we must *embrace a new being* governed by *humility*.

The first goal of our earthly Self should be to redefine itself in transcendent terms: we must align the meaning of our lives with heaven's values. Placing our lives *in sync* with heaven allows us to see ourselves as we are meant to be—who we are and what we're doing here—in relation to God's plan to free us from this earthly exile. The undefined Self—Percy calls it "the Self abstracted out of itself into nothingness"— wanders through life seeking meaning from the world. We must stop viewing happiness as a collection of earthly pleasures; we've said that earthly pleasures alone leave us longing and unfulfilled. The Self must literally "die to the world." To the Self mired in the immanent pleasures of this life, this entire process involves suffering.

In Matthew 16:24ff, Jesus commands us thusly: "If anyone wishes to come after Me [into heaven], let him deny himself [redefine the Self] and take up his cross and follow Me." The cross has a dual meaning here: suffering (from the turning away from earthly pleasures) and death (literally "dying to the world"). In the next verse, Jesus reiterates the futility of immanent pleasures in preparing the Self for heaven: "For whoever wishes to save his life [gaining heaven] shall lose it; but whoever loses his life [relinquishing the dependence on immanent wealth to define the Self] for My sake [to follow Him into heaven according to the divine plan] shall find it [heaven]." Numerous stories, including the parable of the rich man and his full barns (Luke 12:16–34) and the parable of laying up treasures in heaven (Matthew 6:19–24), reiterate this very important and critical necessity for a heavenly directed Self.

The second goal for developing a healthy Self is learning to accept suffering. We'll discuss suffering in a later chapter, but for now, we simply can say we must overcome our natural, presoul, phylogenetic instincts to seek pleasure and avoid pain and grow into a supernatural existence that is consistent with the perfection imbued in the soul by God. This natural, presoul tendency to seek pleasure and avoid suffering has stayed with us and has led to the modern notion that true happiness is possible only in the absence of suffering. Nothing could be further from the truth...at least in this earthly life. There is suffering here in the realm of suffering, and true happiness only comes from accepting suffering as part of our earthly exile.

There are two critical reasons for this: the first is that our happiness here and in heaven is dependent on a soul that can be sanctified only in the presence of suffering and sacrifice, mirrored exactly in the Incarnation of Christ, who suffered for the precise reason to make us heavenly. The second reason suffering is an essential part of happiness in this life and the next is that accepting suffering is a sine qua non for unconditional love. We cannot express true, unconditional love toward others and toward God Himself without sacrifice and the suffering that always accompanies it.

Spiritual growth is driven by the acceptance of suffering. The soul becomes heavenly and learns to express true love only if we are able to suffer as Christ did.

The third goal for developing a healthy Self is spiritual growth imbued with the very unnatural quality of *humility*. Man is not a humble species. People who grow spiritually without humility end up with the very unheavenly trait of self-righteousness. They appear quite holy to the world but soon begin to see their holiness as their own doing and not a gift from God. They are often cruelly judgmental toward others who are different, and acting as self-appointed surrogates for God, they condemn others whom they judge to be sinners. Viewing themselves as god surrogates places them in the same tainted light as Lucifer; it was Lucifer who saw himself as equal to

God and demanded that his followers be *non serviam* to God's will. Humility may very well be the most heavenly virtue, juxtaposed to the most unheavenly vice, *pride*.

At what point in history did mankind become so proud, thus being unable to know himself in true existential and transcendent terms? The most obvious culprit is the modern age, with its technology, science, and ease of everyday life. As technology advanced—especially in travel and communication—man became more aware of others in the world and began to compare his life with those of the rest of humanity. He abandoned his ideal, existential self-identity as a "contributor" with a specific purpose in God's plan to that of a "comparer," so that his identity became dependent not on pleasing God but on besting the rest of mankind.* Man let himself be defined in terms of other humans; the desire to be at the top of the social order trumped the divine will. Yet the beginnings of this mistake are really very old.

The sin of Cain apparently has never left the human race.

To overcome our desire to "win" the pointless game of life, we need to grow spiritually into a transcendent cloak, and humility is the fertile soil in which man can spiritually change into a heavenly species. Humility can be brought forth from the soul and amplified into the conscious mind as a way of life through effective prayer and meditation. Effective prayer does this by establishing an intimacy—a knowing—of the unknowable God. The more we know the magnificence of God, the more we are able to define ourselves as humble contributors to His plan and not as competitors with the rest of the world. This redefinition of the transcendent Self is the meaning of

---

* A contrast using the terms *comparer* and *contributor* is discussed at length in *The Five Pillars of the Spiritual Life* by Fr. Robert Spitzer, SJ.

the descriptive phrase "the poor in spirit" in the first of the Beatitudes heard in the Sermon on the Mount (Matthew 5:3).

The importance of humility, Fr. Robert Spitzer's notion of "contributorship," and of surrendering to God's plan can be found in the familiar story of the Annunciation of Mary, wherein the angel Gabriel tells her she is to conceive a child, not by a man but by the Holy Spirit; the Child will thus be the Son of God. At the time, Mary is only about fourteen years old and unmarried; such a birth would create serious social backlash for her in the small, close-knit village of Nazareth. No one (then or now) would likely believe the angel; indeed, her life could have been in danger—women were sometimes stoned for such scandal and blasphemy. Yet she willingly accepted the dangers associated with contributing to the divine plan and told Gabriel, "Behold the bondslave of the Lord, be it done unto me according to thy word." Sharing the news with her cousin Elizabeth, Mary prayed in the Magnificat, "For He [the Lord] has had regard for the lowly state of His handmaid" (Luke 1:38–55). In other words, God noticed Mary's obedience in the face of danger, her willingness to contribute to the divine will, her trust in Him, and her humility necessary for all of this. God forgets our sins but remembers our humility.

To know the Self requires surrender to the divine plan, and such surrender requires profound humility. Living a life of such humility gives the life of the Self here on earth direction, meaning, and a future of bliss in the afterlife.

A healthy Self opens us up to the power of God through grace freely bestowed on us if we make effective prayer and meditation part of our daily lives. If we rely only on human strengths, achieving a healthy Self can be a nearly impossible task, given the temptations of the modern world. Some of us spend untold sums of money, time, and effort to find out who we are and relieve the pain of failed love, failed personal success, and failed inner peace. Most never bother to seek any change at all and end up living life in an existential angst that imbues the consciousness with free-floating, undefined anxiety and, worse, depression. At this low point of our lives, earthly life is most unheavenly.

The Pitfalls of the Unhealthy Self

A common question asked at the onset of psychotherapy is, "If you could have any three wishes, what would they be?" The answers given nearly always involve money, love, and health. If we expand these broad categories, we want wealth to assure our survival, ease of living, and pleasure; fame and power to assure us of requited love from whomever we wish; and the ability to stay young forever—immortality. We fail to see that these wishes embody the fallacy of modern life: according to it, happiness can only come from things *outside* of the Self. We cannot seem to connect the value and meaning of the Self—who we are and what we're doing here on earth—with true happiness and well-being. In these modern times, happiness seems to be dependent on some sort of external reward. Something else—something besides the Self—is always controlling our sense of fulfillment and well-being.

It's an easy trap, and Satan knows exactly how to bait it.

If we look carefully at the earthly desires mentioned above, we find them to be eerily similar to what Satan offers Jesus in the wilderness after His baptism in the Jordan River by John the Baptist (Matthew 4:1ff). After forty days of fasting in the barren wilderness, Jesus is starving, exhausted, and certainly beaten down to a point so low as to question His desire to fulfill the Father's plan. The devil takes advantage of the situation and tempts Jesus with bread (modern-day money), the inability to die (modern-day desire to stay young forever), and power over the earth (modern-day status and unlimited love). Satan is trying to derail Jesus's earthly mission and plan from the Father to redeem mankind from Satan's prison. The lures of worldly desires mean nothing to Jesus—He has been to heaven and knows that the glory of the transcendent far overshadows the glint of worldly promises. Jesus recognizes Satan's trap of deception and tells Satan in no uncertain terms to "go to hell."

Immanence alone will always fail the true desire of the soul, which by its created nature seeks the transcendent and permanent. Immanence alone will never bring lasting joy to the Self, only suffering from the lies and disappointments—the thorns on the roses—always associated with worldly obsessions. Everything that is immanent (things we know here and now) ultimately destructs, fades away, or changes into what we don't want, leaving us empty and directionless. This not only includes material wealth, jobs, social status, and physical beauty, but love relationships based only on superficial qualities. We chase after earthly desires that are futureless and of no benefit to our transcendent Selves. No matter how strong our obsession—be it with money, status, or a love interest—immanence is mortal and always passes away into nothingness.

Undoubtedly, the worst deception from this immanent world comes from money. Obsessively seeking and fulfilling immanent material desires displace the Self away from its created, transcendent nature in order to seek more and more immanent material pleasure. Like flesh-eating bacteria, obsession with material pleasure erodes the Self out of its transcendent framework into an unrecognizable nothingness. In *Lost in the Cosmos*, Walker Percy writes: "The self in the twentieth century is a voracious naught which expands like the feeding vacuole of an amoeba seeking to nourish and inform its own nothingness by ingesting new objects in the world but, like a vacuole, only succeeds in emptying them out."

Can money really buy happiness? How many "toys" does it take to fill the void in an empty Self, a Self whose real value has been abstracted out and replaced by a desire to have oneself defined by the adulation of others, by possessions and status, by physical beauty, by sexual conquests, and by other fleeting immanence?

In his 1976 book *To Have or To Be?*, psychoanalyst Erich Fromm expands on this notion of losing our sense of Self and the social consequences therein because we define who we are by what we have, and not by our true being—our true existential calling. Since immanence by its nature always fails the soul, trying to establish a true sense of Self by those of us fooled and victimized by the superficiality of this material world always demands more and more of the fleeting, ineffective fix of worldly treasures, or worse, relief from the angst with alcohol, drugs, and other paths to destruction. It is why we drink too much, why we abuse drugs, and why we fail at love again and again.

Those of us with true wisdom know something that seems to escape those of us without wisdom: definitive happiness does not come from our most common desires—wealth, power, and fame. Definitive happiness is one of the descriptors the Catechism uses to describe heaven, and it can be best defined as a state of contentment that does not fade with time, a state of periodic ecstasy without the pain of withdrawal, and a state that never contains boredom or dissatisfaction. Definitive happiness cannot arise from immanent or worldly treasures; sooner or later, time steps in and dulls any joy from what we desire most. At the very least, aging and death put an end to the gleam of immanent gain; more often than not, the very worst happens—a tragic path to ruin and self-destruction. Is this the result of some kind of cruel trick?

It is indeed a trick, and a very cruel one at that. It is a supreme deception that the world in itself can be heavenly, perpetrated against us in order that we turn our backs on the real purpose of our existence:

to escape this world and enjoy a successful odyssey to heaven. Who would create such a painful deception? The answer is none other than the Great Deceiver himself—Satan. In both the Old and New Testaments, we are told that the earth is the realm of Satan (Job 1, John 12:31, and Revelation), and worldly desires are indeed his to promise to anyone. The promises are very effective and seem to be imbued within our free will. Chasing the false promises of the evil demagogue sadly ends with the nothingness of death.

Edward Arlington Robinson's poem "Richard Cory" paints an all-too-familiar picture:

Whenever Richard Cory went down town,
We people on the pavement looked at him:
He was a gentleman from sole to crown,
Clean favored, and imperially slim.

And he was always quietly arrayed,
And he was always human when he talked;
But still he fluttered pulses when he said,
"Good-morning," and he glittered when he walked.

And he was rich—yes, richer than a king—
And admirably schooled in every grace:
In fine, we thought that he was everything
To make us wish that we were in his place.

So on we worked, and waited for the light,
And went without the meat, and cursed the bread;
And Richard Cory, one calm summer night,
Went home and put a bullet through his head.

IV

Love: The Language of Heaven

*It is better to be hated for what you are than to be loved
for what you are not.*

—ANDRE GIDE, *AUTUMN LEAVES*

*Love is the reward of the one who loves, not of the one
who is loved.*

—SØREN KIERKEGAARD

Love is certainly a mystery. In some form or another, it is a strange
attraction imbued into every living thing. It can range from the simplest form, where plants are attracted to sunlight and water sources
in order to survive, up to the highest and most complex level—the
unconditional love God has for His creation. Why is it that only we
humans screw it up?

Perhaps it is because we allow an emotion to overpower and control our logic and reason, whereas in lower forms of life, the attraction of "love" is flawlessly controlled by innate instinct—an absolute
necessity for survival. Yet we humans do have some control over our
other emotions such as fear, anger, and sadness; these can be reined in

by consciously activating logic and reason, at least most of the time, given that our thought processes are intact. If we are afraid or angry, we can, with enough conscious reasoning, talk ourselves down to a level of relative calm. Much more complex logic and reasoning can assuage some forms of depression, although it can be an arduous task; it can be a successful process, however—such rethinking is the basis for cognitive therapy.

But love is a different story altogether...and being smart is no help whatsoever.

Because love often overpowers our logic and reason, it can drive us to make choices and behave in ways that contradict good sense; yet love can persuade us to choose and act in ways that are healthy for the Self. Love can infuse never-imagined joy into our lives, yet it can also be the source of hatred, violence, and despair like we've never known. Love can also reinforce our sense of survival, make us feel whole, and give us meaning and direction in our lives, or it can take all these things away in a heartbeat. Such a fork in the road of loving on this earth is terrifying, yet the innate need to love overpowers our instinctual fear and drives us forward into the exciting and danger-ous unknown.

One thing is certain: all love, no matter the relationship—lover, spouse, parent, child, friend, or God Himself—is initially all about the Self. It is about the lover, not the loved. To think otherwise, as we most often do, is the great deception of the romantic dream.

When we love another as in a lover or a spouse, the love we have is *first* driven by how we think the object of our love will make us happier. We instantly and unconsciously evaluate what we're going to get out of this person—we ultimately seek pleasure on all levels—intellectual, recreational, and sexual. Since love originates in the lover—the Self—an empty, vacuous, or confused Self is frozen in this unhealthy, selfish mode of loving. It is purely *conditional* on how the needs of the lover are to be satisfied. If we base our desire to love solely on physical beauty, wealth, power, status, or celebrity, we must be ready to accept that such anemic loving will die when the conditions fade away. This is the sad, inexorable fate of all conditional love.

We are taught in childhood to love God under the same feeble, rewards-based dynamic: if we say we love God, then we get a reward called heaven; if we say we don't love God, we get a punishment called hell. Sadly, many people go through life loving God *and* other people in this primitive, childish way. The opposite type of loving—and clearly the only way to experience real love—is *unconditional love*. It is the love for another that we all hope for in life; many of us have promised it with a solemn vow: "For better or worse, for richer or poorer, in sickness and health..."

As we said, God, the Perfect Entity, expects no less than perfect, unconditional love from us.

—⋘—

Two things, then, are necessary to begin the quest for healthy love. The first is a healthy, formed sense of Self. In the true existential sense, we must know who we are, why we're here, and that we have choices in life, choices that are completely under the control of our individual selves and not others. The second is a firm grasp on the differences between healthy and unhealthy love. Both of these lofty goals are works in progress throughout our lives. The road is not always an easy, smooth path.

Complete understanding, though, of *all* the workings of love is futile. It remains one of the great enigmas of this life. Throughout the ages, volumes have been written about human love, yet we still lack a firm grasp on its many facets—its origin, its purpose, its mechanics, and why we are in awe that one particular emotion can produce immeasurable joy and pain in the same breath. We hurt when we don't have it, and sometimes the ache is so intense we offer ourselves up on an altar of complete foolishness to get what we crave. Like Jay Gatsby yearning for the green light at the end of Daisy Buchanan's dock, we spend our lives placing our feeble little rowboats of Self against the treacherous current of reality, relentlessly seeking that which is not there. It *is* there, we insist, and "every little feather blown our way" reinforces our colossal illusion about a love we want but do not have; "no amount of fire…can challenge what a man will store up in his ghostly heart."*

Since love is all about the Self, an empty, romantic Self naturally looks to the person loved to become whole. The "ghostly heart" Fitzgerald talks about is the empty Self, confused about its existence but obsessed with finding out, clinging tirelessly to the love relationship like a life preserver on a dark sea. There is a little bit of this in all of us; Binx Bolling, Walker Percy's main character in *The Moviegoer*, is a colorful but sad fellow who lives an everyday life he abhors, but he dreams of his quest—to discover the true meaning of his existence. His loves are thus superficial, self-serving, and empty, like he is. His only respite is to use the characters and plots of movies to fill in the blanks of his reality.

In unstable individuals who never achieve a sense of worthwhile Self, unhealthy, conditional love becomes a necessity for emotional survival and must not be taken lightly; a needy, often-rejected, empty Self is a dangerous and hungry beast with little regard for the well-being of others. Such unhealthy and often dangerous love seems to be everywhere in these modern times of instant gratification and selfishness. The hallmarks of such neediness flash brightly in the world of those looking for love—we must be wary of those who love

---

* F. Scott Fitzgerald, *The Great Gatsby*.

too much, too soon. Healthy love, then, should be a lifelong goal for a peaceful life as well as a meaningful afterlife—the ins and outs of good love may very well be the language of heaven. Even healthy love, however, is a complex thing, often a double-edged sword. In these modern times of comparing ourselves to others and instantly getting what we want, can any love be completely healthy? The fact that a facet of our existence could wreak such turmoil—both good and bad—on our emotional stability certainly suggests at least some hidden pathology in loving another. Pathological or not, love is a force to be reckoned with carefully. Is it an obsessive survival mechanism that has evolved to protect us from the world's bogeymen? For those of us in the throes of a love relationship, the feelings that love evokes seem to overpower our physical and emotional functions. As the song says, "All I need is the air that I breathe and to love you."[*]

Such volatile dynamics make defining love a conundrum for the analytical mind, but the ancient Greeks tried to make the notion of love clearer by using several different terms for the various types of love. The translation and usages throughout history have dulled the precision of the categories, but we will use four of the most common and accepted types: *eros, philea, storge,* and *agape.*

Eros is the first stage of romantic love between two people that is strongly rooted in a mysterious physical attraction; most often it is accompanied by sexual desire, but in some instances such as obsessive love, the desire for sexuality is strangely absent. Such attraction without sexual desire is more intense and sometimes neurotic, where control, manipulation, and reinforcing the low self-esteem of the obsessed lover supersede healthy physical desire. As the first attraction

---

[*] "The Air That I Breathe," a song by Albert Hammond and Mike Hazelwood from their 1972 album *It Never Rains in Southern California.*

between lovers, eros is clearly is the source of the most intense immanent pleasure—even ecstasy—but it also can be the source of the
most pain of loving. The initial attraction of eros can develop in two
ways: it can grow into a healthy, lasting love relationship, or it can
become a seedbed for some very dangerous dynamics.

Philea is love or affection that we *choose* to have for another who is
an equal to us, such as a friend. It is never sexual and can be expanded
to mean love for all of mankind—that is, brotherly love. *Storge* is not
chosen but is the inborn love that is natural to parents, children, and
siblings. *Agape* is the ultimate, perfect love. The Greeks considered
it the highest and most valuable love; it is unconditional love that
rises above sexuality or choice. Agape love between two human lovers is indeed the rarest jewel—it is the prize that all lovers seek but
few attain. It is a perfect description of divine love, and it is generally
accepted that humans can only share agape love with the unknowable God through the divine help of the Holy Spirit.

A good example of the different nuances between philea (chosen
friendship) and agape (unconditional, self-sacrificial love) is seen in
John 21:15–17, sometimes called Jesus's "swan song"—His good-bye
messages to His close apostles. The stage is set for Jesus to "undo"
Peter's denials the night before the Crucifixion; there is even a charcoal fire burning as there was in the courtyard where Peter's faith
failed three times. Jesus asks Peter if Peter "loves" Him. In the original Greek texts, the more precise terms for "love" are used:

> "Simon, son of John, do you **agape** Me?" Peter answered,
> "Lord, you know that I **philea** You." Jesus said, "Tend My
> lambs." Jesus said to him a second time, "Simon, son of John,
> do you **agape** Me?" Peter answered, "Yes Lord, You know that
> I **philea** You." Jesus said, "Shepherd my sheep." He said to
> him a third time, "Simon, son of John, do you **agape** Me?"

Peter was grieved because this was the third time Jesus said this. Peter answered, "Lord, You know all things; You know that I **philea** You." Jesus said to him, "Tend my sheep."

The different Greek words for "love" demonstrate two notions. First, God asks us to love Him at the same level that He loves us—agape. Second, this level of love for God requires the infusion of the Holy Spirit. Peter was still a couple of weeks away from this gift at Pentecost, when the Holy Spirit descended upon the apostles and Mary. Peter simply did not have the spiritual workings to love at the divine level, so he persisted with his offer of friendship (philea) to Jesus, clueless as to why Jesus asked so many times. We are spared such embarrassment—the gift of spiritual strength to love God (and others) as we must, comes to us at baptism—that special moment in time when we acknowledge that we fall short of God's love but firmly commit to change and begin the arduous journey to sanctification and the jewel of agape love.

—⁂—

Without a doubt, love is the language of heaven. If the ability to love others is imbued in our beings, the workings of heaven—including our new, imperishable bodies—will be familiar to us, allowing the ecstasy of the Beatific Vision full reign over our afterlives. The entreaty to love one another, though, is so overused that its impact is dulled; the phrase is repeated over and over from pulpits of all faiths. Loving is a much more difficult and complex undertaking than the simple words depict, and, in these modern times, we are doing a horrible job of loving.

Preached or not, learning to love others by heaven's ways are the sine qua non of a joyful eternity. Jesus Himself said so in Matthew

19:16–22. "Teacher, what good thing shall I do that I may obtain eternal life?" Jesus answered the pious rich man that he should keep the commandments, and when asked which ones, Jesus enumerated some of the well-known Ten Commandments but tacked on "You shall love your neighbor as yourself." He told the man who was wealthy to sell his possessions and give to the poor. The importance of the story is not an indictment of wealth, but a lesson for us that genuine love of others—often involving self-sacrifice—is as important as following the rules etched in the stone tablets of Mount Sinai.

Genuine love for others in these modern times is clearly a work in progress. Learning to love heaven's way is a soul cleansing that involves removing stains many of us do not view as being sinful at all. Through ignorance, we carry thoughts, attitudes, and sometimes behaviors that are clearly not heavenly, namely intolerance, condescension toward others, judgment of those who are different to the point of frank xenophobia, and a host of other maladies that are, in reality, the latent and bastard children of hatred. The modern computer age has been a silent partner in disseminating hate, and, sadly, many of us live with the delusion that our hatred is somehow pleasing to the Almighty.

In a different vein, there are things that are not considered outright sins but leave an unheavenly stain on the soul; we actually admire and extol these attitudes and behaviors as "qualities" in modern living. We live in a competitive, survival-of-the-fittest age where besting others is viewed as a hallmark of worldly success. Again, lightning-fast transfer of information has allowed us to compare and compete with one another in the possession of material wealth, physical beauty, social power and status, aggression thinly masked as "ambition," and, sadly, social dominance over others different from ourselves.

In addition to these subtle stains on our ability to love others, bad love rears its ugliness in a much more blatant and dangerous venue:

the unhealthy love relationship between lovers. Broken love relationships seem so common these days, and the danger of violence and abuse is escalating in those of us with needy and empty souls who look to the sparks of eros in search of meaning in our lives.

Unhealthy Love: The Seductive Mistress of Obsessive Love—Eros Unchained

We are never so defenseless against suffering as when we love.

—SIGMUND FREUD

Of all the ways human love can go wrong and cause suffering, the most common is an insidious and destructive attraction: *obsessive love.* This is love that begins normally enough with the mutual attraction of eros but disintegrates into a living hell of possessiveness, jealousy, control, and ultimately abuse that can be physical, emotional, or both. Obsessive love develops when one lover has deeply rooted and unhealthy needs that are unchained by the passion of eros.

Initially, eros tempts us with a mysterious attraction that is very strong, even overwhelming, and we gradually relinquish our logic and reason for the passion and false sense of completeness the relationship gives us. This can be quite normal; if we are psychologically balanced—that is, possess a sense of Self that reassures us about who we are and why we are worthy of being loved—we can safely depend on the relationship to give us happiness in the form of companionship, fun, and romantic interplay. But if one lover is an empty Self, *needing* more than *desiring* completeness, the dynamics of the love relationship explode into obsession, obsession bloated to the point where companionship, fun, and romance are pushed into the background. The focus of the relationship degenerates into the need for constant physical presence to the extreme of "owning" the loved person and controlling his or her every thought and activity by surveillance, manipulation, threats, and ultimately physical violence. After tasting the passion and false sense of fulfillment of eros, the empty Self is unable to face reality alone. The severity of such neediness varies greatly from mildly irritating to floridly pathological and dangerous. In *The Art of Loving*, Erich Fromm agrees: "Paradoxically, the ability to be alone is the condition for the ability to love."

The unpleasant and dangerous baggage of obsessive love—neediness, jealousy, possessiveness, control, emotional abuse, and physical violence—can lead to the tragic end of murder and suicide in cases where the obsessed lover is depressed, paranoid, or abusing alcohol and drugs. Such tragic extremes are not uncommon; they appear in the news on a regular basis. The platform upon which the cancerous growth of obsessive love begins is the stagnation of an empty and needy Self into a rewards-based mode of loving—the love object initially viewed as a *desire* for joy becomes a *need* to survive. When the love relationship is unable to fulfill the empty Self—as it is never able to do—the obsessed lover, who is already battling severe depression, turns to substance abuse, and the tragic possible outcome becomes reality.*

The only firewall protecting us from the explosion into obsessive loving is the Self. A Self that is empty or only filled with the superficiality of modern times is a poor safeguard against growing up as a

---

* Psychoanalyst Karl Menninger said that homicide is nearly always part of suicidal ideation, especially if the suicidal individual erroneously externalizes the blame for his or her depression onto the partner/victim. About fifteen hundred such cases a year are documented in the United States, although the actual numbers are probably much higher.

hungry, needy beast that must have a lover to feel complete. In fact, it is an inadequate sense of Self—low self-esteem—that creates the need for and drives obsessive loving. The tween and adolescent version of obsessive loving is the "crush." It is normal for kids to have multiple crushes—one-sided attractions for real people in their lives or for celebrities they have never met in real life. Until maturity hopefully occurs in the midtwenties, the Self of the adolescent is truly a work in progress. Children absorb snippets of reinforcement from parents and other role models that gradually reassure and fill the Self with positive notions of acceptability, lovability, and, at the most basic level, survivability. Until the adolescent feels strong and emotionally complete enough to stand alone against the world, the onus for such fulfillment falls on the crush.

The real danger of the crush appears when mature self-esteem doesn't materialize, and the empty or poorly formed Self leaves adolescence for adulthood. Love in such people becomes an obsessive need upon which the very survival of the Self depends. This modern age of techno wonders seems to be a fertile soil in which obsessive love can grow; the perception that we can have every wish fulfilled at the speed of light keeps the poorly developed Self of childhood mired in the muck of fantasy and immediate gratification. There is simply no need to develop the Self into its created purpose—the "forever child" never grows up.* Fromm again wisely observes that "Immature love says 'I love you because I need you'...mature love says 'I need you because I love you.'"

To be fair, modern technology is really just a distraction for the adolescent with persistent low self-esteem; it is not a true cause. Technology fills the immature Self with a temporary fix—a

---

* This would explain why most murder-suicides involve a much younger individual killing an older partner before killing him- or herself.

distraction from what is missing from the developing Self; the trouble starts when this empty sense of self-worth is carried into adult life. There is no exact cause of low self-esteem, but at least some blame can be ascribed to three sources: parenting, genetics, and childhood trauma.

Parents who are a little short on their ability to nurture or communicate praise for accomplishments often hinder the development of self-esteem. Worse are parent figures who are overly punitive or demanding, placing unrealistic expectations of success onto the delicate shoulders of a growing Self. Reinforcement of such patterns sends a powerful message to kids that they are not worthy of love and praise, and they enter adulthood seeking validation from others. The objects of their love become necessities based on control rather than choices based on respect.

The role of genetics as a cause of physical and emotional disease is finally making its way into legitimate research. It is well accepted that genetics plays at least a partial role in the personality disorders commonly associated with low self-esteem, namely *borderline personality disorder* and *narcissistic personality disorder*. These personality disorders contain all the characteristics of someone likely to love obsessively: besides low self-esteem, people with personality disorders are highly sensitive to rejection and abandonment. When the object of his or her obsessive love pulls away from the suffocating neediness of the relationship, the obsessed lover reacts with rage and sometimes physical violence. As we said, since serious depression often coexists with these disorders, such escape attempts from unstable individuals often result in horrific tragedy.

Another cause of low self-esteem that may or may not coexist with parenting difficulties and genetic patterns is childhood trauma. Generally, the trauma to the developing Self of the child occurs as a result of any of three tragedies: abuse—emotional, physical, or at worst, sexual; abandonment by a parent figure, either by death or divorce; or physical deformity from an accident or congenital defect.

Children who are abused grow up somehow thinking the abuse is their fault and is deserved; in light of such belief, these adolescents become adults truly convinced they are not worthy of love. Their adult love relationships only function with constant affirmations that they are indeed worthy of it, and the responsibility to supply such reinforcement falls on the significant other. The relationships are replete with instability and violent arguments—the highs are extreme, when the affirmations of lovability are given; the lows can be dangerous if the affirmations somehow miss the mark in a way real or perceived. The needy, insecure "lover" controls, manipulates, and threatens in order to keep the opiate of reinforcement coming, on an ever-increasing basis. An underlying borderline or narcissistic personality disorder makes things much worse. Borderlines and narcissists cannot tolerate the slightest hint of rejection or abandonment—the horror of childhood that tells them they are unworthy of love is replayed once more. The results of such a breakdown are often tragic. Walker Percy's main character in the novel *Lancelot* muses, "There is no pain on this earth like seeing a woman look at another man the way she once looked at you."*

The psychodynamics of a toxic love relationship sometimes seen in individuals who were abandoned during childhood by a parent figure are exactly the same as with abuse. The low self-esteem from feelings of unworthiness, the obsessive need for affirmations to the contrary, the need for control and manipulation of the significant other, and, of course, the fear of rejection and abandonment are all hallmarks of the need for obsessive love.

The third form of trauma that negatively affects the growth of self-esteem is a physical deformity from a childhood accident or congenital defect. A child so afflicted is treated differently—better or worse—by parent figures; the child is either overprotected by fearful and perhaps guilty parents, or the child is shunned outright by parents in denial. The child's sense of desirability—so important in a mature love relationship—is derailed, and, as adults, these individuals relentlessly seek affirmation of their physical acceptability through obsessive loving marked by control and neediness. When his or her serious relationships fail—as they always do—the lost and wandering lover seeks excessive and casual sex in order to feel physically acceptable. Once the sexual bond is accomplished, the intense attraction dies, and the relationship ends. There is no more need for that particular sex object, and the unfulfilled Self seeks out another conquest to reaffirm its desirability. Repairing a shattered and low self-esteem in this way is a lesson in futility; shattered marriages, broken hearts, and abandoned offspring are the sad remnants of such futility.

Yet obsessive loving seems to require some sort of perfect storm. Not all adults with these childhood signs of trauma fail to develop adequate self-esteem; inherited personality glitches, along with varying degrees of parenting success, surely play roles. Yet whether obsessive loving is confined to adolescent crushes or whether it moves forward into adult life characterized by one failed love relationship after another, one thing is universally present, and that is the *intensity* of the desire for another. Why does this love hurt so much?

The mysterious desire generated by the Self that loves "not wisely, but too well" arises in the unavailability of the love object. The challenge of the crush and obsessed love is to erase the Self's feelings of undesirability. The greater the challenge—the unavailability of the love object—to "possess" the love object, the greater the obliteration of the feelings of undesirability. It may be the basis for the trite saying "We want most what we cannot have."

The pain of the crush and obsessed love is truly eros unchained. If we feel an intense yearning for another to the point that we *must* possess this person, this intense attraction is actually masking an existential fantasy image of ourselves as complete, lovable, desirable, and thus *survivable*. The unhealthy aspect of such obsession should become obvious when we realize that we may know very little about this perfect, fantasy "soul mate"—he or she may be a casual acquaintance or even a public figure like a media celebrity. Yet it is the lack of knowledge about the crush that allows us to create and shape him or her into exactly what we need to feel whole. This process is called *idealization*; it exists in all forms of loving to varying degrees, but it is never healthy.

Idealization is an unconscious process that blocks any potential breakdown of the fantasy of possessing our crush or object of obsessive love. If the object of our obsession is two-dimensional—for example, a celebrity that we only know through the media of photos, videos, TV, or the movies—idealization is easier. Anything we learn about our crush that does not fit our template of idealization—the fantasy notion that our crush is perfect for us—is erased by denial and rationalization, and we are able to continue the fantasy. If we learn something that is a "deal breaker"—a bit of information that cannot be erased—the idealization process simply breaks down, and the obsession painlessly fades away. In this sense, idealization is kind of a safety valve that bursts the obsession once the undesired reality of the love object can no longer be justified or whitewashed. The adolescent crush of a young woman on a popular celebrity quickly fades when she, a staunch supporter of animal rights, finds out on social media that he enjoys hunting baby seals on weekends. No way to spin that glitch.

If the object of our crush or obsession is a real person with whom we are physically and emotionally bonded, any breakdown of our idealized image of him or her—an image we create that is crucial for us to feel lovable and worthy—often causes emotional upheaval and sometimes physical violence. When our lover, whom we've idealized as the only solution to our existential angst of unworthiness, fails at his or her daunting task of making us feel whole, all hell breaks loose. It is the hallmark of an unhealthy relationship, and the scary beginning of a manipulative, controlling, and potentially abusive life.

As bad as all this sounds, this psychopathology exists in all love relationships, healthy or unhealthy—to a varying degree. When obsessive loving becomes a problem in the stability and longevity of a marriage or love relationship, professional help is a must. A life of spiritual growth filled with prayer and meditation may help or even cure what lacks in the "ghostly self," but most often a competent and patient therapist is needed to work through the unfinished business of growing up. The intellect is of no help in easing the pain of love—being smart is no protection against a hungry and needy heart.

—⚍—

There are many types of unhealthy love, but they all have one result in common: they distort the paths we take through life and coerce us into making horrible decisions that always lead us to pain and self-destruction. Chasing the wrong kind of love from the wrong person for the wrong reason wastes our emotional energies, which are better used to develop earthly talents necessary to fulfill our divine purpose. More important, the spiritual growth necessary to know God, the source of all real love—the matrix of the next life—is badly neglected. Our modern trend of basing love on the false gods of money, power, celebrity, and physical appearances distracts us from the true calling of the Self. The modern age, with its increased fluidity of information about the world, fools us into a fantasy belief, a completely destructive notion of how life and love should be. Even the smartest of us unwittingly compares ourselves to those having cheap and fragile immanent idols instead of looking at ourselves inwardly and seeking real values for the Self. These are true values that correctly define who we are and why we exist. Only knowing the real value of the Self can make our last odyssey successful; immanent materialism and sensual beauty will be left behind as discarded ash.

You can get all A's and still flunk life.

—WALKER PERCY, *THE SECOND COMING*

The Hallmarks of Healthy Love: The Difficult Journey from Eros to Agape

Where there is love there is life.

—MAHATMA GANDHI

The building blocks of healthy loving have been described ad infinitum in hundreds of self-help and pop-psychology books, but to avoid overwhelming confusion, we are going to reiterate four of the most crucial aspects of what makes loving what it should be. These four hallmarks are applicable to all love relationships, be they between lovers, friends, family pairings, or, most important, God and His creation. The emotions and characters in these relationships are different, but the dynamics of loving are the same.

Mutual Respect

The first essential quality of healthy love between two parties is *mutual respect*. We discuss mutual respect first because it is the foundation of the other three hallmarks of healthy loving. It is given great lip service by most of us, but its lack or weakness is most often the cause of troubled love. Mutual respect demands that both parties not only accept what the other person is about—and this involves many parameters—but admire and even cherish most of these parameters. Doing this well is the challenge of modern loving, and the heterogeneity of our societies makes this especially difficult. Love that overcomes the challenges of being different from each other has been the fodder for a lot of movies and books. We desperately want to believe that *amor* truly does *vincit omnia*.

It does not.

The complexity and subcategories of mutual respect lend credence to this sad but realistic fact. The parameters that seem to crop up in most relationship counseling sessions are age, beliefs (about children, money, God, and in-laws), life goals, and, less often, ethnicity. Discussing these parameters makes us worry that we are sinking into the basement of conditional love—that is, "I love you because you are X years old, make X dollars per year, believe in God, and are thrilled that my unemployed brother is going to live with us," and so on. It would seem so, but in reality, we are simply trying to establish a relationship rich in peace and accord and to avoid a day-to-day life of pain and arguing. Perfect accord in these parameters is not the basis for the love bond; trying to pair up with a good match is simply a good idea—mutual respect thrives when there is peace and calm. More important, when the conditional veneer of these areas fades away or changes, the unconditional strength of the love comes to the rescue. People get old and sick; they lose jobs or even their faith in God. Healthy love does not abandon such loss: for better or for worse, the love is there. True love is not easy.

Being the same in a love relationship is not always best; being aware of the challenges of being different is much more important. Surprises in marriages are not good.

Healthy Love Is Unconditional

Unconditional love is not just a necessity for lovers in a relationship; it is an innate part of the parent-child relationship and, more important, the sine qua non of loving God. The unconditional love we have for our children is automatic: it is inborn in our nature. Children do their very best at challenging this love: they disobey rules, they rebel, and they whine when they don't get whatever they want, no matter how outrageous the demand. They threaten to make their love for us fully conditional—"Give me what I want, or I won't love you." The wise parent is always respectful in doling out bad news—"I respect where you're coming from, but as I am the parent and responsible for your well-being, you have no choice in this matter." A nine-year-old who wants to trade her Barbie phone for a seven-hundred-dollar smartphone does not deserve a list of the reasons that such a tearful plea is a bad idea. A respectful and sympathetic no is sufficient, along with the notion that her request is not a bad one, just one at the wrong time. If such a strategy is begun early enough and with consistency, the child begins to develop respect for the parent figure. Giving in is not the way to engender respect; neither is it a hallmark of unconditional love. Loving unconditionally is doing what is right in spite of the tears of protest.

Strangely, such a scenario is a mirror image of how many of us deal with God and His wisdom. We disobey rules, we rebel, and we whine when we don't get what we want. To love God unconditionally, we must accept that we are not going to get every prayer answered exactly how and when we want. There is a plan in place to save us from eternal death, and we are sometimes not privy to exactly how unanswered prayers are really blessings in disguise. In order to love God unconditionally, we must have trust in His ways, just like a whiny, demanding nine-year-old must trust parent figures. Trust is the absolute foundation of unconditional love; this is true for love of parent, child, lover, or God Himself.

If we trust the object of our love, then the self-sacrifice necessary for unconditional loving to take place becomes acceptable. Self-sacrifice is part of every healthy love relationship; the lover who is not willing to suffer for the benefit of another is not capable of unconditional love. The self-sacrifice of God toward us is obvious in the Person of Jesus Christ and His passion and death. We must be willing to sacrifice as well, whether it is for love toward God or another human being. And, unfortunately, self-sacrifice always involves *suffering*.

A Healthy Love Accepts Suffering

In healthy loving, parties therein must accept some sort of suffering involved in the necessary self-sacrifice. In some mysterious way, God suffers when we disobey, rebel, or whine when we don't get what we want when we want it. God's plan to bring us out of exile is paramount to all else; this plan is one of the cornerstones of divine love. If the workings of this plan cause us suffering, God suffers with us, but He cannot be blamed for our pain any more than a surgeon or dentist can be blamed for doing what is necessary for our well-being. If we understand and accept this, our love for God begins to shed its conditional, childish aspect and begins to grow into true unconditional love. The same holds true for the children of wise but firm parents who put the welfare of their children first—and avoid the silliness of trying to be friends with offspring. The children rarely understand this…until they become parents.

Between lovers, the suffering of self-sacrifice is a necessary price to pay for the joy of a solid relationship. Someone who is unwilling to suffer is a bad partner; such a dynamic creates a relationship/marriage that is lopsided. The inability to accept the suffering of compromise creates a sick relationship of bully and martyr, and, after a while, the resulting acting out of both parties signals a death knell for the relationship. Mankind is the most advanced of species and, as such, is the most territorial. Territoriality is not just about "this is mine, and that is yours," but also about nearly every decision of daily life. When two lovers cohabit, the lovers face countless such decisions every day, decisions that often threaten territorial boundaries. This is the case when "what I want is not what you want." The only way to assuage the threat is to compromise, and compromise involves suffering to some degree or another.

As we're about to see, accepting suffering on this earth is not just a key facet of healthy love, but it may also be a sine qua non for a successful odyssey off this earth into a perfect realm where there is no suffering...truly a place without tears.

V

Suffering: Accepting It Is the Ticket to the Next Life

To live is to suffer, to survive is to find some meaning in the suffering.

—Friedrich Nietzsche

What is to give light must endure burning.

—Viktor Frankl

Innocent suffering is not something human logic can grasp; it makes no sense. Why does it exist? Why do some suffer much more than others? Are we being punished for some unknown misdeed in a past existence? Trying to answer these questions is a lesson in futility. One thing is certain: we will find out in the next life when all things are illuminated. Until then, we can only speculate; ultimately, however, we must accept suffering as part of our existence.

Can anything good possibly come from suffering? Philosophers and theologians have wrestled with this question for ages, but the answers seem hollow and thin against our pain. Yet streams of thought seem to suggest that suffering is both a cleansing and strengthening process for the soul. Such notions assume the nascent soul is somehow stained and weakened to some degree. Teilhard de Chardin, in his controversial writings about original sin, calls this less-than-perfect state a *privation*, a privation of the divine perfection necessary for the soul to achieve union with God. In this sense, then, suffering may be an effective tool in our sanctification process; it is sanctification that not only gets us into heaven, but makes heaven more heavenly.

This is what our odyssey is all about; it is the end point of God's perfect plan and the very reason we exist. We do not exist to be beautiful, rich, powerful, happy, pain free, or to receive any other earthly, immanent desire. We exist to be one with God; we can achieve part of that unity here on earth as we eschew immanent treasures and grow toward the transcendent—both are unnatural processes and, as such, may involve some suffering. This unity we desire is fulfilled and consummated in heaven at the end of our odyssey. Sadly, for our existence to manifest this totality, we must first die. Suffering is thus enmeshed into our very existence.

We need to make three assumptions that are essential to our understanding of why suffering is absolutely necessary to power our quest for an ultimate, perfect union with our God. The first assumption is that God is not the creator of suffering, nor is He a passive spectator when terrible things happen to us. The common misconception going back to Job is that God "lets" bad things happen to us—as in, He permits tragedy or, worse, sanctions it. This is wrong. "Letting" something happen follows a human or *anthropomorphic* circuit of logic. For example, "If God existed and was all-powerful, He would not let bad things happen" is a human logical assertion. If God were human and followed human rules of logic, then this statement would be true. But God is *not* human, and His ways are absolutely inscrutable and mysterious. They infinitely transcend human logic and reason. The burning question of why there is suffering in the world was never answered in the book of Job. At the end of the book, God simply told Job in no uncertain terms that Job was completely out of line for asking the question in the first place: "Gird up your loins like a man and speak" (Job 40:7–14ff).

Job was silent.

He later admits, "Therefore I have declared that which I did not understand, Things too wonderful for me, that I did not know" (Job 42:3).

Kierkegaard suffered greatly in his young life, and rather than try to understand God's role in suffering, Kierkegaard the existentialist looked into himself, the individual, for answers. We should do likewise. The ways of God are beyond our logic, but we do know some things about man and the world. God created man and the world in a perfect state of dynamic growth. The creation story of Adam, Eve, and the Garden of Eden is an allegory of this. Man was protected from the harmful effects of the changing nature of the world by the perfect, idyllic garden God had prepared for him. In order to love God in the truest sense, man was given a free will—the choice to love God or not to love God. Free will is essential to genuine love. A robot can be programmed to express love or programmed not to express love. Without the choice of free will, any love expressed by an automaton is not genuine love. No one wants to be loved unless the lover chooses to do so. Even our pets love us on a higher plane than this.

Free will has a downside. Free will allows man to choose good, neutral, or bad actions. This power of choice was imparted to man inside the Garden of Eden, and man *chose* to sin. His ejection from the protection of the garden placed man face-to-face with the ravages of the natural world. There were no earthquakes, tidal waves, volcanic eruptions, floods, or horrific storms in the Garden of Eden. Man's chromosomes were perfect from God's creation—the DNA sequences lined up perfectly, producing proteins that protected man from mental and physical disease, and even growing old and dying. In the garden, there was no fear, depression, aggression, criminal behavior, or psychosis. There was no cancer, heart disease, or the congenital anomalies that cause so much of our suffering. Man's choice to sin and his resulting ejection from the protective environs of the garden placed man out in the natural world; man became a victim of the growing pains of the world. His unprotected interaction with a sometimes-violent earth began to affect his DNA—sometimes in a good way that fostered evolutionary growth, but many of the changes were not good. Mutations and resulting polymorphisms in man's genetic code started to fail in producing the protective biochemical processes enjoyed by Adam and Eve in the garden. Because of the choice of sin made in Eden, man was suddenly born to suffer and die. From a perfect creation, the world has become a place of suffering at the hands of man and his free will. We have created our own *Purgatorio*. And so, we suffer, but ironically, it is this very suffering that is our way out.

The second assumption is that we incorrectly connect God to our earthly suffering, mostly because we have the anthropomorphic notion that God should interfere with man's free will and remove suffering from the world. We must remember that free will is a necessary component of loving; if free will is compromised or interfered with, there can be no genuine love. No love...no union with God... no odyssey...no heaven. In the perfect order of creation, suffering is not God's doing; it is man's business. God's connection to our suffering is ex post facto: His only action occurs after we are in pain. That action is comfort and support: we are endowed with the strength and patience to endure until we reach paradise.

Many of us turn to the beloved verse of Romans 8:28 in times of great suffering and sorrow: "And we know that God causes all things to work together for good to those who love Him." Some of us incorrectly assume that since we love God, He will take away our present pain and prevent any further suffering. To correctly grasp what the apostle Paul is saying, we must understand that what man considers as "good" is very different from what the word means to God. We consider "good" to refer to our quality of life here on earth—wealth, security, health, success in love, freedom from pain and suffering; these are immanent qualities. God, however, sees "good" as a transcendent quality—that is, anything is good if it draws us closer to the paradigm of Christ's life of obedience and holiness. Christ suffered, and we must also accept suffering, if we are to successfully morph into the supernatural from the natural.

We know that suffering strengthens and shapes the soul back to its original perfect state—this is the process of sanctification. While God is pleased with our sanctification—it brings us closer to Him—God is not part of the suffering. God did not create evil and suffering; neither does He permit it *solely* to chafe the imperfections of man. Sanctification of the soul is man's responsibility; God provides the grace for strength and comfort during the process. The fact that suffering from evil in the world could bring us closer to God is ironic—it is a mistake of evil itself. Satan made a huge error in tempting the free will of man and thus bringing evil into the world; the suffering engendered by Satan has been transformed into a weapon against him. The very worst of human pain does indeed shape the spirit of man. The scars of human imperfection from man's free will are abraded in some mysterious way, in some earthly time frame known only to the Creator. Man is thus made ready for the perfect union at the end of the last odyssey. The ironic benefit of suffering is shown in a quote by Helen Keller: "Character cannot be developed in ease and quiet. Only through experience of trial and suffering can the soul be strengthened, ambition inspired, and success achieved."

The suffering of innocents and the deaths of children are most vexing problems for us. Suffering is not a punishment for evil; we Christians believe that Jesus paid the debt for evil in the world on Calvary. The suffering of innocents is certainly tragic but also is the most perfect path to union with the innocent, suffering Christ. Jesus chose to suffer a horrendous death not only to pay the world's sin debt, but also to identify with the most innocent of suffering and thus bring man and Creator closer together, culminating in the ultimate union occurring in the afterlife.

The notion that innocents must be sacrificed to suffering in order to reshape the imperfections of mankind is a cruel one, but it is the result of evil and the sin of man in the Garden of Eden. God had no part in such design, but the sacrifice of suffering is a perfect imitation of Christ's fulfillment of the Father's plan. The archetype of such obedience unto death is seen in the story of Abraham's offering of his son, Isaac, on the mountain in Moriah (Genesis 22:1–12). It is the recognition of the sacrifice of innocent suffering shaping our souls—the innocence of both Jesus and earthly sufferers—that is the basis for perfect repentance and forgiveness. It is a ticket into heaven no matter how bad our earthly lives. As the good thief on Calvary with Jesus said, "This man has done nothing wrong...Jesus, remember me when you come into your kingdom. And He said to him, Truly, I say to you, today you shall be with Me in Paradise" (Luke 23:41–43).

The third assumption also concerns our anthropomorphic distortion of God and His ways: it is simply that God is not a helicopter parent. We ascribe qualities to God that are most likely correct: He is present somewhere and hears us, He loves us and cares about us, and, most important, He has put in place a plan to get us to a state of perfect, blissful union with Him in the afterlife. He also freely gives us grace—the flow of His own Spirit—that strengthens us and guides us to find and follow the plan.

Some of us also assume that God is supposed to protect us, rescue us, and keep us from all harm and suffering. We can all attest that such protection has happened hundreds of times throughout our lives. The vexing question is, why are there times when it doesn't happen? Are there times when God stops caring about us or is perhaps forgetful and negligent? As we said before, human logic demands an answer—if God cares, why aren't we rescued *all* the time? We answered before by saying that God is not subject to human logic and that helicopter parenting, by its nature, trumps free will. Trumping free will and helicopter parenting are human things. When my son was seven, those speedy little minibikes were the rage. He cried and carried on to get one. Having worked in an ER, I had seen firsthand the damage done to little bodies when wheels, motors, and speed are not kept in check. His free will was wisely shut off, and he did not get the mini motorbike. At that moment in time, I don't think he even liked me, much less loved me.

We cannot say for sure why God only rescues us, protects us, or prevents loved ones from dying sometimes, but we can guess it has everything to do with His plan to get us home. Certain things in our lives must occur for His plan to succeed—and it will succeed, with or without us. In Luke 1:18–20, Zacharias doubted Gabriel's word about God's plan for the birth of John the Baptist. The angel's retribution was swift: "And behold, you shall not be able to speak until the day when these things take place, because you did not believe my words, which will be fulfilled in their proper time." If something must occur or not occur for the plan to move forward, then we can speculate that God acts in our lives. We must remember, the divine plan is everything…it is why we exist.

Our speculation above about God acting in our lives is bold human pride coming to light and is a dangerous undertaking. By assuming that God acts in our lives, we again are endangering free will. We simply should accept that God's ways are mysterious and beyond our logic and comprehension. Yet most of us hold on to these dangerous assumptions that God acts like our human logic dictates. I read a sad obituary notice where the surviving family of a loved one wrote, "God broke our hearts by taking X too soon." Rational theology was apparently forgotten in this beautiful piece of poetry. But God didn't break anything; neither did God take anyone. Someone died, and his family got sad. That's all there is to it. Death is ugly but gives us respite: without death, there is no joyful end of our odyssey... there is no heaven.

—m—

What can we say about suffering that will both console us and give us hints as to how and why suffering strengthens the soul and makes for a better afterlife? Again, we have to start with some assumptions about ourselves. First, we have to believe there is a God, a heaven, and a joyful end to our lifelong odyssey for those of us who are decent and have such faith. Second, we have to believe that our suffering not only has meaning but is crucial to our sanctification process—the growth process where we become holy for the holiest of places. Faith is everything. Without faith, there is no odyssey, no heaven, no ecstatic union with our Creator—the very reason for our existence. Without faith, our lives have no meaning in the transcendent world. Death is uglier because there is no respite called heaven. Kierkegaard, in his *Fear and Trembling*, describes such a hopeless ending: "If there were no eternal consciousness in a man, if at the bottom of everything there were only a wild ferment, a power that twisting in dark passions produced everything great or inconsequential; if an unfathomable, insatiable emptiness lay hid beneath everything, what would life be but despair?"

Assuming we believe in God and the afterlife of heaven, what is there about suffering that makes it necessary to enjoy heaven to the fullest? And why is suffering so inconsolable—why does the pain linger in our lives, often crippling us with seemingly endless melancholy and sadness? Is the elixir of time the only opiate for our pain? Time, it seems, does not always make it better.

In fact, time may be our worst enemy when we suffer. Time, in one sense, is a man-made construct, a dimension on earth, not in heaven. There is no time in heaven (Aquinas); everything is *right now*. This makes time an immanent or worldly measure, and its function is to create space between events. Let's say a tragedy strikes us at point A in our lives. It is time that delays the occurrence of point B—relief of our pain to some degree. We can't rid ourselves of time here on earth, but we can wait it out...until the pain subsides or until we reach the timeless joy of heaven. Waiting out a stretch of time here on earth requires patience, a virtue few of us have in this modern world. For consolation in suffering, then, we need patience as well as faith. If we are suffering the loss of a loved one, faith reassures us: "I will see him again." Patience reassures us further: "I will see him again soon."

Being patient is the best way of turning our backs on the immanent (worldly) measure of time, but it is only a drop in the bucket; we must let go of all things immanent, sooner or later. Our heavenly experience may depend not so much on our saintliness or the lack of it as our letting go of the immanent world we leave behind—"dying to the world." In Matthew 16:24, Jesus used the cross—a symbol of death—to iterate leaving worldly immanence behind: "If anyone wishes to come after Me [into heaven], let him deny himself and take up his cross." As we'll see, dying to the world—letting go of everything we have and can see around us (immanence) is a lot more challenging than we might think.

Dying to the world is not an easy business. Like all living things, we have evolved to survive. Survival is the strongest natural instinct we have; everything we value, everything we seek, everything we have and keep is based on our desire to stay alive in this world. Yet our main calling in life—our reason for existence—is to become supernatural. To become supernatural, we must first die to the treasures of the natural. Christ put it quite plainly: "Truly, I say to you, unless a grain of wheat falls to the earth and dies, it remains by itself alone; but if it dies, it bears much fruit. He who loves his life loses it; and he who hates his life in this world shall keep it to life eternal" (John 12:24–25).

In order to live out our true destiny, we must turn our backs on all our immanent treasures. "No man can serve two masters… you cannot serve God and the world" (Matthew 6:24). A ticket into the afterlife thus involves tremendous risk. As Kierkegaard said, risk and doubt are part of faith; we must strengthen our faith to be able to take such a blind leap of belief. Peter failed the test of faith when Jesus called him to leave the boat and walk on water. Peter doubted and began to sink. Jesus saved him and said, "O ye of little faith, why did you doubt?" (Matthew 14:25–31). As we'll see, the strength to stay afloat and survive in times of peril comes from effective prayer and meditation, but, more importantly, it comes from suffering.

Exactly *how* does this happen?

In this world and the next, transcendence has complete power over immanence. Because the immanent world is what we see, experience, and prove with science—this includes all material things, natural wonders, and also *people*—we assume it is the only reality, having the laws of physics to back it up. Immanence says with positivity that a weight dropped from a height will fall down to the ground. Transcendence says that if God wants the weight to fly to the moon, it will do so. Such an event would be called a *miracle*. If

God's plan requires a miracle, then a miracle happens. The power of immanence (the world) over reality is only an illusion. We believe in the power of the world because we can see it, but there are things beyond our senses that are much greater. Transcendence that we cannot see is all-powerful over the universe; it is transcendence, after all, that has created the universe. So when we move away from immanence toward transcendence, we are breaking the chains of worldly sensation, getting stronger, and experiencing existential freedom at last. This is a very common theme in many Eastern religions.

Jesus performed many miracles in His ministry, occurrences that were beyond the laws of physics. He always did these things with the help and sanction of the Father—the ultimate Transcendence. Jesus was not taken away by the temple guard in Gethsemane; He *let* them take Him away. Jesus was not scourged, crowned with thorns, or crucified against His will; He *let* these things occur because they were necessary for the Father's perfect plan to get us all home to heaven. He made the power of transcendence over immanence perfectly clear to the mob that confronted Him in the garden: "Do you think that I cannot appeal to my Father, and He will at once put at my disposal more than twelve legions of angels? But it must happen this way that the Scriptures be fulfilled" (Matthew 26:53–54).

So, then, anything that moves us away from immanence toward transcendence strengthens us. As we give up (or lose) our attachments to the material world—all that we can experience, including other people—our lives change in so many ways and become *miraculous*. Things happen to us that defy logic; some ascribe the miracles of our changing lives to serendipity. Both Freud and the fictional detective Sherlock Holmes said that there is no such thing as a coincidence; the miracles in our lives after suffering are real. Dying to the world, however, is a long, painful process, sometimes involving tragedy. Albert Camus said, *"Au milieu de l'hiver, j'ai découvert en moi un invincible été*" ("In the middle of winter, I discovered in myself an invincible summer").

The engine of dying to the world, in some way or another, is *loss*; as such, loss is the basis for all suffering. Loss can be active—a choice of sacrifice, willfully giving up certain aspects of immanent life in order to gain transcendence here on earth. In the simplest sense, active loss might be the fasting and self-sacrifice of Lent, leading us to greater sacrifices down the road of our lives. On a higher plane might be the self-sacrifice of clergy, missionaries, and those unique people who give to others without reward or recognition. On the same high level of active loss would be the cloistered clergy like monks, ascetics, and religious orders in which a rigorous but simple lifestyle is led in order to concentrate on prayer and meditation for the sanctification of mankind.

Most loss, however, is passive—it is something that happens to us against our wishes. It might be the tragedy of a lost loved one or the loss of our health and well-being through disease, accident, or the cruelty of nature. We can also lose our fortunes, freedom, reputations, or, often the worst of all, we can lose the love of another person through death or abandonment. Because we are powerless when passive loss occurs in our lives, we seem to suffer greater pain. In this sense, then, both active and passive losses are heroic. Active loss strengthens the soul through self-sacrifice, but passive loss does it by forcing the Self to survive through the anguish and pain.

Kierkegaard said that if we don't suffer with a path to spiritual transcendence in mind—something few of us do—our pain can begin to hide within ourselves. We must confront our suffering even to the point of despair—despair at the realization that suffering is an integral part of this is immanent life. Clare Carlisle, in an article in *The Guardian*, points out that Kierkegaard saw such despair as a good thing because such existential suffering is a hallmark of our spiritual nature and closeness to God by being torn from the pleasures and security of the immanent world, including people. For many of us, though, a vexing, often-heard question looms, blocking the idea that suffering brings us closer to God: How can God be all-powerful and benevolent and yet create a world so full of misery and suffering, whose victims are often completely innocent?

As I said before (and am about to discuss in detail in the next chapter on theodicy), there may be no logical answer to this question because the question itself may be logically and theologically incomplete due to anthropomorphic assumptions—we assume God decides things after some kind of data input, or worse, that God thinks like a human being. The question certainly is vexing and has turned many away from a belief in God's existence altogether. Kierkegaard dealt with the problem of suffering in the world from an existential perspective rather than an intellectual or logical one. He saw suffering as a means to growth of the Self toward God. The suffering of man is within man himself and has nothing to do with whether God exists. This notion agrees with many Eastern religions. In Hinduism, there are many gods, and in Buddhism, there are no gods, so God is not involved with suffering. In both these religions, it is man's attachment to the world that causes suffering. Every religion seems to agree: to move to a higher level, we must let go of what is below us. Sometimes, suffering does the letting go for us.

—m—

Brokenness

> *God uses broken things. It takes broken soil to produce a crop, broken clouds to give rain, broken grain to give bread, broken bread to give strength. It is the broken*

alabaster box that gives forth perfume. It is Peter, broken
and weeping bitterly, who returns to greater power
than ever.

—VANCE HAVNER

Ever has it been that love knows not its own depth until
the hour of separation.

—KAHLIL GIBRAN

The brokenness of life, the suffering that is to shape and strengthen our souls, comes to us in many, often tragic ways, and nearly always when we least expect it. Two of the most common sources of passive loss that lead to our suffering are a loss of our physical or mental well-being from disease or congenital defect, from injury, from war, or from natural disasters. The other is a loss of love from someone close to us; from death, separation, or abandonment; from love that is not returned; from kids who grow up and leave us; and even from love we wait for that never comes.

Consolation and relief of the pain of any of these losses is a rare jewel to find. It *is* there, but we must, in the midst of our grieving, confront the ugly fact that suffering is a natural part of this world. The opposite of suffering is not joy, says Kierkegaard, but evasiveness and cowardice. We must face our pain and accept that suffering is a natural part of this life. This reminds us that the immanent world is something to let go of, and our supernatural side or transcendent soul is better able to pull us toward God. Our grief drives us to cry, "Foul!" or, "Life is not fair!"—but these words are cries of retreat from the suffering nature of the immanent world. When we accept suffering as part of the world's treachery, we understand why we must shun the world and come closer to God, in the Person of Christ, as He freely and obediently accepted the horrors of Calvary. When we cry out, "Where is God when I suffer?" the answer is, "The same place He was on Good Friday."

When we suffer, the natural and human tendency is to place blame on someone or something. Somehow we feel justice will be served for our pain if blame—even if it is wrongly placed—is put upon the offender. Blame is the impotent little brother of vengeance. Blame is not justice; the only true justice lies in forgiveness. The force behind blame is anger, and anger is a dangerous ball of fire. When it is held within, it burns the holder. When it is passed to another, the hands of the wronged are burned.

The anger that seeks to place blame is the root of depression. When this anger of the sufferer is held inward, depression flares up on top of the depression from the sufferer's loss. The anguish from the suffering gets worse and grows into despair—not the philosophical despair of Kierkegaard, but a soul-crushing destruction of the Self. The only way such despair can be assuaged is through acceptance and forgiveness. It takes tremendous courage and strength of self to forgive in the face of pain, but it is the only way. Such strength and courage come from turning to God in effective prayer and meditation.

Many say the worst pain comes from losing a child. This seems to be true. There must be no anguish like losing the warmth and love of a little child. The strong believer knows there will be a joyous reunion in the afterlife, but there is still a vexing fear. It is the "littleness" and helplessness of a child we endear, and if heaven is timeless, we wonder, "Will my lost little one be still recognizable to me?" The worry is speculative, of course, but our notion of the timeless heaven says that there is no age there, so our lost children will not be young; neither will our lost parents be old. What we will "see" in heaven is only what was transcendent on earth and traveled with us in our odyssey. We will "see" only what was good on earth about our lost loved one and nothing that was bad. The transcendent qualities in little children that we feel on earth are the love bonds, the familiarity of their smiles, the warmth of their closeness to us, and their unseen *essences*—perhaps their souls themselves, the mysterious things that allow parents to pick their children out of crowds. We marvel how many animal species can do this, but humans can do it too. It is a transcendent skill—it will be there in the afterlife.

What is there, then, about the littleness of a lost child that pains us so much? It is because the littleness of our children is a replay of our own inner child. We unconsciously remember the nurturing and love of our own childhoods and bask in the joy of seeing it repeated in the smiles of our little ones. When we lose a child, we lose part of ourselves, and this is the pain we feel. There is consolation—ask any parent of grown children. When such parents look into the eyes of a hulking grown man or a beautiful mature woman, they still feel the joy of a little child's smiles. Heaven, in some mysterious way, mirrors this intimacy.

For some whose faith is weak, who have lost a child, parent, or loved one, or for someone suffering the ravages of mental or physical infirmity, consolation may never come. This is when people, in their anguish and despair, blame God. As we'll see, this is a horrible mistake for so many reasons. We must confront and accept our suffering within ourselves, as part of our existence in this *Purgatorio* created by the serpent's lie to Eve in the garden. All suffering ends at the destination of our odyssey—reuniting with lost loved ones, no more infirmity, no more tears, only unimaginable joy where "the lion lies down with the lamb."

Blessed are they who mourn, for they shall be comforted.

—MATTHEW 5:4

VI

Theodicy and Antitheodicy: Do We Need to Defend God?

God has no control over man's free will; most important,
God never sanctions man's evil acts. Evil is strictly a
human enterprise.

—THE OLD PHILOSOPHER

Unde malum, Domine? Lord, why is there evil?
God creates out of nothing. Wonderful you say. Yes, to
be sure, but He does what is still more wonderful: He
makes saints out of sinners.

—SØREN KIERKEGAARD

In spite of our lengthy discussion on the meaning of suffering on earth, we still face the obvious and unanswered question troubling believers: How can an omnipotent, omniscient, and benevolent Creator allow evil and its tragic offspring, suffering, to exist in the world? We left the question behind as unanswerable after some feeble attempts to come up with an answer using human logic and specula-tion. We put our trust in *pious fideism*—faith in God's inscrutable ways. It is a solid course to take but one that leaves many of us wanting and curious. The uneasiness that comes with the question is from our lingering doubts about God's role in suffering and why He doesn't step in and stop our pain. Such doubts left hanging become subtle and unconscious indictments of an innocent God.

We cannot face God holding a grudge.

If we die without answers that satisfy us, our postdeath consciousness may have some uncomfortable questions for God. Facing God with such a doubt of His all-goodness may make our first encounter with heaven awkward and embarrassing, to say the least. It is a problem we need to resolve now in this life, or our spiritual growth toward heaven may suffer. We must deal with the doubt now or deal with it later; it is not going to disappear by itself. If our answer is only that we trust and believe in God no matter what and that there is no answer we can grasp, and if we really believe what we're saying, we will have struck heavenly gold. In such a case, we love God unconditionally. This pious fideism will be enough to settle the matter, and as long as our faith is strong enough to be sincere, God will gladly accept such humility. In fact, we'll see after our laborious discussion that pious fideism and *eschatological hope*—simple faith and trust in God as well as the reassurance that life after death is free of suffering—are the best and least troubling ways to explain the existence of suffering and evil in the world. For many of us, though, they are not enough to settle our grudge with God.

For nonbelievers, the problem is simpler: there is evil in the world; therefore, the God we describe as omnipotent does not exist. Yet, for some believers, the question of why our benevolent and all-powerful God would permit suffering and evil in the world weighs down faith and clouds any defense that might be launched against unbelief in God's existence. Many of us turn to human logic and reason for an answer. The result is centuries of like-minded believers who have felt compelled to defend the Almighty against this vexing paradox of logic. These well-intentioned thinkers are the *theodicists*—those who try to defend God against the indictment of permitting evil and suffering in the world. To many believers, this seems like a good idea. Defending God against this obvious paradox of good allowing evil using human reason and logic seems like something that must be done to silence those who deny God's very existence.

Theodicy is an extraordinarily complex topic. There is no way a few well-intentioned words can do the problem justice. We shall merely skim the surface of what might be considered an ocean of thought and present a few notions that may or may not satisfy our curiosity beyond the reassurance of pious fideism. Our ideas are aimed primarily at suggesting answers to *unde malum*—why God permits evil and woe in His creation.

The *antitheodicists* strongly believe that any attempt to defend God is impossible and even profane. The only answers we are entitled to on this earth are pious fideism and eschatological hope, the message of Job. They correctly believe that a feeble and inadequate defense of an innocent God for the sufferings of man worsens the problem and belittles the suffering of innocents. They also correctly point out that trying to defend God for the evil in the world requires two distasteful assumptions: the first is that God and evil in the world are somehow connected, and the second is that God is not omnipotent after all. The antitheodicists contend that arguments of theodicy are not strong enough to answer the question with certainty, because human logic and reason cannot explain the workings of God. The logic used to defend God makes sense, but the assumptions necessary to complete the logical circuit require God to have human qualities; this is the fallacy of anthropomorphism. The antitheodicists say we should leave the question alone—we should trust God and let pious fideism extinguish our human curiosity.

The antitheodicists who trust God unconditionally know that imparting human traits to God is dangerous territory. Anthropomorphism—making the unknown mirror ourselves—can derail any train of logic and reason we put forth. God is not a He; God is not a She; neither is God an It. God is not even a Being—a being has to have been created, and God has not been created. "God always was, is now and ever shall be" (Catechism 212). God is...well, God. The words in Exodus 3:14 are explicit: "*I AM who I AM.*"

God, then, must be viewed as an unknowable Entity. If we view God as a humanlike, personable kind of guy—not unlike the nice fellow down the street—we then are faced with the notion that God knows things just as we know things. We assume that God "finds out" about human suffering and then makes a decision to do something or not do something. It is how we work; it is a natural process. Our *supernatural* God, however, by the very definition of supernatural must be infinitely more complex. For one thing, ascribing natural and thus physical qualities to God in the face of the vast dimensions of the visible universe—literally trillions of trillions of light-years—creates an anthropomorphic fantasy that God must be *very big*. To human logic, such a notion seems downright silly. Again, God is not big; neither is God small. God simply *is*.

The omniscience of God is transcendent (beyond our understanding) and very different from the immanent data input into our feeble minds—humans "know" things after input through the senses. The data flows to the mind, where it becomes cognition, and the mind then decides to act or not act on the cognition. This series of events in human knowing are governed by, among other things, time—a human construct. But God is timeless. God does not "know" things through any kind of input familiar to us. To us, knowing about something could be considered a "cause," and our decision to act or not act would then be an "effect." By our own definition of God as omnipotent, God is not constrained by cause and effect. The timelessness of God allows us to speculate that God knows all things in all eons (in our time construct) before they occur. To interfere—for example, to prevent bad things from happening—would disrupt the fabric of creation and thus our existence, our sanctification, and ultimately a successful odyssey home. Like the warning to fictional time travelers, that which has not yet happened must be left untouched.

What or Who God is, and how He works or acts, are complete mysteries and will remain so. We can safely assume that the notion of *Deus absconditus* (the hiddenness of God) is somehow part of His plan to get us home with him and is thus for the good of our very salvation. The notion that God has any culpability at all and needs defending is completely based on the human need to follow a certain order consistent with human logic and reason. Is God a common criminal who needs a good lawyer? Modern Christian theodicists recognize this inane image and have scaled back their efforts, concentrating not on arguing whether God is innocent or guilty but on demonstrating that belief in God's existence is perfectly rational in the face of evil. The focus now is on showing that God's existence is not contingent on anything man does, good or evil. Man exists because of God; God exists in spite of man.

Throughout history, there have been countless volumes written about the existence of God and the presence of evil in the world. After the author of Job, thinkers and saints such as Irenaeus, Augustine, Anselm, and Aquinas through writers like Luther, Calvin, Leibniz (who first used the term *theodicy*), Hume, Kant, Teilhard de Chardin, and countless others have wrestled with various forms of theodicy. Secular literature is also replete with the theme from Milton, Pope, Voltaire, Goethe, Tennyson, Dostoyevsky, T. S. Eliot, Camus, and holocaust survivor Elie Wiesel. We shall discuss only a few ideas pertinent to our needs; hopefully, we will be able to face our Creator with complete love and admiration, free of accusatory wonderings. Like polite guests at a buffet, we shall fill our plates only with what we need...but this buffet is really huge.

—⚹—

Deep within every man there lies the dread of being alone in the world, forgotten by God, overlooked among the tremendous household of millions and millions.

—SØREN KIERKEGAARD

Why do we need an answer to a question that may have no answer? It is because we are afraid of being alone in the universe. If God is totally disconnected from the evil in the world as the theodicists say, is He also disconnected from us? Is this why bad things happen to good people? If God is distant from our needs and not up close and personal with us when bad things happen, are we really *that* alone in the cosmos? Is God completely out of touch with us? It is a terrifying notion that seethes with existential angst.

If the opposite is true, that God is up close and personal in our daily lives, then we are thrown back into the circuitous logic of the original question of why God doesn't protect us all the time. Is God really supposed to do this? Some of us think so, because Jesus said, "But the very hairs of your head are all numbered" (Matthew 10:30). The statement really says that God knows of our sufferings and is there, by our side, to comfort us in our pain. His disconnect with evil in the world is intact, but He is fully connected to us in every time of need and pain. He is connected to us in our suffering with the same love that He showed at Calvary.

So, who is right, the theodicists or the antitheodicists? Both are right, as long as their arguments do not infringe on the indisputable fact that an omnipotent and all-loving God exists in the presence of evil in the world, and this same God is always there to comfort and strengthen us in time of suffering. But the ugly paradox of *unde malum* persists.

Three Speculative Answers to Unde Malum

Classic and contemporary religious thinkers have amassed a dozen or so notions that attempt to explain why it is perfectly rational and sane to believe in God's existence in the presence of evil and suffering in the world. Three of these notions shed light on the argument. The first, we've already discussed at length: that evil is an unfortunate side effect of free will; without free will, there can be no true, meaningful love of God. The second includes the obvious pious fideism and eschatological hope: that evil cannot be explained and we must have faith and trust in God that all suffering will end in the afterlife—basically, that the argument cannot be decided in this life and that we shouldn't worry about it, because a better life is coming.

The third notion is the most interesting. It is that there must be another, outside, transcendent force that continually tries to pump evil through the portal of man's free will. For some, this transcendent evil force has no name or persona, but in the Bible, especially in Genesis, Job, the Gospels, and the rest of the New Testament, most notably in Revelation, this transcendent evil force is personified as Satan.

For many, Satan is the logical solution to our problem of *unde malum*. The question remains, however, as to *how* Satan manages to accomplish his evil intent in the presence of God's power and will. Even more pressing is *why* God allows Satan such free rein. To answer these questions, we must change course and look at the creation story in Genesis and the dialogue in Job as allegorical; a fundamentalist or literal interpretation of this scripture cannot support our logical but speculative notion of what really has happened between God and Satan. As we'll see, the events in Revelation need not be considered as completely allegorical; they can be taken as literal to some degree and still support our answers quite well.

We know that Lucifer was a powerful angel with an intimate knowledge of God; in addition to this power, Lucifer, along with the other angels, had the gift of free will—they knew right from wrong and could choose either. Lucifer, along with a band of like-minded angels, chose the sin of pride—in colloquial speech, they got a little too big for their britches. As their pride grew, they felt they no longer needed to bow down before God; their notion of *non serviam* was based on their self-proclaimed equality with the Almighty. This is exactly the temptation that would be later placed before Eve by the serpent in the Garden of Eden: "On the day you eat from it [the forbidden fruit tree], you will be like God" (Genesis 3:5).

The resulting conflict was swiftly dealt with by heavenly forces—Michael and his archangels defeated Lucifer and his minions. God's punishment was just: the rebelling angels were banished out of the realm of God's abode of heaven to a dreary exile in a place called earth. From then forward, Lucifer takes on his true nature as Satan, a fallen angel who has been condemned to "roam about the earth" looking for trouble. This image is embellished in Revelation 12:7–12, which describes the great war in heaven in which Michael the Archangel and his legions fought the "dragon and his angels." *Unde malum* becomes clear in verses 9 and 12: "The serpent of old called the devil and Satan who deceives the whole world, was thrown down to the earth, and his angels were thrown down with him" and "Woe to the earth and the sea, because the devil has come down to you, having great wrath."

Here we must speculate that Lucifer took the newly created but fallen man with him to the exiled outpost of earth. In order for this to have happened, the creation of mankind in the Garden of Eden must have occurred in some place other than earth, perhaps in a physical realm similar to earth but closer to heaven and free of all evil. In this sense, then, mankind was literally kidnapped by Lucifer and his henchmen and taken hostage to this world—a world of disasters, disease, suffering, and, worst of all, the constant presence of Satan. Satan at last had his captive subjects to worship him and reinforce the sick, prideful notion that he is a second god.

Is our beloved earth, then, really a precursor to hell, the place of sulfurous lakes of fire? What about the Second Coming of the Lord, the Rapture, and the Eternal State of the New Jerusalem that scripture tells us will take place on earth? In spite of our natural love for this planet, the earth is not an eschatologically viable place: science tells us with reasonable certainty that in a measurable amount of time—4.7 billion years—the sun will darken. The news is worse for our planet. In less than a billion years, the sun will begin its metamorphosis into a red giant, a dying star that expands as its energy wanes. In this same time frame, the dying sun will have already expanded to engulf Mercury and Venus, with Earth as its next target. In less than five hundred million years, the proximity to the dying sun will render the earth a burned-out cinder incapable of supporting any life at all...perhaps a literal sulfurous lake of fire.

These facts of science seem to create a conundrum about what we read in scripture. The doomsday of our dying sun puts any notion of an Eternal Kingdom on this planet in a very precarious position. Of course, it is perfectly rational that the Rapture and Second Coming of Christ will occur before the end of this earth, but the Eternal Kingdom—the New Jerusalem—will require a more viable option. Scripture resolves this dilemma in Revelation: "And I saw a new heaven and a new earth; for the first heaven and the first earth passed away, and there is no longer any sea" (21:1).

The word "sea" in this verse is a metaphor for all that is evil in this world—from natural disasters and disease, or from the hand of Satan himself. This world is, after all, Satan's realm and place of exile from heaven. This lends credence to our notion that there must be another physical place like this earth—a place closer to heaven or perhaps part of heaven itself, without evil and suffering—where God planted the Garden of Eden,* where He created man, and where He fully intends mankind to end his odyssey.

The "apple" that Adam and Eve ate is simply an allegory for their decision to join Satan's rebellion against God—to become like God and be *non serviam* to God's will. When they were caught, ejected from the heavenly Garden of Eden, and left to roam, suffer, and sweat on the "heavenly earth," they were easy recruits for Satan's exile to this world; assuredly, he lied and promised to return everything they had lost. We can't be sure whether Adam, Eve, and the rest of mankind were forcefully moved to this earth after their ejection from the heavenly garden or were lured by Satan's "apple." Whatever the case, the entire race of mankind became captive hostages of Satan and his minions on this, our beloved earth but future hell. We became immersed in a "sea" of suffering because we were in a place of suffering.

The "kidnapping" of mankind was successful, but our loving Creator was not going to stand by idly and let His beloved children suffer in captivity. Satan set the ransom demand, and God paid it to

---

* In Genesis 2:14, the Garden of Eden is physically placed somewhere in an ancient, lush valley in Mesopotamia between the Tigris and Euphrates Rivers. To the Genesis authors, this lush valley must have seemed like heaven. There was ubiquitous vegetation, a countless number of fruit trees, and water for irrigation; it was a huge oasis in the Arabian Desert. Not knowing of the "other heavenly earth," the writers simply placed the Garden of Eden in the only logical and appropriate spot familiar to them.

set us free. The ransom was steep: Satan demanded that God Himself come to earth and, as a man, be subject to the same temptations plaguing mankind—wealth, power, and immortality. It was Satan's intention to make the God-Man—Jesus Christ—fail at the divine plan for the redemption of mankind; God Himself would be thus vanquished and be forced to bow down before Satan the victor. This temptation is beautifully described in Matthew 4:1–11.

Jesus the Man was strengthened by His divine nature, and through the presence of the Holy Spirit, the "Spirit" in Matthew 4:1, Jesus the Man emphatically put Satan in his place. Although Satan failed at this first attempt to vanquish God's plan to rescue or redeem mankind, Satan still had mankind as hostage. But the presence of God on earth—Jesus Christ—gave mankind another chance after Eden to choose God's way or Satan's way. Jesus mirrored His life on earth exactly as expected of a human, even to the point of taking on the role of a sinner at His baptism in the Jordan. Even though Jesus was sinless, he knelt down and let John baptize Him in the Jordan River in order to show us by example the essence of perfect repentance—"to fulfill all righteousness" (Matthew 3:15). Jesus needed no repentance; He was perfectly obedient to the Father's will—the joys, sorrows, sufferings, and ultimate death were a perfect paradigm to how Man could escape Satan's grasp. The promise of the Resurrection and odyssey back to the "heavenly earth" would be the reward for choosing God's way of living. Such segments of mankind choosing God would be of no use to Satan and his plan to be worshipped as a second god, so such souls would be released from the realm of Satan. Mankind choosing Jesus's way of living would still have to endure the suffering and death of life with Satan but would enjoy a resurrection and escape to eternal life.

When some say that God does not act in the face of evil and our suffering, they are thus completely wrong. The familiar passage in John 3:16 says it all: "For God so loved the world, that He gave His only begotten Son, that whoever believes in Him should not perish, but have eternal life." This notion that God rescues His children from evil and suffering and then returns them to their true home is depicted typologically throughout scripture. There is the familiar story of Moses parting the Red Sea and leading the children of Israel out of enslavement in Egypt around 1400 BC, and then, after wandering in the Sinai desert for forty years, into the Promised Land. The Babylonian Captivity, beginning somewhere around 580 BC, ended with the Jews being allowed to return home, after Babylon was conquered by Cyrus the Great of Persia in 539 BC. In the New Testament, the story of the Prodigal Son in Luke 15:11–24 tells of a son who leaves his father's house—an allegory for the heavenly Garden of Eden and man's fall—and, taken in by the lure and deceit of worldly pleasures, finds terrible suffering; truly penitent, he returns to his father's house, where a loving welcome awaits.

In this our earthly exile, we not only have Jesus's exemplary life to guide us to freedom, but we also have God freely bestowing His grace upon us in times of pain. We Catholics also believe that God has given us free access to Mary, the Mother of Jesus, as well as the saints who can intercede and pray for our safe and successful return home. In the midst of our suffering in this life, God has not forsaken us at all but has given eschatological meaning to our pain. God, always aware of our suffering natural to this earthly exile, has taken our pain and allowed it to strengthen and sanctify our kidnapped souls. Our suffering tempers the desires of our free will to turn away from God and fall victim again to the lure of the world as we did in the Garden of Eden on the "heavenly earth." Without this sanctification, we are doomed to die in this prison; with this sanctification, our escape home is guaranteed.

More Facts of Science and Our Speculative Theory of Unde Malum
In this chapter, we have, in essence, been left with three choices for the answer of why there is evil in the world and why an omnipotent God would permit it. The first choice is the mantra of atheists who claim there is evil because there is no omnipotent God. The second choice is for strong and humble believers who affirm God exists, is indeed omnipotent, and has no hand in the suffering of man. The solution to the paradox of how God and evil can exist is unknowable now and is to be revealed in the afterlife of heaven. Such eschatological hope is fueled by pious fideism. The third choice is our speculation that mankind has been kidnapped from the Garden of Eden to an exile called earth, the realm of an evil third party—Satan—and, as such, is subjected to the sufferings inherent therein. God has allowed this travesty through some kind of cosmic "deal" hatched before time began between God and Lucifer, a fallen angel. God has permitted some suffering because the agreement has demanded it; the makings of this deal are portrayed in the first chapter of Job. God has used the sufferings inflicted on man by Satan as a means to sanctification—the somewhat weak argument of the theodicists called "soul-shaping."

Fundamentalists who hold to the literal interpretation of *sola scriptura* and do not believe in evolution find this third choice perfectly reasonable. The rest of us, however, who believe in the stark reality of science and DNA evidence, must turn away from any literal interpretation of the creation story and accept the allegorical nature of Old Testament stories. Yet such acceptance in no way undermines the feasibility of our theory of a cosmic kidnapping.

Allegory is a reliable literary device used in all forms of art to illustrate complex ideas in understandable ways. It has been used throughout history, including the Genesis story of Sarai and Hagar and the birth of Abram's son Ishmael; the allegorical nature of this event is affirmed by the apostle Paul in Galatians 4:21–24. In Plato's

The Republic, published around 380 BC, the complex notion of conscious awareness of reality is expressed in the Allegory of the Cave. Allegory, then, is the key to understanding the complex symbolism of Adam, Eve, the Garden of Eden, the infamous apple, and, of course, the serpent in the Genesis account of man's beginnings. With this key firmly in hand, we are ready to face the arduous task of reconciling our speculative theory of Satan's role in *unde malum* with new science. Such a task requires enormous speculation approaching fantasy, but we must remember that it is but one theory of many possibilities; the real truth awaits us at the end of our odyssey.

We have seen science tell us the earth is not an eternal place and that there must be a "new earth" at some future time. Science, along with DNA technology, has debunked many other beliefs, and, in our theory of the fall of man, we seem to be facing new theories about man's earliest existence. Controversies abound over which theories are closest to the absolute truth. As such, we have reassurance that clearer guesses are as good as ours, giving license to our speculative story of why there is evil in the world.

We must rely on the allegorical nature of the Genesis account of Adam and Eve in order to reconcile what the Bible tells us about the beginnings of man and what seems to be a rare point of agreement in the many, often conflicting, findings of science and DNA. Clearly, there was not just one Adam; neither was there just one Eve. We have a population of Y-chromosomal Adams from a hundred twenty thousand to a hundred eighty thousand years ago, another population of mitochondrial Eves from ninety-nine thousand to two hundred thousand years ago, and several other hominids from much earlier times arising in East Africa or, according to a conflicting theory, multiple places out of Africa. These early "Adams" and "Eves" produced many offspring of differing subspecies. Natural selection culled out the many, less viable subspecies, and somehow, modern man, *homo sapiens sapiens,* came to be our latest and true ancestor. The *homo sapiens* subspecies lived somewhere on earth starting in the late Pleistocene era around 195,000 years ago; the natural selection of less viable *homo sapiens* subspecies continued as late as 15,000 years ago,* leaving our true ancestor, *homo sapiens sapiens,* as the dominant species. Modern man was a long time coming.

Without succumbing to phylogenetic gobbledygook, we must simplify what is known down to a notion that, at some era in time, perhaps lasting thousands of years, man developed rational thought and cognition sufficient to make a moral choice between good and evil. Newborn man, using his gift of free will, chose evil. Allegorically, Satan convinced Eve to eat the apple of pride and become *non serviam* to God.

What about the Soul?

Then we have the problem of our immortal souls. When did God breathe His perfection into us as He did in Genesis 1:27? Here, we must speculate on a grander scale than before. We know the soul is a perfect creation, made in the image and likeness of God. Such perfection would be made in a perfect place like heaven—the all-perfect abode of God Himself. We must surmise that all the souls of mankind were made at once, awaiting placement in less-than-perfect bodies. We rely on the Augustinian notion that the soul is perfect, but the body is capable of evil. Perhaps it was at this point of soul creation that God and Lucifer had their little chat about man, as depicted in Job 1ff.

Lucifer may have challenged God that His creation wasn't so perfect after all, and when the soul was placed in a less-than-perfect body

---

* The well-known *homo sapiens neanderthalensis*—Neanderthal man—died out about thirty thousand years ago, but surprisingly, DNA from this extinct subspecies has been found in modern individuals.

in a less-than-perfect place called Earth, the soul of man would turn away from God. God agreed to the challenge and only asked that Satan not kill man off. Newborn man's choice to follow Satan and his promises of a godlike existence doomed man to an earthly slavery under the cruel mastery of Satan. The plagues of Job are analogous to the sufferings of mankind, to be endured until a ransom could be paid. Our all-loving God paid the ransom with the life of His only Son, Jesus Christ. The Redemption by Christ's Passion would free mankind from the slavery to evil and its suffering; the Resurrection of Christ was mankind's ticket home.

The earlier hominids, starting with multiple subspecies of *Australopithecus afarensis* from about 3.5 million years ago, were not human in the theological sense; their souls or animating spirits were those of animals—mortal, able to sustain life until death, but not capable of rational, moral decisions. When the pure, or nearly pure, *homo sapiens sapiens* established itself on earth with superior powers of survival, rational thought, and moral choice fifteen thousand years ago, the challenge to God from Lucifer placed the perfectly created souls into new man for the test depicted in the book of Job. Thusly exposed to Satan's worldly lures, mankind as the allegorical Eve succumbed to the allegorical apple—sin. This original sin has kept man captivated by the temptations of the world. Man has been truly kidnapped, but the ransom has been paid by an all-loving God with His own blood.

It is both interesting and ironic that our reconciliatory scenario takes place very close in time to the Genesis story, at least in paleontological dimensions. Our little fantasy story puts man's arrival on earth at fifteen thousand years ago; the Genesis account may be as old as five thousand years.

—⁂—

We have done our best to explain the presence of evil and suffering on earth, blaming Satan and the free will of man while acquitting God of culpability. Our acquittal, of course, is predicated on the firm notion that, while God is all-powerful, He is also all just; He is the ultimate paradigm of honor and justice. And such justice demands that He honor the challenge from Lucifer.

Such anthropomorphism borders on the inane, but it's all we have.

To say that we have simplified the argument is a tremendous understatement, akin to a fifth grader explaining theoretical physics's string theory. The debate as to why there is evil and suffering in this life has been around for a very long time. It started with the book of Job, written sometime in the second millennium BC, and has continued through the church fathers, especially Saint Irenaeus, then to Saint Augustine forward. Science and evolution didn't enter the fray until Darwin in the middle of the nineteenth century, and any attempt at reconciling evolutionary theory with biblical theology was viewed by Christianity as heresy. Then, in the early twentieth century, Pierre Teilhard de Chardin, a Jesuit theologian and paleontologist, started a firestorm of controversy.

Until evolutionary theory became too important to ignore, Teilhard was branded a quasiheretic and was moved around and silenced by the Vatican in order to quell the raging debate over the origin of man and original sin. When DNA technology supported science, the last three popes reexamined Teilhard's work, extolled much of it as revolutionary, and praised his Christology—the role of Jesus as ransom-payer/redeemer for mankind. In a very limited way, our little theories and scenarios about the Bible, science, and the origin of evil have channeled a tiny bit of the enormous volume of his writings. Our speculation that borders on fantasy is just that—speculation. In no way is it intended to rattle anyone's Christian beliefs. It's all been just a well-intentioned theory.

More important, none of it is terribly important to the real truth awaiting us in the afterlife.

What is important is that God created man in the perfect image of God Himself, man had a free will, and man chose evil. The consequences are those of man and man alone. Hopefully, we have, in our own minds, satisfied our grudge against the Almighty Lord and are ready to face Him. We shall do just that in the next section, when we die and find out what happens next.

Part II
Departure and What Happens after We Die

VII

Death: An Inconvenient Necessity

*Look, Paisley, we had some fun times...but all good
things must come to an end.*

—Existentialist sixth grader Olive Doyle to
her friend Paisley Houndstooth in Disney's
A.N.T. Farm TV series

*I'm not afraid of death; I just don't want to be there
when it happens.*

—Woody Allen

*Good night sweet prince:
And flights of angels sing thee to thy rest!*

—William Shakespeare, *Hamlet*

We said in the beginning that this is a book about what happens
after we die, and we quickly narrowed the topic down to a treatise on
individual eschatology and the affirmation that the afterlife, for most
of us, is a joyous experience called heaven. We Catholics, known for

covering all the proverbial bases of moral justice, have added the logical idea of a *final cleansing* called purgatory, based on the obvious fact that some of us are better candidates for a heavenly reward than others. Hundreds of writings have discussed this scary topic, many without mentioning the purgatory thing, but the books that are fun to read tell us we are in for an eternal smorgasbord of our earthly desires. Most, however, seem to overlook two unsettling notions. One is that we have to die first in order to get in, and the second is that each of us may have very different experiences once we arrive. Another notion about heaven that is not unsettling at all but curiously forgotten is that the heavenly experience may begin *right now, in this life.*

The first notion is the most troubling, and when someone we know passes on, we wonder what happens to him or her after that final heartbeat. Where is he or she now? What's left behind in front of us is no happy answer—the cold, lifeless body *looks* like the person we knew and perhaps loved dearly, but something is clearly not there. Those of us who are believers quietly assume that the unseen essence of the good among us will enjoy a mysterious passage—a transcendent journey, so to speak—into a joyous afterlife called heaven. Respectful viewing of the deceased is no place to think about any unpleasant stopover, traditionally held to be a temporary, purgatorial charbroiling to perfection.

We want our dead loved ones to be in a better place, which is an unconscious wish that we also want to be in a better place after we die.

Usually, getting away from our daily routine is fun; it's something we look forward to. This is not the case, however, with our trip to heaven. We who are old and find ourselves standing at the departure gate know very well it's a one-way trip; even worse, we have no idea where we're going or if the accommodations there are comfortable.

We get the sinking feeling this is not the fun trip it's supposed to be—the ticket agent is, after all, a scary figure draped in a black hoodie. What should be the best vacation of all is ruined by not knowing what we're in for and having to die first to get there.

As kids, we heard a lot about heaven but very little about death. In second grade of Catholic school, we learned that the good children—namely, the girls—went up into the clouds to be with Jesus. The bad children—namely, the boys—did not. This was very unsettling for me, as I was not only a boy, but a wiggler and a talker who was often on the receiving end of ominous glares and stern words from Sister Mary Grace for my uncontrollable ebullience. Death might not have seemed like an issue to us boys, but missing out on the meeting-with-Jesus-in-the-clouds thing was. Friday confessions with the monsignor relieved our angst, and, having been cleansed of our evil ways, we could once again look forward to our trip upward.

Having to die before meeting Jesus in the clouds never bothered us much. Dying really wasn't something we little kids thought about unless we had to, and if confronted with the tragic loss of a parent or even a beloved pet, our innocent but pure faith restored our equilibrium. Innocent faith is strong faith, and we believed as absolute truth what we were told about tragic loss—that our beloved merely traveled to another, much better place and that we would be with him or her very soon. Somehow, age brought with it the ugly notion of *cynicism*—a nasty effect of knowing too much that eroded our innocent faith from within, leaving us with the terrifying idea that dying is a last voyage into nothingness.

And so, in this computer age—a time when we expect to know more than we should—we ask more and more, "What happens after we die?" Our curiosity is quite natural: we first want to know if dying hurts, or if it's as peaceful as people say it is; and then we want to know if there is life as we know it now after death. Our clergy and psychologists tell us that such things are matters of faith, and we are circuitously returned to childhood when innocent faith took care of such things. Our interface with the world has weakened our faith, and any answers with certainty seem beyond our reach. Søren Kierkegaard, a nineteenth-century existentialist, reassures us that matters of faith always contain doubt. But modern man does not like doubt and finds it increasingly difficult to trust faith; we seem to know everything else, so why can't we know with absolute certainty what happens after we die?

This seemingly insoluble conundrum drives many of us away from the spiritual growth necessary to strengthen our faith and leaves us empty and nearly hopeless for any conscious reality beyond our final exit. But as we explore this mystery in some detail, we'll see there's a lot of perfectly sound thinking that can reassure us there is life after death and quench our existential angst. It is probably not a place in the clouds, but it is very real, and it is called heaven. Dying, heaven, and the trip there are really not as mysterious and scary as we might think.

Are We Afraid of Dying? Can We Feel Better About What We All Face?

In open conversation, we rarely admit it, but we all are afraid of death. Young people boast that they are not afraid of growing old or dying...until *they* grow old and start dying. It happens to all of us. It is the great equalizer: rich or poor, famous or not, we all face the same final curtain. We squirm and writhe, trying to avoid it. We do live in the silly age of Botox and little-blue-pill rebirth, but every day, the mirror tells us it's happening. Then, one day, the image in the mirror becomes downright scary—*who is that?*—and we ask the familiar question of being old: where did our lives go? Our bodies' machinery seems to be breaking down: we can't see or hear so well, we bump into things more, we can't remember stuff from a few minutes ago, every move brings dull pain, and, like old dogs, we seem to sleep a lot.

The physical side of aging can be quite ugly and frightening, so we ask, *quid nunc?* When we accept the autumn of our lives, when people's smiles have a hint of pity rather than amity, the natural question is, now what? To vanquish the fears of aging and dying, we must first accept them as natural events in our lives.

Why is it we are so afraid of death? For one thing, it is a fear imbued in our very nature. Our physical and emotional structure is custom made for the avoidance of death and for survival. Phylogenetically, we have evolved to survive: walking upright and having a larger brain, forward-facing eyes, keen senses, the ability to reason and process sensory input, and an inherent need for territoriality—all are key components of a strong inner drive to live. We do everything to survive: we work to survive, we play to survive, and through the most advanced gift from creation, we even form bonds of love with others whose ultimate goal is to help us live on with a sense of peace and calm.

Yet we are not afraid of death as much as we are afraid of dying—or, better put, *dying badly*. Fears about *how* we die have been around for a long time. Throughout the ages, mankind has exploited this fear, attempting to dominate and control others, and has engineered innovative and horrible ways to inflict death—the sadism of ancient but supposedly civilized cultures, the engines of war that kill large numbers of us at once, and the proliferation of portable but sophisticated weaponry that is easily acquired by the most unstable of us. From ancient societies onward, political regimes bent on preserving order have made killing into an art form: executions of criminals have purposely been gruesome and public in order to preserve social obedience. The Phoenicians knew this well; indeed, they invented crucifixion.

Since we all face death, we wish for a peaceful and painless pass-ing and, more important, we want to leave this earth with our bodies whole. Our disdain for our mortality is manifested in many Western funeral practices, where our deceased loved ones are made up and dressed up to appear as if they've fallen asleep on the way to a dinner party. The intended effect of such practice is to assist in the grieving process—to say good-bye to the lost loved one as we knew him or her in life. These postmortem antics, however, have the unfortunate effect of reinforcing our denial about what really happens when we die. Yet we persist in our denial. We just want to fall asleep and lie in peaceful repose—exactly what we see when we gaze down at an open casket.

For most of us, sleep is a peaceful thing, and this gives us com-fort about dying. The New Testament writers use the term "falling asleep" when referring to the death of the faithful; the Greek term used is *koimao*. The passing of the Blessed Virgin Mary, the Mother of Jesus, "assumed" into heaven body and soul, is called her "dor-mition," or death that resembles falling asleep. But Mary did not die—her sinless state spared her from the sentence of death earned by Adam and Eve in the Garden of Eden, so a more correct term for her passing is the Greek word *koimesis*—literally, "lying in repose," without death. Historically, then, falling asleep is a blessing for our last exit, and dying badly is something to be avoided.

We can get some relief from the statistics of dying. The vast major-ity of us die from *senescence*—we just get old and die from a host of medical failures associated with aging. We do, literally, fall asleep. In developed countries, well over 90 percent of us die from senescence; in poorer countries, the percentage is lower, with infectious disease and the lack of proper medical care leading senescence by a third. So, most of us can look forward to a peaceful end: our *koimao* will be painless and uneventful, and our bodies whole.

Our advancing technology and unstable world politics, however, have exposed us to a greater risk of a violent end, an end where we do not die in peaceful sleep or with our bodies whole. Modern travel, terrorism, mass killings, and an increase in mental instability in society have all put us at risk for violent deaths with physical obliteration. Is such a horrible fate the end of our desire for a peaceful afterlife? Do we need to be whole and "look good" at death in order to get into heaven?

Of course not. For one thing, the earthly shell we see sleeping peacefully and looking so good in the casket begins to disintegrate a few minutes after its death. Within a half hour of our last breath, ordinary houseflies up to a mile away know by smell about our demise and begin the journey to find our "sleeping" bodies—hopefully a source of nutrition for maggots, their developing offspring. The decay of death is a natural thing; the sole traveler in our odyssey into heaven is the soul, the essence of our being—the part of us we cannot see and the flies cannot smell.

Sadly, our bodies as we have them now will not be making the trip.

This is a most disturbing notion. Yet the words *terra es, terram ibis** ring in our ears at the beginning of each Lenten season. Our trip into the afterlife, supposedly a state of great joy and peace, suddenly becomes worrisome. No body? Few of us have bodies we're totally happy with, but still, our bodies are *us*. They're what we see and feel. How can we be anything without our bodies? Yet we know our bodies decompose after we die; exhumations show us what is left behind, often fragments of bone and dust...*terram ibis*, indeed.

Fear of such a fate for our beloved bodies makes us shut our eyes and avoid facing the temporality of our existence. It is one reason

---

* Declared to penitents on Ash Wednesday when receiving ashes in the form of a cross on the forehead: "Thou art dust, and dust thou shall be."

we avoid talking about death. Our references to death when talking with others are slathered over with polite euphemisms: "He passed." Passed what?

This denial can be counterproductive and even destructive. It seems to hinder our quest for the spiritual growth necessary to experience real joy here and to strengthen our faith about heaven. Deep down, we don't want to die, but if we must, we want *some kind* of body after we die. We all hope the afterlife is a familiar, physical place of beauty and peace, free from the ravages of time—no Botox or blue pills up in the clouds. We want heaven to be Earth 2.0. Each of us wants a "super body" to transport our consciousness effortlessly throughout whatever dimension of pure joy awaits us. To those of us with age-worn, broken, or defective bodies, the desire for a heavenly super body makes perfect sense. In the next life, however, it's obvious that such a body will be under the complete control of the soul—exactly the opposite of how it is now—because the soul is the only part of us that will live on past death's door, and because our souls' true power will be released in the presence of God and out of the grasp of worldly desires.

Since it is our souls that will be the masters of our new bodies in the afterlife, how well we condition our souls on this earth by growing spiritually may very well determine how super our new, heavenly bodies will be. Hopefully the idea of spending eternity in a physically perfect state can assuage our fears about the *terram ibis* thing. Suddenly, dying isn't so scary anymore.

But how certain can we be that this is true?

The Gifts of Maturity: Wisdom and Faith Give Us Power over the Unknown

Knowledge is different from wisdom. At the simplest level, knowledge, as we understand it, only comes with experience through our senses. If we can see it, hear it, smell it, taste it, or touch it, we can accept with certainty that something is real, and everything we experience about something is true. This is the mantra of science, and, as we discussed at some length before, it is called empiricism. Wisdom takes empirical knowledge and subjects it to human reason and faith, and this deeper, more profound awareness enables us to formulate images of and amass knowledge about things beyond experience. Wisdom helps us to know the supposedly unknowable—it reassures us that truths not only *exist* outside of what we can see and prove by science, but that we can *know* a good deal about such truths.

Atheists and agnostics are card-carrying empiricists; atheists staunchly insist that nothing exists—particularly God and heaven—unless we can experience it with our senses, or science can prove it. Agnostics are a bit softer; they admit that there may be reality beyond our senses and science but indicate that we cannot know it or accept it as truth until it is experienced. Both these cynical bedfellows seem to overlook the glaring truth that science and our senses can be fooled into falsehood, a fact that has played out hundreds of times over mankind's existence. On the simplest level, magicians throughout the ages have made their living fooling our sensory awareness. Science has likewise been duped. Six hundred years ago, we all accepted as truth that the earth was flat, that the sun revolved around the earth, that disease was caused by bad vapors, and that we could easily see and touch the smallest particle of matter. The list of empirical blunders about the truth is nearly endless. Granted, science has corrected its mistakes with more complex empirical methods, but science is still not infallible, only busier.

There is obviously truth beyond our senses, and this is where *wisdom* vanquishes ordinary knowledge. We normally think that wisdom is a perk of being old, but this is not necessarily true. Young people who have developed maturity beyond their years can possess greater wisdom than others of any age. Such maturity among the young is a rare gem, however. Most young folks, products of this computer age of empirical knowledge, disdain matters of faith. They seek to amass facts to support their immediate wants and needs of self-gratification, self-aggrandizement, and sophomoric pretentiousness among their peers, to the detriment of a faith-guided life. They are truly missing out on the wonders and mysteries of the beyond.

Those with knowledge are in awe of how much they know; those with wisdom are in awe of how much they don't know.

Wisdom and the faith it engenders allow us to carefully observe the mechanisms of life over time and marvel at that which seems impossible. If we are to ponder the question of what happens to us after we die, we must have the faith to look to and believe what is beyond our senses. Such faith, along with human reason, allows us to look at the complexity and perfection of the world and man himself and correctly conclude that such intricacy could not possibly fall into place by mere coincidence and chance. The stronger our faith, the more we can believe in miracles. We can grasp and accept that serendipity and coincidence simply cannot explain everything. As our faith in the unseen strengthens, we begin to believe and know that reality and truth far transcend what we can see and touch. Kierkegaard may have been wrong about doubt and matters of faith. Knowing with certainty about what happens after we die may be a truth closer than we think. Human reason is stronger than human doubt. Or, as Hamlet put it, "There are more things in heaven and earth, Horatio, than are dreamt of in your philosophy" (*Hamlet*, act 1, scene 5).

If we believe what the Danish prince is saying to Horatio, we can proceed with some seriously educated speculation on what is next in our odyssey.

VIII

Heaven: A Picture of the Afterlife

Eye has not seen nor ear heard...all that God has prepared for those who love Him.

—1 CORINTHIANS 2:9

As we begin this attempt to create an image of what heaven will be like—a physical place, a spiritual realm, both, or neither—we must also consider what our resurrected "bodies" will be like, since we believe that our immortal souls will be united with new and imperishable bodies (Catechism 999). As we proceed, we'll encounter a lot of roadblocks as well as forks in the road that go nowhere. Some of the answers to our questions will be wild, speculative guesses. By the very nature of the topic, we will not be able to see with absolute certainty that which is invisible and exists in the unknown future. Yet, logic, reason, and revelation will allow us to reach a conclusion—a conclusion tainted by speculation and guesswork, but a conclusion nonetheless.

We will see with some frustration that our sources of transcendent knowledge—scripture, the Catechism, and the Councils of the Church—confuse us with ambiguous phraseology and paradoxes, but it is no fault of theirs. It is our language that lacks the power to convey the truth about the afterlife. After a great deal of circuitous logic, we'll see that heaven and our bodies in the afterlife will have both physical and spiritual characteristics. The exact nature of this combination is a deep mystery, but the truth uncovered will hopefully be sufficient to satisfy our existential curiosity.

Why are we subjecting ourselves to exploring this confusing and transcendent mystery? We want to firmly establish that an odyssey into heaven is a really, really great way to follow our death. More importantly, we want to understand and accept that making heaven truly heavenly starts with changing key aspects of our earthly lives to be more…well, heavenly.

Is There a Heaven? The Mystery of Individual Eschatology

Eschatology is a theological term that comes from the Greek *eschatos*, translated as "final"; the suffix *-logy* means "the study of." It is a broad area concerned with what happens at the end of the world, when and how that happens, and theological events involving man's existence. Our concern is *individual* eschatology. We want to know about our personal fates; we want solid, reliable answers to some very vexing questions: What is going to happen to my conscious self after I die? Does life as I know it now exist after my death? Will life be better? Will all suffering end? Will all my unfulfilled earthly wishes be granted in heaven?

Our definitions of the terms *transcendent* and *immanent* tell us that immanent words cannot be used to accurately describe the transcendent, especially God and heaven. Yet, paradoxically, that is exactly what we are attempting to do; we have no choice. But we can manipulate our immanent descriptions to form a hazy image of what the afterlife might be like. Immanent terms are words describing things that we've experienced (or someone else claims to have experienced), but can we say with absolute certainty that heaven is up in the clouds, at the edge of the universe, or even in a blinding, white light at the end of a tunnel? Heaven may be all these things or none of them. We just can't be sure, if we rely solely on our experiences thus far—that is, immanent proof.

Of late, however, a new immanent proof has made its appearance. We may have come close to an empirical description of what happens after we die that seems credible. There have been many reports of near-death experiences (NDEs), where individuals, mostly reliable and sincere, have been declared dead and resuscitated back to consciousness. Upon awakening, they have given eerily similar accounts of conscious thoughts and "visions" of out-of-body existence—floating down a tunnel toward a white light, meeting lost loved ones and sometimes Jesus Himself—along with an overwhelming sense of peace and calm. In some cases, these accounts have been consistent across cultural boundaries, and they have been frequent and compelling enough to spur serious scientific inquiry into their validity. Unfortunately, thus far, scientific and peer-reviewed research has shown these events to be immanent phenomena of the dying brain and *not* transcendent visions.* The universal nature of the phenomena cannot be denied, however, and the exciting possibilities of such occurrences must be studied further. Until more evidence arises, we must rely on scripture to tell us what we cannot see, because sadly, the fact remains that *the immanent cannot prove the transcendent; we cannot see what we cannot see.*

Before we try to visualize what heaven might or might not be like, we face a far more basic question: Is there a heaven? Since heaven is transcendent (we can't see it), knowing if heaven exists requires transcendent knowledge. As we said, our sources of transcendent knowledge in this life are faith, reason and its tool logic, and revelation. For

---

* Peer-reviewed research is the gold standard for scientific exploration. The methods and results of research papers are scrutinized for any detail of fallacy by other established researchers in that field of study. Every research paper published in legitimate scientific journals must pass "peer review."

this basic question, we only need revelation. For some reason, many of us living in this modern age resist accepting the certainty of our sources and insist on immanent proof of heaven's existence, beyond what scripture tells us. We want to see it. Our skepticism is perfectly natural; it is easier to believe what we can see than to believe ancient written words.

For all believers, however, the absolute truth of heaven's existence and what happens after we die can be clearly seen in two simple premises. The first is that God Himself said so; the second is that Jesus Christ acted out in real time exactly what happens to us when we live and what happens to us after we die. It could not be any plainer.

God Says Heaven Exists

We have another tool that can bring some certainty into focus, and that tool is the absolute truth of God's word. There are at least five hundred references to heaven or phrases that implicitly denote an afterlife of joy in both the Old and New Testaments of every Bible. Even if we believe the Bible is better interpreted by theologians, scholars, and trained clergy, the presence of so many literal references is compelling evidence that heaven does indeed exist. "Let not your hearts be troubled or afraid…in My Father's house are many dwelling places" (John 14:1). Equally compelling is the account of Jesus's Transfiguration on Mount Tabor in Matthew 17:1–11. The event is not a metaphysical hallucination, but scholars agree it is the one instance in the New Testament, other than the actual Incarnation, where heaven *physically* touches earth. If we don't believe in God or the transcendent origin of scripture, the issue of the existence of heaven is totally irrelevant. If we live our lives as if death is really the end of our existences and the beginning of a black nothingness, then the questions we ask are meaningless.

Jesus Christ Acted Out the Answers to Our Questions for Us

Here, the proof of the existence of heaven arises from our reason and logic acting on the revelation of scripture. If we follow Jesus's life in its entirety from His poverty-ridden birth in a cave to His Ascension into heaven, we see that it was God's intent to have Jesus mirror our lives in every detail (minus the sin, of course). It was critical for the divine Jesus to also be a *fully human* Jesus for the Redemption of mankind to be valid and acceptable to the Father, "to fulfill all righteousness" (Matthew 3:15). It was, after all, man's sin that had necessitated the Redemption. The Lord's humanity was indeed complete: He was born dirt poor without any immanent treasures. He was baptized (He acknowledged being a sinner in need of repentance—even though He wasn't a sinner); He worked hard all His life for God's plan without immanent reward; He made friends and socialized, ate and drank, and even partied and danced (at the wedding at Cana). In addition, many less important details were not written down: "And there are also many other things that Jesus did, which if they were written in detail, I suppose that even the world itself could not contain the books which were written" (John 21:25).

Throughout His life, especially at the end, He suffered humiliation, rejection and pain, and ultimately death, clearly mirroring our own suffering lives. If we fear that death is the end, what about His Resurrection and Ascension into heaven? We must assume that such a perfect imitation of our lives would include the power over death for the faithful and a return to heaven. Reverend Charles Stanley, echoing Aquinas, asserts this notion: "If God imitated everything in earthly life, especially suffering, it makes perfect sense that He would include the truth of the Resurrection." In addition to this logical conclusion, we should consider another, less obvious point. If we fear that death is the end of earth's good times, if we truly believe this life is some sort of epitome of happiness and fulfillment, why wouldn't Jesus have stayed longer? He was, after all, the King of Kings, Lord and Master of the universe; He would certainly have had the power to possess and enjoy everything imaginable, even if He had wanted to fast-forward time to live in some future utopia full of technological miracles. But He chose to go back to heaven. Heaven must certainly be better than anything that exists or might exist in the future on this earth.

So, our worries that heaven doesn't exist can be put to rest. Now we want details about what happens after we get there. Our conclusions about what heaven is and what heaven is not as well as the nature of our new bodies in the afterlife will require that we sift through the some-times-confusing verbiage of scripture and the Catechism of the Catholic Church, but we must first deal with the paradoxical notion that some of us may have very different experiences in the afterlife than others.

Do We Really Want to Go?

Before we discuss what heaven is like, we need to address the paradoxi-cal notion that some of us may not want to go, or, better put, some of us may find certain aspects of heaven less than pleasant. How could this be? Isn't heaven a place of extreme ecstasy for everyone? The answer lies in the possibility that heaven may be very different for some of us than others; the deciding factor may be how well we have acclimated ourselves to the values inherent in heavenly life. Our souls are the travelers on this odyssey, and how well we condition our souls to the values and lifestyles of heaven may determine how heavenly heaven will be. Heaven is a state of perfect holiness—sanctification—and it doesn't take a lot of reflection to see that these modern times have pulled us away from the values inherent in holiness. It is holiness that is the normal agenda in heaven, not worldliness.

What are the values and lifestyles of God's Kingdom? Sancti-fication is a lifelong growth process that pulls us away from atti-tudes, behaviors, and beliefs in this life that we erroneously think are important. Gradually, we learn that heaven's way is very different from the world's way. At times, the growth process is painful, but the results—gradual but clear changes in ourselves—accustom us to what life will be like after we die. Our earthly lives will slowly become heavenly. We will be happy right here on earth, making heaven a very familiar and peaceful place.

Another word for happy is *blessed*; it is the first word of the beloved verses of Matthew 5:1–12 known as the Beatitudes. These are not commands, but are clear-cut descriptions of what life in the heavenly realm will be like. As we'll see later in some detail, the verses describe a very different lifestyle from the one we know now in these modern times. Gone will be self-centered and selfish ways, gone will be vengeance, gone will be the hatred and intolerance, gone will be the self-deception of the arrogant, and gone will be our human tendency to maintain contentious postures, fight with others, and ultimately wage wars that kill so many of us.

We live in an era of technology that gives us a tragic path to hatred. Our intolerance and merciless speech—two bastard children of hate itself—shackle us to this world of suffering and tears. Hate cannot exist in the heavenly heart. If we fail to rid ourselves of this scourge, heaven—if we find ourselves there at all—may be a most uncomfortable and merciless place to spend the afterlife. Hatred is a slap in the face of the suffering Christ, a pounding on of the piercing nails of Calvary; it is the sin of sins, while considered by many to not be a sin at all. So, for many, even those of us considered to be moral in the sense of following the commandments etched in the stone tablets, heaven might not be a place we want to go, *unless we change how we live our lives here and now.*

Incomplete sanctification—holding on to distinctly un-Godlike attitudes and behaviors—is going to be a big problem the moment we die.* We can complete our sanctification now by learning the lost

---

* As we said, the Catholic Church handles the question of incomplete sanctification at death with the notion of purgatory (Catechism 1030). Souls that have obeyed the written rules but lack the sanctification necessary for heaven undergo a final

art of kindness, changing our attitudes toward status and material treasures, learning the saintliness of being gentle souls, and, most importantly, by truly accepting that the pillars of real love are mercy, forgiveness, and tolerance toward our fellow travelers.

So, What Is Heaven Like?

*In Himmel gibt's kein Bier, drum trinken wir es hier.**

Siegel and Neubach

My personal quest to learn what heaven was all about began at a very early age. The Internet was light-years away, so I asked my father, a quiet and proper man, about it. When I was seven years old and had two years of Catholic education under my belt, I asked him what heaven would be like. He said he didn't know and that he too wondered. After a pause, he sighed and said he wondered if there would be golf courses "up there." I didn't push the question any further; I was left wondering what golf courses had to do with heaven. In first and second grade, the nuns left me thinking that heaven was a place where the good children went after they died; bad kids like me—impulsive and outspoken—ended up in the "other place." By the time I finished Catholic high school, I was ready to give up; the lure of the flesh had convinced me that hell had a special niche waiting just for me. But in college, soporific Jesuit

---

purification after death but before heaven. While it is not the hellfire-like cleansing of our souls as many of us have been taught, it is still a state to be avoided. We can do this by living our lives full of heavenly values now and conditioning our souls for the heavenly realm through the spiritual growth afforded by effective prayer and meditation. We will discuss purgatory in greater detail later.

* "In heaven there is no beer; that's why we drink it here." From a German song by Ralph Siegel and Ernst Neubach about the existential pleasure of drinking beer.

philosophy classes almost convinced me that the "other place" didn't exist as we feared, and heaven was some sort of ethereal and existential spiritual state where we all ended up. Understandably, this disturbed me. I wanted to know if there were *girls* in heaven, but I was left with the possibility of being a floating ghost for all eternity. It was not a pleasant idea for a libidinous twenty-year-old virgin.

I was not alone in my curiosity. Having some idea about what happens after we die would certainly take the edge off dying. Literally hundreds of scholars have debated this question over the centuries, starting with the ancient Greeks, the Eastern mystics, the early Church fathers, Saint Augustine, Saint Thomas Aquinas, the authors of the Catholic Catechism, many Reformist biblical scholars, and the latest, Pope Saint John Paul II. All their scholarship and intellectual wondering funneled down to the very same question my father had: Is there golf in heaven? At the risk of being sacrilegious, I suppose we should add beer and sex to the wonder pile.

People in general all want their own version of golf in heaven; the thought that we might not get our way leaves us less than enthused about heavenly life. It does beat the other possibilities, but we place such deep mysteries onto the back burners of our conscious thoughts. We do this because we just don't know for certain what happens after we die. We know what makes us happy here and now, and we want that never to end—we want heaven to be heavenly, *but really earthly too*. It's natural that my father would find wearing angel's wings, carrying a harp, and walking up in the clouds a lot less inviting than dropping a six-iron shot a foot from the pin surrounded by his friends, beautiful landscape, babbling creeks, sunshine, and, of course, a cold brew. Huckleberry Finn would totally agree.[*]

---

[*] After Miss Watson and the Widow Douglas convince Huck that all that he cherishes in life—including Tom Sawyer—would not be in heaven, Huck says, "OK, then I'll go to hell."

As I grew older, past my father's years, his question-answer got louder and louder in my ears; as I approached my own moment of departure, it was time to find an answer. There were three things I was pretty sure of: One, heaven exists and death is not the final event in our consciousness. Two, heaven—no matter what the details are about life there—is inconceivably better than we can ever imagine: "The eye has not seen, nor the ear heard" (1 Corinthians 2:9). The third is that all of us will be somehow different from our earthly forms: "We shall be changed" (1 Corinthians 15:51). We'll see that this last statement disturbs us the most. Yet these three truths alone should be enough to satisfy us for now and assuage our fears of death. We must rely on pious fideism—goodly trust and belief that it's God business and not ours. It is a humbling potion to swallow, and it does not satisfy our existential angst. We are not a humble species.

So we push forward, bent on knowing the unknowable. Trying to create a detailed image of the transcendent is like trying to picture a one-ended stick. Logically, we know such a fluke could exist; we just can't picture it. Like the mathematical concept of infinity, we can use it in equations, but our limited intellect draws a blank when we try to describe it in real terms.

Trying to know the unknowable is not a new thing. An anecdote about Saint Augustine walking along the seashore one day describes him meditating on the mystery of the Holy Trinity, trying desperately to understand It. The story goes that he comes upon a small child with a seashell. The child is carrying water from the sea and pouring it into a small hole in the nearby sand. Augustine asks him what he is doing so earnestly. The child replies, "I'm trying to fill this hole with all the water in the sea." Augustine replied, "It's impossible. You can't fit all the water of the sea into that small hole." The child snapped back, "It's no more impossible than what you are trying to do—to comprehend the immensity of God with your small intellect." The child, of course, was an angel, who promptly disappeared. To this day, the seashell is an image associated with Saint Augustine and his philosophy. The lesson from this story is that pride often stands in the way of simple faith—pious fideism.

But, pride be damned, we still want to know.

The unseen heaven may be—and I emphasize *may* be—very different from what we're used to: everyday things in this immanent (worldly) life may or may not exist in heaven, or if they do exist there, they may be radically different. On this earth, we have arms, legs, eyes, and ears because survival in this realm requires them. It is somewhat unsettling to think about, but virtually everything we have and experience here on earth may not be necessary in heaven and therefore might not exist. Surely, everything we need to thrive in the new realm of the afterlife will be provided and will no doubt be a lot better than what we have now, but facing something very different is not easy for us.

We are not creatures of change. We like what is familiar. We expect things to be a certain way, and when they are, we somehow feel safe and secure. We prefer the company of friends over strangers, we travel the same routes to a destination, and we hold on to lifelong beliefs, even though they may be wrong, because they have become part of us. We sometimes curse routine—we even take vacations to escape it—but it is our security blanket. We always return to what is familiar: our friends and loved ones, our employment, our play activities, our bedtimes, our meal preferences, our clothing styles, our news and entertainment TV shows, and even our supermarkets—items we want are where we expect them to be. Routine and familiarity are lairs of safety and security, safe rooms where we can survive free of worldly predation.

Since we want what is familiar, it makes perfect sense that our ideal for the afterlife would be a heaven exactly like earth, a *physical place*, but without the bad stuff: sin, aging, disease, sadness, or suffering. In such a realm, everything we enjoyed on earth along with everything we weren't able to enjoy would be waiting for us in heaven. The Catholic Catechism (1024) says heaven is "the ultimate end and fulfilment of the deepest human longings, the state of supreme definitive happiness," so this notion seems perfectly logical. It seems illogical that God would create this world as such a complex physical realm and then make heaven something completely different.

For some, the notion that heaven is *not* like earth is a deal breaker. There is the story of a devout woman in a Bible-study class where the topic was a description of heaven. The study leader was not careful with his words and said that heaven was definitely not a physical place but a spiritual state of ecstasy for our souls. The woman was so upset at this that she left the Bible study and never went back to church. She wanted to meet her lost loved ones again, and she wanted heaven to be familiar place where everything wrong with her life would be fixed. Her feelings were perfectly understandable.

Thoughts of heaven as a perfect, earthlike physical place that lasts for eternity dance in our heads and leave us hoping. When we interpret the Catechism's descriptive phrase "deepest human longings" as the answer to our earthly wish fulfillment, we feel some relief about having to die. We expect there to be people we knew or wanted to know but without any irritating traits; lost loved ones perfected from all bad immanence, there to touch and hug; unlimited food and drink without health worries; music, literature, and art there to enjoy with the complete understanding we never had on earth; and no worries about money, children, war, sickness, or death.

Sadly, the logistics of a perfectly earthlike heaven filled with billions—perhaps trillions—of resurrected but revamped, purely physical bodies seems unrealistic. But if we think more about what our resurrected bodies will be like in the afterlife, we might see a better image of what heaven itself will be. The Fourth Lateran Council of AD 1215 and the Catechism of the Catholic Church describe our bodies in the afterlife: "all of them will rise again with their own bodies which they now bear..." (999). Unfortunately, the matter is not as straightforward and reassuring as it sounds; the second half of the above quotation is "but Christ will change our lowly body to be like His glorious body, into a spiritual body." Could this mean that we will be floating ghosts in a purely spiritual realm for all eternity, or could we have both physical and spiritual characteristics in heaven? If the latter is true, then heaven must have some sort of physical structure to hold our new "polymorphic" bodies. Saint Thomas Aquinas, though, adds to the confusion: "Incorporeal things are not in place after a manner known and familiar to us, in which way we say that bodies are properly in place; but they are in place after a manner befitting spiritual substances, a manner that cannot be fully manifest to us" (*Summa Theologiae*, Supplement to Part III, question 69).

During a General Audience in July of 1999, Pope Saint John Paul II modified and expanded Aquinas's statement on heaven as a familiar place: "The language of '*place*' is inadequate to describe the realities involved, since it is tied to the temporal order in which this world and we exist." The pope said later that heaven "is neither an abstraction nor a physical place in the clouds, but a living, personal relationship with the Holy Trinity." In this last sentence, the Holy Father said heaven is not a figment of our imaginations—that is, a really super mental phantasm existing only in our minds—nor is it a state of walking about the clouds in fluffy white stuff, carrying harps and wearing oversized angel wings. We must be very careful in interpreting these words. It sounds as if these two very learned men were dancing around a truth they could not pin down. *They didn't know for sure either.*

What Can the Nature of Our Resurrected Bodies Tell Us About Heaven?

From the ancient Greeks forward, there have been dozens of differing theories about the soul and a body in the afterlife, and the arguments have been sometimes vehement—and diametrically opposed. Some say neither the soul nor the body is immortal, and both are gone forever at death. Most say the soul is immortal and exists after death, but they differ greatly as to whether the body, the earthly flesh we know, is resurrected in some way. Saint Augustine, who before his conversion lived a dissolute life controlled by the flesh, vehemently condemned any idea that a heavenly body could consist of resurrected earthly flesh, apparently because the perfection of heaven would be no place for a body capable of terrible sin. He would certainly know about such activities. So, our earthly bodies as we know them would have to be somehow changed. This is exactly what the Catechism and the Fourth Lateran Council say about the matter.

Scripture gives us clues, though, that point to some type of physical environment for our resurrected bodies. In John 14:2, Jesus consoles the apostles about His impending death: "In my Father's house there are many dwelling places." In some Bibles, the term for "dwelling places" is also translated as "mansions," "houses," or "abodes." It is unlikely that spiritual beings lacking physical matter would need specific dwelling places; ghosts would have no use for fancy condos. Some could argue, though, that this passage, along with John 14:23 ("My Father and I will come...and make Our abode with him"), is an allegory for heaven to be a state of perfect union with God and not necessarily denoting physical being. Still, these passages are compelling, and we must take Jesus's words in some literal sense.

The case for having some type of physical body requiring a physical environment can be strengthened with two dogmatic facts: Jesus's Ascension and His mother's Assumption into heaven. Jesus ascended into heaven from Mount Olivet in the same resurrected body seen and recognized by several hundred people over forty days after the Resurrection. During this period, Jesus walked, preached, socialized, ate, and even retained the scars of the Passion in order to reassure the disciples that he was not a ghost (Luke 24:41). Furthermore, two angels at His Ascension reassured the people there that Jesus would return in the same body at His Second Coming: "This same Jesus... will return in the same way..." (Acts 1:9–11). It seems unlikely that Jesus would become a ghostly phantasm upon reaching heaven but keep His earthly "cloak" at the ready for the Day of Judgment.

Or is it?

Since the Blessed Virgin Mary was born sinless, she was exempted from death, the price of sin owed by all of us (Romans 5:12), and the Church refers to the end of her life as her "falling asleep" or *koimesis*. In the Assumption, Mary was "assumed" into heaven, body and soul; the force behind this doctrine is not just her sinless state but the fact that she physically carried Jesus, and, as such, was the "Ark of the New Covenant." The Ark of the Old Covenant was so important to the history of God's chosen people that it was taken into heaven (Revelation 11:19); the old ark in its earthly role contained, among other things, a jar of the manna, the bread from God that saved the Jews wandering in the desert (Exodus 16:1–36). Mary, as Ark of the New Covenant, physically carried Jesus, the new manna from heaven. Jesus asserted this several times—"I am the bread of life" (John 6:48)—in His Eucharistic discourse. So, as the Old Ark was assumed into heaven physically intact, so was the New Ark, Mary; it was her earthly body that carried Jesus, not a glorified phantasm.

The notion that Jesus and His mother are the only two physical entities in heaven while God the Father and everyone and everything else lack physical matter seems untenable. Heaven is clearly some kind of glorified physical and spiritual state. Could Mary, like Jesus, possibly change back and forth from a glorified spiritual state to a glorified physical state as conditions (and locations) demand? Will we be able to?

A really good guess is yes.

So we sigh with relief that we will have some sort of physical existence in heaven, but the troublesome last few words of the Catechism's entry on the glorified body persists: "Our lowly earthly bodies will be changed...into a spiritual body" (999). This phrase does not necessarily mean we're going to be ghosts in heaven. It means our changed heavenly bodies will have supernatural characteristics and powers similar to those of Jesus during the forty days *after* He was raised from the dead. As we said, Jesus did many things in His resurrected, glorified body that were perfectly immanent (earthly)—he walked around, talked, was recognizable as Jesus, and, on two occasions, ate food (Luke 24:41ff and John 21:12ff). However, He also demonstrated the power of transcendence over immanence, being able to walk through solid, locked doors (John 20:19), being able to change His physical appearance and ultimately vanish into thin air (Luke 24:16ff), and perhaps being able to be multilocational (to be in several places at once). He also filled the apostles' fishing nets with 153 large fish after a night where they caught nothing (John 21:11ff).*

Jesus's daily activities after the Resurrection, then, give us a clue about what our glorified bodies might be like. As we said, they could look perfectly normal except that a body patterned after Jesus's post-Resurrection body would have the supernatural powers we just

---

* The significance of the number 153 in John 21:11 has been debated. The simplest explanation is that Peter took the time to count them. A great miracle was performed, and Peter wasted time counting his immanent treasure as the transcendent, glorified Christ waited patiently? As Kenny Rogers would sing twenty centuries later, "You never count your money when you're sitting at the table."

mentioned. Heaven would have to be more of a physical than spiritual realm in order to support such a body. Would heaven have gravity, an atmosphere, unlimited food and water, cities as well as open countryside, and even transportation vehicles? Did the post-Resurrection Jesus really need the things he used during His forty days of final preaching: food and drink and a normal-appearing body? Or did He disguise His appearance to reassure His followers that it was the crucified Jesus before them and not a ghost (Luke 24:37–43)?

Another clue from scripture shows a very different Jesus from the meandering, eating, and drinking Savior in the forty days after His Resurrection. In the sixteenth chapter of Matthew, we see the apostles gathered together after witnessing Jesus miraculously feeding five thousand men, not counting women and children, from just a few loaves and fish. Jesus asked them, "Who do you say that I am?" After seeing such a miracle, Peter was confident in answering, "Thou art the Christ (Messiah)." But to a first-century Jew, the Messiah would be a political savior, and Peter assumed that Jesus would miraculously produce a massive army to drive out the Romans just as easily as He had produced food for so many from virtually nothing. Then the Kingdom of Israel would be restored with Jesus as King and perhaps the apostles as governors of the twelve tribes. Images must have danced in their heads of all the immanent perks of such governorship. Jesus burst their immanent balloon by telling them He was soon going to die at the hands of sinful men.

Peter was aghast. "God forbid it Lord. This shall never happen to you!" Jesus (perhaps a bit harshly) rebuked Peter: "You are not setting your mind on God's interests [the transcendent], but man's [the immanent]." Jesus then realized that His inner circle (Peter, James, and John) needed a visual demonstration (thus immanent proof) of the afterlife. They would see and hear with their senses an image of a normally unseen, transcendent state, in the only instance in the Gospels where heaven physically touches earth.* The immanent hopes of the apostles for a perk-filled life of wealth, power, and celebrity associated with a restored kingdom on earth were dwarfed by the indescribable power and beauty of heaven. Jesus took them to a high mountain—most scholars agree it was Mount Tabor in Galilee—and showed them a vision of the transcendent in the *Transfiguration* ("transfiguration" literally means "transformed"). The three apostles were rendered speechless at this preview of the afterlife. They saw wish fulfillment: the restoration of the Kingdom of Israel in the form of Moses and Elijah talking to their King, Jesus. They saw an image of the transformed Jesus in His glorified body, which the Gospel writers could not describe in immanent terms—similes and allegories were used to describe the transcendent, transformed Jesus: "His face shone like the sun, and His garments became **as** white as light." This reinforces our notion that immanent words cannot portray the transcendent.

Yet they recognized the transfigured, transcendent, and glorified Jesus as Jesus. This was not an apparition—it was *physical reality*. One proof of this is that Peter was ready to set up shelters for the three figures, Jesus, Moses, and Elijah (Matthew 17:4). If given the go-ahead by Jesus, Peter might have started a fire to cook a meal, but the presence of heaven disappeared into the clouds, leaving only the earthly appearing Jesus.

The conundrum of two different bodies of Jesus is solved by the Catechism, which says that Jesus's true, heavenly glorified state was "veiled in humanity," referring to His post-Resurrection body familiar to His disciples (645, 659). As we said, this "veiling" was done to reassure the disciples they were not seeing a ghost and, more importantly, to show the disciples that He really did come back from the

---

* The instances of heavenly images in Revelation are in a vision, not physical reality.

dead. The same Jesus who died on the Cross was now alive in a fully earthly manner, still bearing the wounds suffered on Calvary. But, most important, the Catechism goes on to say that Jesus was not resurrected back into a mortal body—one that would have to die again, as did Lazarus and the others Jesus raised—but an imperishable, glorified, and immortal body (646). The veiling mentioned in the Catechism 645 was indeed a "disguise."

But is there sufficient reason for us to be "veiled" as Jesus was?

What about Human Sexuality?

In spite of what the Catechism says about our heavenly bodies being very earthlike—"All of them will rise again with their own bodies which they now bear" (999)—passages in scripture tell us in plain language that our glorified "bodies which we now bear" may be less earthly than we would like. In the Gospel of Matthew, Jesus answered the Sadducees' trick question about marriage in the next life by saying, "At the resurrection, they neither marry nor are given in marriage but are like the angels in heaven" (Matthew 22:30). A footnote to this verse in the Catholic Study Bible simply says, "sexuality as we know it on earth is *transcended* in heaven." As we defined *transcendent* to mean "beyond," "above," or "better than," we must assume that scripture is telling us the pleasures and intimacy afforded by human sexuality are fully present in heaven, but the means to such joy would be by a far superior interaction than we enjoy on earth.*

---

* Such methodology was portrayed in Ron Howard's 1985 film *Cocoon*. A humanly cloaked alien named Kitty (played by Tahnee Welch, Raquel's daughter) and a fully human Captain Jack (portrayed by Steve Guttenberg) make love in a pool after Kitty removes her human disguise. Only their fingers touch, and they share a mystical, spiritual force between them; the transcendent nature of Captain Jack's pleasure says it all—his ecstasy clearly surpasses any earthly experience.

In addition, the phylogenetic purpose of human sexuality on earth is procreation—producing new members of the species to replace the dying, in order to prevent the extinction of humanity. The immortal, glorified body would have no need for procreation, but the intimacy and fulfillment of sexuality embedded within the soul would likely be carried forward into the afterlife.

More verses in scripture also suggest a more spiritual aspect of our glorified bodies in heaven rather than completely earthlike physical personas. In addition to Jesus saying "we shall be like the angels in Heaven" in Saint Matthew's Gospel, there is a very plain passage by Saint Paul in his First Letter to the Corinthians that further suggests our glorified bodies will be more similar to what Jesus had at the Transfiguration. The entire passage is worthy of careful reading; it is found in 1 Corinthians 15:35–50. Some of the verses bring up the notion of a *perishable body* versus an *imperishable body*. Here are some important snippets:

> But some will say, how are the dead raised? And with what kind of body do they come? There are...heavenly bodies and earthly bodies, but the glory of the heavenly is one, and the glory of the earthly is another...it is sown as a perishable body, but it is raised an imperishable body...it is sown in dishonor, it is raised in glory; it is sown in weakness, it is raised in power... And just as we have borne the image of the earthly, we shall also bear the image of the heavenly...Now I say this, brethren, that flesh and blood cannot inherit the Kingdom of God; nor does the perishable inherit the imperishable.

This passage by Saint Paul does not say we will be ghosts or that our glorified bodies will be totally devoid of any familiar, physical characteristics, but it aims to clear up two common points about our bodies in the afterlife: the first is that our resurrected bodies are not the result of a mere reconstitution of the dust in our graves but new creations; the second is that our new, heavenly bodies will be closely related to our earthly bodies. Yet there will indeed be significant change to what we are on earth: "Our lowly earthly bodies will be changed by Christ to be like His...into a spiritual body" (Catechism 999).

This places our usual images, impressions, and notions about God, the afterlife, our lost loved ones, and all that is transcendent in a most delicate position. As we said before, all these things may look totally different from what we have come to expect from our lifetime of everyday and religious experience. This is a frightening notion, but we should take heart. If everything about us and our surroundings is different from what we encounter on earth, it will be the same for everyone in heaven and will seem familiar to us. Religious icons, so important to many of us for meditation and prayer, may very well be completely inaccurate in their depictions. The common image of God as a white-haired old fellow who walks about on the clouds above us is thus suspect. Is God really a completely spiritual entity? Does He have a human form? Does God look like us and speak our language? And, more important to our earthly hopes, will our lost loved ones look the same? We must tread carefully and with an open mind lest we fabricate ideas about heaven to satisfy our earthly hopes. Yet our theory about the heavenly, imperishable body being a myste-rious combination of a spiritual being and "super-physical" entity in heaven is quite logical. As we press onward, however, we'll find that looking at how the afterlife might be *different* from our immanent lives here on earth may give us a fresh perspective.

Like Sherlock Holmes, we may have to describe heaven by what it isn't.*

---

* In "The Second Stain," Holmes ingeniously finds a very important lost letter. Watson asks him how he knew where it was. Holmes answers, "Very simple, Watson, I knew where it wasn't."

What We're Not Sure Of

As we've said many times, the Catechism tells us that heaven will "fulfill our deepest human longings" (1024). This is a very broad statement; we assume it refers to things we know we want on earth. If our "deepest human longings" exist in our conscious minds—we know what we want and have mental images of these entities—then these earthly longings are stored in our memories. This is where we encounter trouble. Short- and long-term memories are stored throughout the cortex of the human brain; the switchboard for routing these memories is in a limbic-system structure known as the hippocampus.

The problem is, when we die, all this fancy wiring turns to dust—the *terram ibis* thing.

We must not lose heart, however. Some memories are so important to our essence that they have become etched into our very souls throughout our lives as transcendent images—transcendent longings. Since the travelers in our odyssey are the souls, we will have these memories of our most treasured experiences in our new, heavenly consciousness. Besides the ecstasy of the Beatific Vision, we will be aware of all transcendent images etched into our souls while on earth. People with whom we shared love—our children, parents, ancestors, spouses, lovers, and perhaps even pets—will be instantly and mutually recognizable. Even those who perhaps touched our hearts but did not or could not return our love will recognize us and return our transcendent feelings. All things wrong with our love relationships on earth will be fixed in heaven; in the presence of God, heaven will be the place of perfect love for everyone. There will be no longing for love in heaven. The broken heart is strictly an earthly thing.

So people we knew on earth that touched our souls in some way will be in heaven, but what about things that have given us joy and respite on earth? Can immanent (earthly) pleasures and joys exist in the transcendent realm of heaven? Our definitions and logic tell us no, because the pleasures from immanent things are the results of desires originating in an immanent body and milieu. The immanent body seeks out immanent pleasures because only immanent pleasures can really satisfy earthly desires. The earthly body is interested in only earthly things: "There are...heavenly bodies and earthly bodies, but the glory of the heavenly is one, and the glory of the earthly is another" (1 Corinthians 15:40).

Yet again, there is another viewpoint. Our pleasures from earthly experiences—things—may be immanent in origin, but after a lifetime, they would certainly be part of our true essence. The soul, after all, is the main part of both our earthly and heavenly being. If God so wills it, the pleasure we felt on earth from certain things will somehow be infused into our new heavenly consciousness and glorified bodies, whether or not those things exist in the heavenly realm. How can this happen if earthly things do not exist in heaven? The answer is that pleasures we experience on earth originate and exist in our conscious minds, not in the portals of the senses. If we are unconscious, the most wonderful food (including, I suppose, beer), the finest music, a friend's laughter, and even sex give us no pleasure at all. This metaphysical gobbledygook is supported by the image of someone pouring beer down our throats while we're asleep—we would wake up with a terrific headache and not have the faintest memory of any party. Likewise, if we were unconscious but still able to play golf, a hole in one would bring no cerebral joy. We would still have to endure congratulatory backslaps and buy a round of drinks but wouldn't know why.

If we accept this guess of some kind of cerebral infusion to feel pleasure in heaven, which is pure speculation at best, the familiar polka song that says, "In heaven, there is no beer / That's why we drink it here" may very well be wrong. It's just that we wouldn't have to drink the stuff to feel the buzz. My guess is that this theory is too metaphysical and illogical; all things are possible with God, so we must assume there will be some type of interaction between our glorified bodies and physical things. So I have to ask the question, "Is my father quaffing a cold one on the twelfth tee, or is it all in his heavenly mind?"

I vote for real beer and real golf; the sex thing isn't nearly as important.

But There Are Things We're Sure Of

There is no speculation or doubt in saying that nothing bad we know on earth (bad immanence) can exist in heaven. A little thought about our daily lives will show that heaven will be a lot better than life here on an earth full of bad immanence. Bad earthly immanence is anything we can personally experience that causes us pain and suffering: fear, pain, injury, disease and birth defects, suffering, loss, sadness and depression, anxiety, injustice, rejection, personal strife and anger, betrayal, and worries about death. The world itself has plenty of bad immanence—sin, war, genocide, misguided and dangerous religious ideologies, natural disasters, poverty, famine, prejudice, intolerance, and the myriad of sufferings stemming from the world's lopsided distribution of wealth. Bad immanence is allowed to exist because, as scripture says in Job 1:7 and 2 Corinthians 4:4, the immanent domain of earth belongs to Satan. In this earthly realm, then, all good things transcendent sometimes take a backseat, so to speak, to forces of bad immanence—but only in this earthly realm. In the transcendent realm of heaven, there will only be good immanence,* and it will be under the complete control of the transcendent forces of heaven, most notably God Himself.

This brings up a disturbing notion: since the domain of earth belongs to Satan, are we in hell?

---

* Our repeatedly stated notions that the transcendent heaven could contain earthly immanence are obvious paradoxes. They are some of the many contradictions we face in dealing with our quest to "know" the afterlife.

It is not inconceivable to those of us enduring great suffering that we now exist in some sort of hell—earth is, after all, part of Satan's realm. We needn't look far to find terrible suffering around us. One of the greatest pains of this earthly life is losing someone close to us. Whether the loss is through homicide, suicide, accident, disease, or just senescence, the pain of such loss is devastating to the surviving loved ones, affecting the survivors for the rest of their days. Yet our suffering thusly is mirrored in scripture.

The awful pain of losing a child was endured by the Mother of Jesus on three separate occasions. The first was when Jesus was twelve years old and stayed behind in Jerusalem at Passover. After a full day's journey, she and Joseph returned to the city to look for Him, and the panic she felt was vividly portrayed in Saint Luke's Gospel (2:39–50).* The second occurred at Calvary when, at the moment before He died, Jesus literally and sadly said good-bye to His mother: "Woman, behold your son" (John 19:26). The third time was probably the saddest for Mary, but it occurred at an event that we associate with joy and hope: the Ascension of Jesus into heaven (Acts 1:9). Here, Mary watched her Son disappear into the clouds and realized He was physically gone from her life; she would not meet Him again until she herself died. Everyone who has lost someone dear to him or her knows this horrible feeling only too well; without the assurance of faith for a heavenly reunion, despair is the only result.

---

* Since Luke, a physician and writer to the Gentiles, was not one of the chosen twelve apostles, his apostolic credentials were given to him by Mary, the Mother of Jesus herself. Luke was aware of Mark's Gospel, the earliest written manuscript sometime in the AD fifties, which contained the bulk of Jesus's teachings and formed the template for the other synoptic Gospels. Luke's Gospel was completed in the early AD sixties; Luke incorporated Mark's Gospel along with the tutelage of Mary. It was Mary who, sometime in the late AD fifties, gave Luke details about Jesus and her own life that are specific to Luke's Gospel.

In heaven, this pain of lost loved ones will end. We will see those we've lost and recognize them in a new, perfected, but indescribable glorified state. Beloved children, parents, grandparents—all our ancestors—will be there to welcome us; their glorified state will have freed them of all physical and emotional shortcomings. The parent whose love and approval we craved but never got will be in a state of complete understanding and limitless love, free of the emotional chains that kept him or her from expressing love to us. Our sick children who suffered so much on earth will be there, whole and full of life. Lost loves from divorce or abandonment will be there to reconcile; even people we loved so painfully who did not or could not return our love will be there to give us what we may have spent our lives craving. No love in heaven—the state of all love—will be unrequited.*

A *Glorified Body That Can Change: The Heavenly Miracle of Polymorphism*

If all the phases of Jesus's earthly life mirror ours exactly (and we can safely assume this to be true), then our odyssey into glory after we die will be into a somehow-changed body that must reflect all the forms Jesus exhibited in His glory—namely, the Transfiguration Jesus and the many faces of the post-Resurrection Jesus. The Catechism affirms this: "But Christ will change our lowly bodies to be like His glorious body" (999). Since Jesus actually exhibited many different forms during these two periods, we can say He was *polymorphic*—from the

---

* Do dogs and cats go to heaven? The rebel Jesuit theologian Teilhard de Chardin says they do, if we want them there with us. I agree. I have had my heart broken more than a few times by the death of a beloved pet; in moments of reverie, I still remember their best moments that gave me so much joy. There are no broken hearts in heaven—none.

Greek for "many forms." In all His forms, Jesus was initially not recognizable until He allowed it, affirming that His glorified appearance could change at will. On the road to Emmaus, two disciples did not know it was Jesus who walked with them: "Their eyes were prevented from recognizing Him" (Luke 24:16). After Jesus broke bread with them, He changed His form once again: "Their eyes were opened and they recognized Him" (Luke 24:31). On Easter Sunday night, His disciples were startled by His sudden appearance in their midst behind locked doors: "They thought they were seeing a ghost" (Luke 24:37). At the tomb on Easter morning, Mary Magdalene did not recognize Him until He said her name: "She turned around and...did not know it was Jesus" (John 20:14). And during the seven disciples' failed fishing expedition on the Sea of Galilee, Jesus once again was not recognized until their nets were filled with 153 large fish: "The disciples did not know that it was Jesus" (John 21:4).

The point of these scriptural passages is that Jesus was somehow "different" and recognizable only if He allowed it. We will be different as Jesus was different, just as the Catechism says. We must entertain the possibility that we might look like the Transfigured Jesus—that is, changed and both mysteriously spiritual and physically real but also fully recognizable and apparently not needing sustenance or shelter. More important, we may also have the Lord's post-Resurrection power to be polymorphic; in this sense, then, heaven may consist of many different realms or dimensions, some glorified spiritual realms and some glorified physical realms. The world of quantum physics tells us, with some mathematical certainty, that we may be living in a multidimensional universe right now!

Whatever the state of our existence in heaven, there are some things about the afterlife that we can deduce with certainty. Saint Thomas Aquinas in his *Summa Theologica* describes some of the supernatural aspects of a glorified heavenly life. Heaven, he said, is perfect in its infrastructure and is also *atemporal*—that is, the human construct of time does not exist in the afterlife, so the glorified body would be immune from aging, pain, and death. This brings up the interesting notion of age in heaven. How old would we be?

Since we would have supernatural powers that at the very least would be similar to Jesus's abilities to change His earthly appearance, we can assume that we would be able to be any age we wanted to be at any given time. The young child who died and left grieving parents would be able to appear at the heavenly reunion exactly at the age of the child's death. The heavenly child would then be able to transform to whatever age he or she wished. The same would be true for elder parents and grandparents who passed with infirm, sickly bodies; when familiarity of the joyful reunion was established, the heaven dweller would be able to return to a more comfortable and appealing stage in his or her life.

Our notion of a glorified, spiritual, but somewhat physical body that can change back and forth is perfectly compatible with the dogmatic facts of Jesus's Ascension into heaven with a "veiled" post-Resurrection body that did some very human things, including eating and drinking as well as appearing completely "normal." And Mary, in order to preserve the earthly body that was the "Ark of the New Covenant," was assumed into heaven in that earthly body, in no need of an earthly veiling as Jesus had. In light of our theory of polymorphic powers, we must assume that, upon reaching heaven, Jesus was returned to His fully glorified state as on Mount Tabor, and Mary was given a glorified body somehow consistent with the heavenly milieu and her earthly status as Ark of Jesus. The logic tells us that, should either of them be sent back to earth—Jesus at the Rapture and Mary during her many apparitions—they would have the power of polymorphism from God to veil their heavenly glory in a comforting, earthly form familiar to us.

Could we really have such power from God? Are there immanent or earthlike parts or dimensions of heaven that require an earthly shaped body? Is heaven an immense, infinite expanse covering infinite numbers of dimensions or "places"—some earthly physical and some heavenly metaphysical? If there is golf and beer in heaven—and our theory suggests there certainly is—we're going to need something to swing the club and raise the mug.

In addition, once we reach the glorified state of heaven, does God ever send us back to earth—thus needing an earthly "veil"—in order to influence the living into bringing about His divine plan, as he did with His own Son, Jesus? After all, we do pray earnestly for the Father's will to be "done on earth as it is in heaven"; are there citizens of heaven walking among us, assisting mankind with this task? It is a favorite theme in our entertainment genres, and such divinely sanctioned returns to earth certainly would explain a lot of the unknown.

Support for such extreme possibilities come from Jesus's own words, "like the angels in Heaven." Saint Thomas Aquinas in his *Summa Theologica* discusses angels in some detail. He says that angels are spirits who, by their nature, are not created with bodies, but, in the service of God and at His behest alone, they are fully capable of assuming physical bodies, fully visible as normal human people. The most notable appearances of humanlike angels are at the near sacrifice of Isaac by Abraham, the visit to Zacharias by the angel Gabriel in Luke 1:11, Gabriel's message to Mary at the Annunciation,* the presence of "two men dressed in white" in Jesus's tomb on the first Easter (Luke 24:4 and John 20:12), and at the Ascension (Acts 1:10).

---

* Was Mary's being "troubled" at Gabriel's appearance due to a "ghostly" appearance or simply because a strange man addressed a fourteen-year-old girl with the theologically significant title "full of grace"? The same question arises in Luke 1:12 when Zacharias is "gripped with fear" at Gabriel's sudden appearance in the temple.

If we are, as Jesus said, "to be like angels," then it makes sense that we too should have the transcendent power of polymorphism—to be both humanlike and heaven-like. Changing back and forth might very well be a perk of the afterlife. Our state in heaven would be a glorified, spiritual-physical presence as Jesus exhibited at the Transfiguration, but a state with the transcendent power of changing into an imperishable, immortal body, just as Jesus exhibited after the Resurrection, and it would depend on what dimension of heaven we found ourselves. In such a scenario, access to golf courses, beer, and whatever else that would add to our happiness would be a given. My father would be happy, and so too, I imagine, would Huckleberry Finn. Even the weather would be perfect and worry free. A Mark Twain quote agrees: "We go to heaven for the climate; we go to hell for the company."

Accepting the Notion of a Glorified Body That Is Different from What We Have Now

We said that, since Jesus was different in His glorified state after the Resurrection, we too will be different. If we have trouble with the notion of giving up our earthlike bodies, two ideas may help us accept what happens to us after we die. The first is the obvious fact that the bodies we have now are *perishable*. All things on this earth are perishable, from the most inert rock formations to the most fragile of butterflies. All things will disappear at some point in time. This is especially true for things with moving parts, like machinery and, yes, the human body. These disturbing facts are one of the foundations of nature; there are no perpetual-motion machines or systems on this earth. Even the sun, an energy source that runs on fusion physics, is going to run out of gas in a few billion years. The earth, as we know it, will be a burned-out cinder in less than half a billion years as the sun morphs into a red giant and swallows up the planets.

Such is our fate too. No matter who we are, what we have, or what we do, including the postmortem silliness of cryonics, we are going to end up as piles of dust—*terram ibis*. If we're young and fit, it's natural that we would want to keep the bodies we have, but for those of us past the "beautiful" twenties, the descriptive "perishable" takes on real meaning. As we get closer to the last decades of our lives, our body machinery simply winds down. Activities that used to give us a measure of joy in our lives—socializing, entertainment, sports, and vacations—take a backseat to ordinary physiology: locomotion, sleep, waste elimination, sexual prowess and desire, and for some of us, the more basic functions of breathing, seeing, hearing, and remembering simple stuff. The older we are, the better able we are to look back on our lives and see our broken bodies as ugly, troublesome vehicles for our ever-young souls. Death is a perfect time for a trade-in and upgrade.

The thought of a new body that is paradoxically identical but different and imperishable compared to what we have now can only bring hope and excitement about the afterlife. Scripture reassures us our new bodies will not be epoxied and duct-taped versions of the dust we left behind but new, immortal essences—both physical and spiritual and capable of wondrous powers. Our new existence will have infinite power from our eternal union with God Himself and will be free of every possible immanent defect.

Will we be bored in heaven? Noted humanist Isaac Asimov answers the question for agnostics and nonbelievers: "For whatever the tortures of hell, the boredom of heaven would be even worse." What will we do for all eternity? God is never bored, and in our eternal, mysterious union with the Trinity, we will enjoy the same unlimited potential in our existence. As we'll see later, boredom due to an incomplete Self is a source of much of the suffering on earth, and there is no suffering in heaven. Agnostics and atheists do not believe in the existence or power of a heavenly God, so the fantasy of an afterlife for them is nothing more than a temporal extension of earthly time.

Another approach to accepting our new heavenly bodies is to overcome our very human tendency to fear and disdain the unknown. We feel safe with what we know, yet most advancements of our human experience have been into the unknown. Sixty years ago, the telephone was a large, scary black object with a fearsome ring; it seemed miraculous that we could talk to others—albeit with marginal audio quality—by simply putting a finger into a dial and twisting out seven numbers. Today, we can control much of our lives by simply speaking into a device smaller than a deck of cards and telling a mysterious nonperson exactly what we want, from locking our homes to checking on sneaky kids to starting our cars to getting information on virtually anything. The fearsome black ogre from the early twentieth century has become a comfortable and necessary way of life.

A more visual analogy of overcoming the fear of the unfamiliar is seen in the evolution of another electronic miracle, the television. As late as 1985, we watched in amazement as Marty McFly Jr. talked to a huge window-shade screen and ordered up channels from a selection of thousands. This was truly science fiction to those of us who experienced the birth of home TV; the first sets were bulky, heavy pieces of furniture sporting ten-inch black-and-white screens. The arrival of colored television in the midfifties was considered the ultimate in viewing—the "massive" twenty-one-inch screens left us agape. Back then, we couldn't imagine television as we now know it. Within a generation, we will no doubt have life-size holographic media celebrities interacting with us in our living rooms, acting out dramas, making us laugh, or scaring us worse than the ring of an old telephone.

The point of these two electronic analogies is that we needn't fear the unknown of our heavenly bodies. However, unlike the constantly expanding wonder of technology, our glorified bodies will indeed be the *ultimate*; nothing better will be able to surpass our heavenly existence. Our heavenly bodies will have reached the final stage of evolution—there will be no miraculous advances for them as there will be with today's electronic miracles. With this in mind, we should proceed and rest assured that heaven and the bodies we will have there will be far better than anything we could ever imagine.

A Preview to Heaven Is All around Us

Heaven is under our feet as well as over our heads.

—HENRY DAVID THOREAU, *WALDEN*

Our curiosity about what happens after we die can be quenched somewhat if we make the effort to appreciate what happens before we die. We are so wrapped up with "stamping out fires"—as a neurotic friend once said—that we fail to notice and actually savor the miracles occurring around us. The modern, frenetic pace we have set up for ourselves drains us of our psychic energy and prevents us "seeing" a piece of heaven right now. Heaven may appear in something very simple, like a child's laughter, a freshly opened flower, a deep azure sky on a calm day, or the existential peace of silent prayer.

I remember times long past when my life was a twisted mess of complex agendas obsessively kept as a price for success. Such chaos worked, but I went through much of my life missing heaven. Burnouts were regular events, and I remember one summer evening when I crashed in a heap sitting in the yard. I sat perfectly still—numb, really—and stared ahead. Eight feet away was a fountain lazily dripping water into lower pools; a portly robin came and stared back at me. The bird then plopped into the water of the largest pool and promptly took a bath. I watched and realized sadly that in my nearly five decades of life, I had never actually seen a bird take a bath in real time! A great sense of peace and calm overshadowed me. That was years ago; I have since learned that "seeing" heaven starts with opening our eyes here on earth.

This is not really a book about heaven. It is a book about making life simpler so that *getting* to heaven is easier. It is a book about an odyssey up a mountain where the trail is made of smooth stones, not jagged rocks. Our odyssey will tell us who we are, what we're doing here, how to love without hurting, and how to live with suffering. Once we learn these things, we will begin to "see" the invisible heaven we all crave so much. If we learn to pray and meditate effectively, the images will get sharper and sharper, and the end of our odyssey—heaven—will be as peaceful, calming, and familiar as a bird taking a bath on a summer's eve.

> *If we are able to comprehend and enjoy properly the*
> *graces and good things that the Lord showers upon us*
> *every day, we will already have begun to experience that*
> *joy and peace which one day will be completely ours*
> *in heaven.*

—*L'OSSERVATORE ROMANO*, 28 JULY 1999

IX

Theosis: The Final Cleansing

If we fail to cleanse ourselves of the world's chaff and die worshipping the false gods of immanent values, we are not ready for heaven. Within such a misguided and unheavenly value system lie many traits that are the seedbed for evil but are often overlooked in asking forgiveness and promising repentance. Loving the world too much forces us to adhere to the world's rules for survival and success—namely aggression, intolerance, prejudice, bigotry, xenophobia, selfishness, cutthroat competition, and many other sugarcoated forms of hatred. As we've said, heaven is the realm of all love, and it has no place for hatred of any kind. To find heaven heavenly, we must "take up our cross" and "die to the world" and its false idols of materialism and power that inherently engender hatred.

This process of putting the world and its treasures into proper perspective is the foundation upon which we can build our sanctification. Sanctification is a lifelong growth in spirituality through daily prayer and meditation whereupon we introspect or "look into ourselves" and digest exactly how, down to the smallest detail, we have fallen short of or strayed from God's wishes. While heaven is the realm of perfect love, it is also the realm of perfect justice, *ad res minima*—every single unheavenly thought, word, or action of our lives is to be answered for.

As we accomplish this indictment of the Self, we change; there is a metamorphosis of the soul that takes us to a greater intimacy with God. The entire process—letting go of the world, embracing prayer and meditation, and undertaking a spiritual growth toward God—is called *theosis*. It is obvious, though, that some of us need more of this heavenly transformation than others. There are the devout among us, and then there are the less than devout. The latter run the gamut of the truly rotten apples who have little interest in the transcendent to the perfectly decent folks who follow the rules for the most part but have never seen the inside of a church or never sincerely prayed unless something was wrong. It seems illogical that both the devout and less than devout would enjoy the same reward in God's presence. Either the experience of heaven is different for each, or there is some kind of "further" sanctification for the slackers.

This creates a host of questions, the most obvious of which include these: How much sanctification is necessary for man to "qualify" for heaven? Is man destined to be perfect on this earth? Can man really be completely free of his tendency and weakness for all sin? Another set of questions is even more curious: When and where does sanctification take place—in this life, the next, or both? Is a suffering stint in purgatory—considered by many as hell with a back door—the equalizer in the sanctification of man? Does purgatory even exist?

It is important that we keep the process of sanctification—the "soul-shaping" model of theodicy—in a positive light. We are, after all, defending God. We who are basically decent folks are all going to heaven eventually; the point of this book is that the greater our *theosis* in this life—getting close to God through prayer and meditation, leaving worldly values behind, and accepting our suffering—the smoother our odyssey and, more important, the more heavenly our afterlife. Those of us who have neglected *theosis* in this life may very well face the process after death but before heaven. We must remember *ad res minima*: everything is accounted for in the heavenly court of perfect justice. We pay up now...or later. This brings up the unpleasant notion of purgatory.

Theosis and a Place Called Purgatory

The notion that we get a second chance at sanctification, forgiveness for minor and often forgotten faults, and *theosis* beyond this life is not accepted by most non-Catholic Christians. When we die, that's it—game over. This brings up the tedious and circuitous arguments for and against *sola fide*—complete sanctification and justification by faith alone. There are as many scriptural references supporting this notion as those rejecting it, so we shall not partake of such a contentious buffet.

Protestants correctly point out that man, in no way, can pay the sin debt owed to God. No collection of good works by a human can pay back a divine debt. *Sola fide* was Luther's reaction to the widespread corruption in the early Church regarding indulgences, a system that placed some sort of immanent value on prayers and good works that could be used for transcendent favor. Promises from monks and clergy for a purgatory-free afterlife with a preapproved passage into heaven were often exchanged for money or even sexual favors. This was a horrible distortion of the real intent of the *Indulgentiarum Doctrina*, which was created to get people to pray, do good works, and succeed at personal sanctification and spiritual growth. Luther was correct in his indictment of the corruption,* but

---

* In 1205, Saint Francis of Assisi was praying in the chapel of San Damiano when Christ appeared and told Francis to "fix my church." Saint Francis gathered bricks and mortar, misunderstanding the divine request, but later realized that Jesus was referring to the widespread corruption eroding the reputation of Catholicism.

some Reformists have stretched the notion of *sola fide* into the claim that no effort is required by man to grow spiritually closer to God as long as a sincere statement and commitment to faith in Jesus Christ are made.

Many really fine Protestant clergy begin or end their services with the familiar mantra, "Do you accept Jesus Christ as your Lord and Savior? If you answered 'yes,' then you are saved and guaranteed a place in the glory of heaven." This promise of *sola fide* irritates Catholics as well as the followers of the other two monotheistic religions, Judaism and Islam; all three religions are replete with laws and regulations that guide their faithful in the lifelong process of spiritual growth. Some Protestants feel that the doctrine of *sola fide* gets them off the hook for the rigors of personal sanctification. They are dead wrong, but not because the affirmation accepting Jesus as Lord and Savior is wrong. It is dead right. The word "accept" in the statement of faith is loaded with meaning, meaning that demands every bit of effort to gain spirituality as all the laws and regulations written down in other religions.

To "accept" Jesus Christ is to assimilate and appropriate His existence into our existence, just as He emptied Himself of the glory of heaven to perfectly imitate man's existence. If we accept Jesus Christ as Lord and Savior, we must imitate Jesus Christ in His existence, actions, thoughts, attitudes, and especially His prayer life. If we live our lives as Christ did, we then are truly guaranteed the passage into glory. Living the life of Christ in toto is not easy. It demands that we change from our world-driven values to those of heaven—this is a de facto definition of the personal spiritual growth of sanctification.

We Catholics assimilate and appropriate the Essence of Christ literally by eating His flesh and drinking His blood, as commanded by Jesus Himself in John 6:51–58. This is the doctrine of the Real Presence—that Christ is physically present in the Eucharistic sacrament.

In one very important sense, the Protestant call to "accept Jesus as Lord and Savior" is the Reformist version of the Eucharistic sacrament. In both cases, the Essence of Christ is assimilated into our essence. Interestingly, at the onset of the Protestant Reformation, both Luther and Calvin accepted the doctrine of the Real Presence; the present-day call to accept Jesus is a very real callback to this notion. In any event, all Christians must absorb Christ through the spiritual metamorphosis of sanctification *before we die.* If it doesn't happen now, it happens later.

It's obvious that some of us are less repentant than others, some of us pray less or not at all, and, as such, serious soul shaping and sanctification are necessary after death if we are to enjoy heaven to the fullest. The Catholic Church calls this the "final purification."

"Purgatory is a state or place for those who die in God's friendship, assured of their eternal salvation, who still have need of further sanctification to enter into the joy of heaven" (Catechism 1030).

The scriptural basis for any redemption and forgiveness after death comes from Christ's words in Matthew 12:32: "Whoever shall speak against the Holy Spirit, it shall not be forgiven him, either in this age, or in the age to come." The logical conclusion is that there is some form of cleansing in the next life, and we must believe the Catechism and assume that some sort of postdeath, preheaven sanctification takes place. Final purification certainly makes sense based on what we see in ourselves and others, and by the apostle Paul emphatically reminding us that "we all have sinned and fall short of the glory of God" (Romans 3:23).

—⚬—

The notion of a purgatory is unpleasant, to say the least. The problem is that the mechanics of purgatory—how we are finally purified—have been blown way out of proportion and have frightened many believers into turning away from God altogether. The scary part of purgatory seems to be the notion that it involves a hell-like fire over a certain length of time, like a cosmic prison sentence in a blast furnace. The more purification and sanctification we need, the longer our time in the fire. But God is not a cosmic bogeyman who would create such torture for those destined for heaven. For one thing, it seems illogical that charbroiling the soul—a physical phenomenon upon a metaphysical entity—would have any positive effect on our desire to be intimate with God. In addition, there is no time after death; time is a human construct that ceases to exist in the realm of eternity. Any final purification in the afterlife would have to be timeless, either eternal or instantaneous. We know purgatory cannot be eternal, so the only option is that any stint in purgatory must be very brief in earthly terms.

The Catholic Catechism has toned down the rhetoric to a necessary final purification or cleansing of the soul. The need for our souls to be cleansed after death but before heaven was first described by Pope Saint Gregory the Great in his *Dialogues*, written around AD 600. His use of the word "cleansing" was again based on a very liberal interpretation of Saint Paul's fire metaphor in 1 Corinthians 3:15 and 1 Peter 1:7; Gregory added the simile "cleansing as with fire." At the time of the Council of Florence in 1490 and the Council of Trent in 1563, the word "as" was lost in copying and translations, and purgatory became a "minihell." The tradition persists to this day, even though the Catechism explicitly states that the final purification is "entirely different from the punishment of the damned" (1031).

We need to suggest a new notion of purgatory, one that is consistent with defending a loving God that only wishes to bring His prodigal children home. There will be suffering, but of a very different kind—suffering from awareness, an awareness of every thought, word, and deed in our lives that strayed from God's will, whether such shortcomings were forgiven sins or just times when we fell short of the perfect paradigm of Christ's life. Our consciousness in the afterlife will be overtaken by a brief but very intense opening of the mind to every instant of anything less than perfection in our earthly lives. Such awareness alone will not "cleanse" us to a state where we are worthy of intimacy with God in heaven. The awareness of all our faults must take place in the presence of the innocent, suffering Christ.

So purgatory, then, does not take place in a cosmic furnace but at Gethsemane, at the Tower of Antonia, in the garrison of the entire Roman cohort, on the Via Dolorosa, and lastly on the little hill of Calvary. We will be vividly shown every instance in our lives where we fell short of God's expectations while we kneel at the rock of Gethsemane and watch in agony and terror as the blood of Jesus drops; while we stand next to the pillory of Antonia, watching the flesh be torn from His body by soulless torturers; while we watch the same fiends spit on him, slap Him in derision, and puncture His scalp with a mocking crown of thorns; while we walk the Via Dolorosa and watch Him marched naked through the streets and fall forward onto the stone pavement with arms lashed to a crossbar; and finally, when we kneel at the Cross and see His blood dripping around us into the dust and hear His final utterance of our redemption, "*Kalah.*"*

The "burning" we feel will be our own guilt for the hatred in our lives in the presence of His absolute innocence and love. Somehow, we will be cleansed, fully knowing we deserve what He is enduring. Our debt of gratitude to the suffering Christ will overtake our consciousness, and it is a supreme gratitude that must begin in this life. Since there is no time in the afterlife, our lessons on exactly

---

* Hebrew word uttered as the last lamb of Passover is slaughtered: "It is finished."

what we have done wrong and whom we hurt—down to the smallest event—will not be measured in years in a furnace but in the intensity of our shame. Like the good thief whose confession from his cross exemplifies a perfect *Purgatorio*, every single thing we have ever done short of God's will is going to burn us in the presence of His innocence and may only require a single dying breath of time.

"And we indeed justly are receiving what we deserve for our deeds; but this man has done nothing wrong...And Jesus said to him...Truly I say to you, today you shall be with Me in Paradise" (Luke 23:41–43).

This notion that there is no time construct in purgatory and that our entire postdeath final cleansing occurs in the blink of an eye certainly relieves our fears about what may happen to us after we die, but, in the sense of *ad res minima*—that heaven is a realm of perfect justice and we must answer for every single occurrence in our lives of unkindness, hate, intolerance, and other human faults—such a notion sounds unfair. It seems illogical that we could repay a lifetime of unheavenly attitudes and feelings with only an instant of conscious awareness; a lifetime of hatred and intolerance needs a lifetime of payback. Logic demands that cleansing from any such life not only would involve a time span, but, more than mere awareness, would require actually experiencing the unkindness we have dealt others. This conundrum has no easy solution. We must wait and see.

What About the "Other Place"?

This is not a book about hell, and the debates about eternal damnation are insufferably circuitous and complex. It is a nasty buffet we shall avoid entirely. Discussions in all religions throughout history run the gamut from hell not even existing to the traditionally held notion that hell is a place of eternal suffering somehow involving unquenchable fire. Defending the infinite mercy of God, the Catholic

Catechism regards eternal damnation as a willful choice, "a turning away from" the boundless love of God. The Catechism (1033ff) does affirm that hell is a place of eternal suffering with fire—there are simply too many scriptural references to ignore this long-held notion.

The frightening images of hell should not concern us here; neither should we decide who is guilty enough to deserve such a fate. Culpability of evil is God's business, not ours. The very worst of the worst of humanity—those responsible for untold death and suffering of mankind—must be judged by God alone. Only God knows the workings within the human heart. Hitler thought he was doing the world a favor in ridding the world of Jews by murdering six million innocents, and his twisted megalomania started a war that killed fifty-five million more. Jihadist suicide bombers kill and maim countless innocent people, but they truly believe they are doing God's work. It is natural that we desperately want these misguided souls to suffer horribly for their deeds; *if* and *how* this happens are not in our control; only the Supernatural Judge of creation has this onus.

One thing should concern us, however, and this notion is very important. We must stop glibly judging others by saying this one and that one are "going to hell" simply because they are different from us. What is different can range from someone's religious beliefs, ethnic origin, nationality, gender orientation, or even political beliefs. Many of these things are intrinsic and not choices, and we are horribly amiss in judging and damning our fellows for traits over which they have no control. To do so is the definition of sinful pride and utter ignorance. If we fear eternal damnation ourselves, we must not wish it on others who are different. Pride is the evil twin of hate. If we fail to purge these worldly poisons from our soul, we may have a very tragic end to our own odyssey.

Hate is the most unheavenly trait of fallen man.

Part III
A Heavenly Odyssey through Spiritual Growth

X

Prayer and Meditation: First-Class Passage to the Afterlife

The function of prayer is not to influence God, but rather to change the nature of the one who prays.

—SØREN KIERKEGAARD

We've established that we are creatures of want; on this earth, we get some kind of fleeting and plastic sense of happiness when we get what we've desired so badly. Yet, like children on Christmas morning, we leave the baubles and toys we've asked for on the floor, losing interest before the morning is over; the things we wanted so much now bring boredom and a sense of wanting more. This very human and selfish cyclic tendency often drives us to foolish and destructive behaviors throughout our lives. As we've said, unfulfilled longing is the result of trying to fill our empty Selves with *stuff.* Sometimes, the same dynamic of dissatisfaction is the basis for our unexplained obsession with people. The desire for worldly treasures, including other people, can be maddening, and when the longing is severe enough to disrupt the flow of our daily lives, we resort to prayer. We pray with the hope that we will get something we want, or we pray to not get something we don't want.

While this seems logical, we are faced with very unsettling situations when our prayers are not answered exactly the way we want them to be answered. We react with two possible outcomes to divine refusals. The first is the most common and dangerous: our faith in the whole "ask-and-you-shall-receive" notion, engineered by a loving and benevolent God, is shaken; we become, as a result, more skeptical of an absolute truth.* The second outcome is reliance on faith—pious fideism—to reassure us that God's ways are mysterious and that we must accept unanswered prayers as part of the divine plan for our salvation.

The first outcome is a big mistake; the second outcome, while praiseworthy, still leaves us unsatisfied and wanting because faith always contains some element of doubt. Neither outcome gives us a sense of complete satisfaction. There is a third way, however, to look at our longings, our chronic dissatisfaction, and our prayers that may give us hope and an end to the yearning that seems to plague us throughout our earthly exile. That way is found interwoven into the idea of heaven and what it means for our wish fulfillment. We are not referring to the cynical "suffer now/pie in the sky later" mantra of asceticism but to getting what we really want now, here on earth, as a mirror to what happens after we die and complete our heavenly odyssey. Strangely, it is earthly prayer and meditation that bring this new perspective into view. If we understand correctly the dynamics between prayer and our earthly desires, we begin to get a clear picture that heaven does indeed begin on earth. Our doubt disappears with this new picture, and we can be reassured that our deepest longings can be satisfied here on earth and, most certainly, in heaven.

---

* We quoted Søren Kierkegaard earlier: "There are two ways to be fooled. One is to believe what is not true; the other is to not believe what is true."

There are several caveats to this uplifting statement. First, we must understand the psychological nature of our desires; second, we must accept the paradoxical statement that we may not really want what we think we want; and third, we may not fully understand the nature and purpose of prayer. All three of these notions must certainly raise red flags among believers.

The psychology of wanting things or people is a complex subject, but it can be reduced to the simple idea that getting what we think we want makes us feel whole, complete, and secure. Excessive need to feel whole, complete, and really survivable is the hallmark of an empty Self desperately in need of fulfillment. The accumulation of stuff—adult toys and, more important, money—gives us a sense of power that we can overcome whatever troubles the world throws at us. This includes people; sometimes our love for others has the unhealthy perspective of neediness. We erroneously think that if we utterly possess the heart and soul of another person, we can endure any suffering from this life. In heaven, all this aberrant psychology dissipates; we are fulfilled in the majestic presence of God, and the Self is no longer an empty, needy chasm. Yet, as we'll see, the very same fulfillment can be had on this earth with effective prayer and meditation. Prayer takes us into heaven right now so that we, as well as our desires, change. This is exactly what Kierkegaard said two centuries ago.

The paradox that we may not really want what we think we want is an offshoot of Kierkegaard's statement. Heaven will be a state of total awareness; we will have a clear understanding of the universe, creation, God's plan, and our own transcendent structure. In such a state of completeness, the Self will be no longer empty but will fully understand why some of our longings are good and justified and why others are downright silly. Since effective prayer and meditation take us into heaven and God's presence right now, we can begin to see with clear transcendent eyes what we *should* want and what we *should* get.

For our purposes here on earth, the third caveat is the most critical. We must learn what effective prayer is and how it works. The reassuring thing is, the whole metamorphosis occurs automatically.* We only need to begin to pray effectively, and the magic of heaven begins to appear clearly, overtaking our consciousness. We will truly get what we want.

—⁂—

I was watching our local football team on TV the other night, and a question—really a paradox—arose in my mind. It was a very important game that both teams desperately wanted to win. At the start, the camera showed our kickoff returner awaiting the kick. He sighed deeply, exhaled, made the sign of the cross, and then pointed skyward. I assume he was pointing toward heaven, and that could mean only one thing: the guy was praying! Undoubtedly, he was asking God for a successful runback, perhaps even a touchdown. Then the camera showed the opposing team's kickoff specialist, who also sighed, exhaled, made the sign of the cross, and pointed skyward. His prayer must have been praying for a perfect kick that would stymie the receiver deep in his own territory, away from any decent scoring chance.

Does God hear these prayers from young men who may be the very last people we would expect to be prayerful? I'm fairly sure God hears such prayers—He hears *all* prayers. He just doesn't always answer them in the manner expected. Are earthly sports displeasing to God? Or are the athletes (and really, all of us) praying for

---

* In Eucharistic speak, *ex opere operato* ("out of the work worked").

the wrong thing at the wrong time, in the wrong way, and with the wrong attitude? The answer to the last question is all of the above.

What Are the Right Things to Pray For? And What Are Prayer's Right Times, Ways, and Attitudes?

> *There are two great tragedies in life. The first is not getting your heart's desire. The second is getting it.*

—G. B. SHAW

We are often told from the pulpit to pray for anything we desire—God hears all prayers and answers them according to His divine will. Being human, we often hear what we want to hear, and we twist and reduce the mysterious and complex divine nature into a Santa Claus–like dynamic that gives us what we want and protects us from suffering if we are good. This distortion is reinforced by personal interpretation of scripture; without careful analysis, we hear Jesus saying exactly what we want to hear. At first glance, Jesus seems to promise us whatever we want, whenever we want it.

"If you abide in Me ask whatever you want and it shall be done for you" (John 15:7); "Ask and it shall be given to you" (Matthew 7:7–11); and "Give us this day our daily bread" (Matthew 6:11).

A more accurate translation of two words in these texts gives us a clearer picture of the real intent of Jesus's words; the ones to examine more carefully are "want" and "daily." "Want" is better translated as "need." The "right things" for which to pray are anything we *need* to get through this life, as long as that need doesn't pull us away from God and His plan to get us home to heaven. The word "daily" as it is used in Matthew 6:11 is not found anywhere else in the New Testament. The Aramaic phrase is best translated as "give us just enough material sustenance for this day." It is a clever way that God gets us to pray every day.* The purpose of both words is to develop our dependence on God as part of our spiritual growth; such dependence brings us closer to the Unseen Almighty and forces us to not only relinquish our arrogant notions that we are survivable by our own actions and wits but also to acknowledge our trust in—and thus love of—God. This change from prideful self-survivor to humble servant is the crux of spiritual growth and exactly what Kierkegaard meant when he said, "The function of prayer is not to influence God, but rather to change the nature of the one who prays."

The correct attitude we need to have when praying is absolute humility; it is the sine qua non of successful prayer. Humility keeps our petitions to God in the proper frame of coming from a humble servant, not a spoiled, demanding heir to the throne. In addition, we need to know that all the words of Jesus that center about the "ask and you shall receive" verses refer to the qualities of good discipleship—being a humble servant. Such a humble servant in God's Kingdom needs transcendent gifts—the guidance of the Holy Spirit, grace, the tools of effective discipleship, mercy, tolerance, forgiveness, strength, comfort, and a life of holiness.

"Blessed are those who hunger and thirst for righteousness [holiness], for they shall be satisfied" (Matthew 5:6); and "But seek ye first

---

* Every parent with a child away at college knows this dynamic. The standard operating procedure of every offspring living at school away from home is never to phone, text, or e-mail parents unless there is an urgent need for further funding. If our prodigal child spends $20 a day on junk food, snacks, movies, or, heaven forbid, beer and weed, and we respond with $100, we will hear back from said offspring in five days. If we only forward $20, we will be rewarded with another communication in twenty-four hours. The math is simple—and the Lord is undoubtedly very good at math.

the Kingdom of God and His righteousness [holiness], and all these things [worldly needs] shall be added unto you" (Matthew 6:33).

Yet God Does Bestow Immanent Gifts

Oh Lord, won't you buy me a Mercedes Benz?

—JANIS JOPLIN

We must not think, however, that God does not want us to ask for immanent or worldly needs that crop up throughout our daily lives. The student who prays for a passing grade on an important exam, the parents who pray for the safety of their child out with friends, the breadwinner who prays for help with the monthly bills, the family who prays for a successful medical outcome for a loved one—these are all perfectly legitimate and immanent desires that, when prayed with humility and sincerity, are pleasing to God. They are all heard; they are answered in accordance with God's complex plan to get us home at the end of our odyssey.

Praying for Wealth

Praying for wealth and success in our earthly lives is precarious business; some clergy go as far as to say we are never given license to pray for great wealth. This does not seem to be altogether true—God doesn't care if we are rich or poor; He only cares that we love Him unconditionally. The outcome of such prayer depends on our motives for wealth and how we live our lives should money and power be given to us. Sometimes, the person blessed with wealth and power remains a humble servant to God and uses his or her position and money to further God's plan. More often than not, however, sudden wealth and status completely derail spiritual growth, and the fortunate but really luckless recipient begins a tragic and destructive spiral into physical and emotional ruin. We only need to look at the lives of people who seem to have everything "under the sun" (cf. Ecclesiastes 6:1–2ff)—namely celebrities, athletes, and heirs to family fortunes—to see the vanity and futility of great immanent riches. We are all foolishly and naively convinced that money, power, and fame are the keys to happiness and satisfaction, yet many of these people who are so happy and satisfied end up checking into a new kind of hotel for modern life—celebrity rehab. Something very important to the existential Self is clearly missing in "having it all."

If the desire for wealth supersedes our efforts to follow God's plan for our lives, our hopes for a successful odyssey into heaven are erased. We will die holding a load of cash, an impressive obituary, and not much else. *The end will be the end.* We must keep our attitudes about what we need and want in line with God's plan for us. We must be very careful and thoughtful before we pray for wealth. The roses that seem so beautiful in this life often have very sharp thorns and lead to misery and suffering.

> *If you want to know what God thinks of money, just*
> *look at the people he gives it to.*

> —Dorothy Parker

What we pray for and what we should pray for are often very different things. A few lines from a prayer by an unknown Confederate soldier quoted by Rabbi Marc Gellman from Wayne Dosick's book *When Life Hurts* give us a heavenly slant on not getting what we want:

> I asked God for strength that I might achieve; I was made weak that I might learn to humbly obey.

I asked for health that I might do greater things; I was given infirmity that I might do better things.

I asked for riches that I might be happy; I was given poverty that I might be wise.

I asked for power that I might have the praise of men; I was given weakness that I might feel the need for God.

—ɯ—

Unanswered Prayers

Yet when *what* we pray for is very important and the outcome is not what we want, we experience suffering. Especially vexing are the occasions when we pray to save a loved one from serious illness, harm, or even death, and the prayers are seemingly unanswered. We must not blame God; how He deals with the suffering in this world is a complete mystery. The anger at God over losing a loved one or bearing the suffering of a child can be especially acrid and consuming; we must keep our faith and bow down in humble submission. We must surrender. We can never assume we will be free of pain because we are believers. Faith is such a precious gift; we must never let it be tainted by pride. It is a *gift*, not a ticket that guarantees God's plan will always go our way, even if it means the excruciating pain of losing a loved one. It is saintly humility that silences such arrogance. It is the ultimate test of unconditional love for God. In this sense, a horrible and untimely death of a loved one—an event resulting from this life in Satan's realm—has meaning: God may be asking us the ultimate question, "Do you really love me as I ask?" Such unconditional love is vividly portrayed in Jesus's three desperate pleas in the garden of Gethsemane: "My Father, if it is possible, let this cup [suffering] pass from Me; yet not as I will, but as Thou wilt" (Matthew 26:39).

Death is a universal and natural part of life. The death of a loved one, especially someone who is young and in his or her prime, always leaves soul-wrenching pain in those left behind. Time, in spite of the adage, does *not* make it better. Everyone dies, but the tragedy and pain come from the fact that death sometimes arrives at horribly inopportune moments. Is this the work of Satan, who has been given dominion over this immanent realm, or is it part of God's complex plan of which we have no grasp? Job wondered too. Scripture gives us no answer but only reminds us that such pain is a natural part of living on this earth.

> *There is an appointed time for everything. And there is a time for everything under heaven—a time to be born and a time to die.*

> —ECCLESIASTES 3:1–2

Praying to Ease the Pain of a Lost Loved One

We know that prayer is a way to communicate with and get to know God intimately. It is the portal for the immanent to transcend the material world and travel into the unseen afterlife. Many people who are firm believers ask, since we communicate with God and the saints who are in a transcendent realm, can we use some form of prayer to communicate with lost loved ones? It is a legitimate question. The effects of losing a loved one—a child, parent, spouse, lover, or friend—are greatly underestimated by those of us spared this pain. For the rest of their days on this earth, survivors' lives are changed, and never for the better. The loss of a loved one is a ragged amputation of part of the soul that never completely heals.

Strangely, the ability to communicate with deceased loved ones may very well be real. The evidence that we can do this in some way is speculative and anecdotal but is nonetheless very strong. Over the years, psychiatry and medicine have given me the opportunity to talk at length with many people who have suffered personal losses. Many of them—and by many, I mean dozens—have told me secrets about how they have dealt with the grief. One way is to "talk" to the lost loved one using a written journal. The act of writing down whatever is in the broken heart seems to work through the grief, and the warmth felt afterward is a sign of healing. But sometimes, strange things happen beyond the serendipitous.

Unlike charlatans who claim to have the power to relay messages from the dead, these people do not get answers, at least not right away; neither are they in words. The answers come, but always in a mysterious way. People describe receiving insights or new thoughts—graces, perhaps—as if light bulbs go on above their heads. They firmly deny that these are coincidences; these are new thoughts that they claim they would never have had on their own, and such insights always seem to answer the questions put to the lost loved one. People also describe events that occur after communicating with a loved one, events that seem quietly miraculous. The following is a well-known anecdote that's been around for a few years; whether there is truth in exactly what happened is open to argument, but the tale is compelling. It's the outcome that is so remarkable.

She was a stoic woman who had lost her son in war. She was a believer, but a skeptical one, and a scientist by trade—her business was empirical proof. Her son's death turned her life upside down; there was no more joy in her soul, and simple daily tasks became burdensome. She visited her son's grave regularly, and something happened one Christmas season that was beyond science.

It seems the grave next to her son's had a string of battery-run Christmas lights on it; these types of lights stay on during darkness and are made to last the weeks around Christmas. She had seen the lights on a previous visit to the cemetery, and they glowed steadily. She had been writing a journal to her son for some time, but on this latest visit to his grave, she told him in a soft voice that the best Christmas present she could receive would be to know that he was OK. She finished her visit, and there was only silence. She turned to leave, and the lights began to blink on and off. She stood there in awe until the lights once again glowed steadily.

It was a Christmas present from her dead son that brought her back to life. She began to feel joy again and ate and slept better; her work and social lives began to heal. It was perhaps a gift from his soul to hers, a gift that was a signpost for her odyssey to come.

How to Speak With God

Through the study of books one seeks God; by meditation one finds Him.

—Saint Padre Pio

Prayer can be both active and passive communication with God and is of three types: prayer using words (spoken aloud or spoken in the mind), meditation, and contemplation. Although different from each other, all are very effective in achieving our goal of becoming transcendent in this immanent world—a goal that will certainly make heaven a joyous and familiar place. The first type of active prayer—spoken words—can be created within ourselves in simple language we understand well, or it can be formed prayer that has been written by others. Most notable of formed prayer is the Lord's Prayer, composed by Jesus Himself, answering the apostles' questions about how to pray (Matthew 6:5–15). Besides the Hail Mary, Glory Be, and other familiar prayers, there are many more written or translated by Church scholars in prayer books. These prayers can be part of the Eucharistic Liturgy of the Mass, structured Novenas, or prayers composed by saints. All Christians recognize Mary's prayer, the Magnificat; this prayer spoken in front of her cousin, Elizabeth, during the Visitation of Mary, contains all the components of an effective prayer we mentioned—especially humility. It is worth a review and daily recitation; it is in Luke 1:46–55.

"For He has looked upon [noticed] His handmaid's lowliness… He has shown might with His arm, dispersed the arrogant of mind and heart" (Luke 1:48, 51).

We should mention a couple of points about prayers written *for us*. Catholics need to make sure that prayers are consistent with the Church's teaching by looking for an official sanction by the bishop of the place where the prayer book (or any book involving Church dogma, for that matter) was published. These sanctions are called the *nihil obstat* and the *imprimatur*. The former simply means, "There is no problem with what has been written"; the latter is, "Let it be printed." Throughout the ages, the Church has been plagued by freethinkers, some outright heretics, who sometimes put their own religious opinions into print that are outside the bounds of accepted teaching and are not consistent with what the Gospels and Christ said. One familiar example is the placement of "novenas" and other prayers in the personal sections of newspaper want ads purporting to "never fail" if prayed fervently for a period of time and then sent forward in other ads. These pseudoreligious chain letters may be well intentioned, but they "test the Lord"* and are very misleading about how prayer really works.

The second point about prayers written for us is that we must understand what the prayers are saying. I can remember going with my mother and her friend to Wednesday-night Novenas offered to Mary and the Miraculous Medal: "O Mary, conceived without sin, pray for us who have recourse to thee..."† In the Novena prayer book, we read aloud, "And so, I consecrate myself to the Miraculous Medal and to thee, O Virgin of Virgins." Being only eight years old, I had no idea what the words "conceived," "recourse," and "consecrate" meant. I was a little shaky about "virgins" too, but I figured it must be really important.

I needed to understand that this Novena was getting me into a lifelong commitment of tremendous importance and responsibility. "Recourse" meant we were asking Mary to pray for us because we trusted in her power and privileged relationship with her son. To "consecrate" ourselves to Mary and her Medal is to anoint ourselves as trustworthy servants, agents, or representatives of devotion to her from the rest of the world. The terms of commitment are for life. I had no idea of the importance of those words, but they certainly have had a profound effect on my later life. Understanding the full meaning of our formed prayers is thus critically important.* If our prayers

---

* "You shall not put the Lord your God to the test" (Deuteronomy 6:16). This was Jesus's response to Satan's promise of immanent immortality in Matthew 4:11.

† I actually had no choice in the matter. I was only the in third grade and could not be trusted home alone with my brother.

* My mother was a devout woman, a Catholic all her life and quite well read, but when it came to Latin, she was completely baffled. Her formative years were pre–Vatican II, when the Mass was entirely in Latin. She, like everyone else, knelt quietly during Mass as the priest—his back turned to the crowd as if he were in the middle of something nefarious—mumbled the prayers. The only respite came when the choir would sing a prayer out loud. The prayer before communion was what we now pray

commit us to a lifetime of responsibility, it's best to know what we're agreeing to.

—∞—

Of the remaining two types of prayer, meditation and contemplation, meditation is active prayer, something we initiate and do. Contemplation, on the other hand, is passive prayer—it is a special, higher form of meditation initiated by God. Since we cannot initiate contemplation ourselves, the obvious starting point for us is meditative prayer—we actively read, review, and think about the people and the stories in the Bible, particularly the New Testament. The basis for such meditations is the Christian tradition of *lectio divina*—literally, "divine reading." Our first step is to get a good study Bible, one with detailed footnotes and references. I use the Catholic Study Bible and the Catechism of the Catholic Church. The Catechism is a massive and detailed text of nearly a thousand pages that not only references all the prayers and dogma of the Church but also clarifies many issues beyond what we learned in Catholic school.

Prayer for most of us is limited to active, formed prayer like the Lord's Prayer and short, personal petitions to God in times of trouble. But the real backbone of effective Christian prayer is meditation on the life of Christ in the Gospels and on the details of God's plan for the salvation of man throughout the entire New Testament. There

---

together as "Lamb of God, Who takest away the sins of the world," but in the Latin Mass, it was sung as *"Agnus Dei, qui tollis peccata mundi."* One day, she said, "OK, college boy, tell me, what was it that Jesus told us?" I said, "Excuse me?" She said, "That song before communion, you know, the one that goes 'On this day, He told us'...something I can't figure out. What did He tell us?" After I explained the Latin, she said, "Well if they meant 'Lamb of God,' they should've *said* 'Lamb of God.'" Rome agreed, and the Second Vatican Council introduced the vernacular Mass.

are several goals in meditation. One goal is to connect our knowledge of God's plan to our own lives—all the joys and sorrows, triumphs, and trials of our daily life. This gives us a perspective on how God would deal with our problems and whether God would truly rejoice in our achievements. Another goal is to change ourselves—to at last define who we are and what we are doing on this earth by using the life of Jesus Christ as a perfect paradigm. Connecting the teachings of the Gospels to our daily lives will ground our floundering Selves—giving us a path of smooth stones on which to walk through life. Knowing who we are—children of the Almighty God and faithful participants in His plan to get us home—gives us the structure to act as such. The resulting effects on our morality, our suffering, our love lives, and our odyssey homeward into heaven will be nothing short of miraculous.

Contemplation is a higher form of meditation that is strictly passive—we cannot initiate contemplative prayer. It is meditative thought and images placed into our consciousness by God Himself. It is reserved for people who have been praying daily for a while and have mastered the art of completely shutting out the world. It is not an answer to our requests—these are given in ordinary prayer. Rather, contemplation is a view in our mind's eye of the transcendent world of God and heaven. It is firsthand knowledge of what we supposedly cannot know. The level of intensity and passion in contemplative prayer varies greatly among those fortunate enough to experience it; some describe ecstasy in the midst of a trance-like state. Most experience an overwhelming state of peace, calm, and fulfillment. Anyone who is faithful to daily prayer and simple *lectio divina* meditation can experience the transcendent joys of contemplative prayer. It is a gift from God for those of us who can effectively turn away from the world's distractions during our prayers and who place daily prayer and meditation first on our lists of priorities.

Throughout the centuries, the Church has recognized apparitions to dozens of saints—Saints Augustine, Jerome, Gregory the Great, Dominic, Catherine of Siena, and Teresa of Avila, to name but a few—that have added timely and transcendent truths to our faith; their visions occurred during contemplative prayer. The dozen or so recognized apparitions of the Blessed Virgin Mary, including at Lourdes, Fatima, LaSalette, and Guadalupe, are also the result of extreme moments of contemplative prayer. Some would argue that these apparitions were not contemplative visions but physical visits by Mary; this seems unlikely, since Mary was not visible to everyone.*

A Very Easy Way to Pray and Meditate
A perfect prayer would be one that combines spoken words with meditations on the life of Christ and that opens the gate for contemplative visions. Both speaking with God and thinking about the life of Jesus and how His life connects to our daily needs, accomplishments, joys, and suffering can be effectively achieved through what is considered to be the perfect prayer by the Church: the Rosary of Mary. Even though its power is well-known, many Catholics avoid this special prayer, claiming the Rosary is tedious and repetitive droning of little

---

* Certainly, Mary's appearances were miraculous, but if she were imminently present in the truest physical sense, others would also have seen her. A true physical presence of Mary on earth would be the transcendent existing in the immanent. In the Old Testament, this occurred many times—e.g., the burning bush and Moses on Mount Sinai—but in the New Testament, the only occasions of a physical presence of the transcendent in this immanent world are the Annunciation to Mary by the angel Gabriel, the Incarnation of Christ, the Transfiguration, the post-Resurrection Jesus, the Descent of the Holy Spirit at Pentecost, and the Real Presence of Jesus in the Eucharist.

consequence. In fact, most non-Catholics openly despise it, wrongly believing it is a prayer to Mary and not to God Himself.

Both groups could not be more wrong. Throughout this book, we will refer to the *meditative aspects* of the Rosary—the most important but neglected part of the prayer—and how these meditations, called *mysteries*, connect to our daily trials in living, loving, suffering, and ultimately hoping for a successful odyssey into the afterlife.

Meditations about the Direction and Meaning of Our Lives Here on Earth

If we focus on the direction and meaning of our lives and superimpose these personal insights upon some sort of paradigm of perfection, we will evoke a vivid image of how close we are to a happy, well-lived life and a successful odyssey. We have discussed at some length how this modern age has pulled us away from a life of spirituality and heavenly purpose. We have become, as Walker Percy says, empty, vacant Selves that have no idea who we are or what we are doing here, and many other modern thinkers, like psychoanalyst Erich Fromm, agree that the empty or ill-defined Self is a principal cause of our modern angst, especially concerning relationships with others. Developing a sense—indeed a lifestyle—of spirituality will breathe life back into our neglected souls; such growth will literally reprogram our interface with the world and change our lives.

Exactly What Do We Meditate About? Where Can We Find a Perfect Paradigm?

We know that the life of Jesus is a perfect mirror in which we can see exactly how to live our lives. In order for the redemption of mankind to be valid, the divine Jesus had to empty Himself of the glory of heaven and live the life of a man. He did just that: He was born in poverty, worked hard according to God's plan, lived without worldly riches—He was basically homeless during His ministry—suffered humiliation and rejection, and ultimately died a most painful death. He lived a life of extremes; His poverty and suffering exceeded what most of us might have to endure on this earth. He did not seek wealth, celebrity, beauty, or power as ends in themselves; such things came to Him as a result of His obeying the Father's will, just as such things should come to us.

His mother, Mary, was also a perfect paradigm, not just for women to emulate, but all who are parents, teachers, guardians, and common workers in the fields of the Father. She did this not seeking power or glory, but in absolute humility: "For He has looked upon His handmaid's lowliness" (Luke 1:48). Her role in the divine realm is that of the Ark of the New Covenant—she brought the Word of God into reality in order to bring about salvation for God's children. Her role in the human realm is twofold: she is an *advocate*—her position as Mother of Jesus allows her to place the needs of mankind before their King;* and second, she is a paradigm of the only perfect *creature*—another mirror that can reflect how we should live our lives.†

Our meditations, then, in seeking to make our earthly lives more "heavenly," must center on God's written Word about these two perfect paradigms. The New Testament is just such a source of actual

---

* The mother of a king enjoys certain privileges, archetypically portrayed several times in the Old Testament. Mary's role as a powerful advocate is strengthened by this privilege. One scenario that we'll discuss later is the story in 1 Kings 2:13–22, which demonstrates the special place and influence of the mother of a king. It is the story of King Solomon; his mother, Bathsheba; and the attempted treachery of Solomon's half brother, Adenijah.

† Jesus was not a creature.

day-to-day events that mirror our own joys, sorrows, and hopes. The Old Testament contains many references to both Jesus and His mother, but these are archetypical and prophetic in nature, often in allegorical form. The New Testament, however, gives a clear picture of how our lives should be lived *now*. This is the miracle of *lectio divina*—reading divine instructions for our earthly odyssey.

There are, however, twenty-seven books in the New Testament; reading the entire scripture on a daily basis is not realistic. The Church has solved this problem by selecting twenty events in the life of Jesus and, to a lesser extent, the life of Mary and her role in God's plan for our salvation. The secret to success in meditating on these events—called mysteries—is to connect them, every day, to what is happening in our lives: our joys and successes, our sorrows and sufferings, and our hopes for the future. The twenty mysteries are divided into four groups of five each. The Joyful Mysteries describe Jesus's early life and how it shows us who we are and what we're doing here. The Luminous Mysteries describe Jesus's teachings about how to make our earthly lives heavenly. The Sorrowful Mysteries describe the suffering of Jesus and how it can help us through our own trials. The Glorious Mysteries are truly the happiest; they describe what we can expect at the end of our odyssey—relief from our earthly suffering, unending completeness of Self, and absolute joy.

These twenty events are, of course, the meditations of the Catholic Rosary. Again, we reiterate that it is the meditations on the Rosary's mysteries that are the crux of this prayer. So we will spend the next chapters explaining each set of mysteries in some detail, and how these mysteries connect to our modern lives. The meditations on these mysteries—the key to a well-lived life—can be part of a complete Rosary; the background is made up of the well-known recited prayers, the Lord's Prayer, and the Ave Maria. For those wishing to pray the complete Rosary, the history and mechanics of the background prayers are described in the next chapter, as well as a very easy way to meditate effectively, using the background prayers as a "canvas" onto which our thoughts and wishes can be displayed before the Lord.

Without a doubt, however, the Rosary has gotten some bad press from all sides. People who pray the Rosary swear by it, yet many non-Catholics hate it. Surprisingly, many Catholics, even devout ones, are not fans of it either. They avoid the Rosary because they don't realize how complex it really is—they perceive it as meaningless droning and repetition. They fail to understand that the heart and soul of the Rosary are the meditations and not the repetitive, recited prayers.* They also greatly underestimate the Rosary's power and place as a perfect prayer. On top of all this, many Catholics have absolutely no idea how to pray the Rosary correctly and effectively.

Mixed feelings about the Rosary have been developing for a long time. Since its creation about a thousand years ago, the Rosary has been increasingly viewed from only one perspective—that of devotion to Mary, the Mother of Jesus. Mariology—the study and promotion of devotion and honor to Mary—has been a hotbed of debate, not only in the Protestant world but within the Catholic Church itself. Non-Catholics seem to have a universal disdain for any devotion to Mary, including the Rosary; many bristle with anger at the mere mention of Mary as a legitimate path to the Lord. As un-Christian as all this sounds, it is perfectly understandable in light of some of the extremes that have developed in Marian devotion. Yet those

---

* As we'll see in the next chapter, the recited prayers are not merely droning repetitions; they have meaning in themselves that are often connected to the meditations. This is true even when the "easy" way is taken—when the recited prayers are part of the hundreds of media presentations on TV, the radio, or the Internet.

disdaining all devotion and honor to Mary need to consider the possibility that bad-mouthing the Mother of Jesus in this life might be a bad idea.[*]

Devotion to the Mother of Jesus began in the third century and steadily grew throughout the ages. It was promoted and augmented by the Dominicans from the eleventh century onward, and some of these clerics reached the papacy. The importance of Marian devotion reached the hands of the great masters of the Middle Ages; their paintings and sculptures depicted the Virgin Mary as a powerful figure perched in the full glory of heaven, surrounded by angels, holding the Child Jesus. The extremes of Marian devotion climaxed in the nineteenth century with hundreds of supposed apparitions by Mary herself—physical appearances of a Mary who spoke, engendered miracles, gave ominous warnings about a reign of hell, and strangely passed secret messages to the visionaries. The Catholic Church began to put the brakes on the extreme exuberance embraced by some of the faithful—exuberance that bordered on excessive and that was no doubt fueled by the "magic aura" around these apparitions. The Church has never officially sanctioned any personal appearances of Mary but has handled the matter with delicacy—it has wisely dubbed them "private visions."

Yet we must accept that visionaries who see Mary are not charlatans motivated by earthly desires; they are really in the presence of the Mother of Jesus. Even though it appears to be a physical presence to the visionaries, it is probably a vision of contemplative prayer—images sent from heaven, but only to the visionaries. If Mary were physically present in the sense of matter displacing matter, she would be visible to all, and, as such, might even have stayed for lunch.

---

[*] Christians believe they will face the Glorified Christ in the next life. Undoubtedly, Jesus will bring up one's unkind, earthly words about His mother. It may be a very awkward scene.

In a 1978 document, *Normae Congregationis,* the Church set up strict criteria for permitting the faithful to honor Mary at these apparition sites—never admitting that the apparitions really occurred but only "not objecting" to devotional shrines being built and new titles being bestowed on Mary. In the last two hundred years, there have been 295 requests to the Church for review of alleged apparitions; only twelve have passed all nine criteria and are "not objected to" by the Church.

In reality, we need not laboriously travel to a far-off apparition site to experience the miracles of Mary's help through her advocacy. A private, quiet place in our own homes will work just as well. If we pray diligently and often enough, the miracle of Mary appearing to us in contemplative prayer is a real possibility.

The extreme growth of Marian devotion and the impetus given to it by the apparition frenzy have created a divide in the attitude of the faithful toward Mary. The *maximalists,* without saying it outright, believe Mary to be on the same plane of Jesus as far as our salvation is concerned. This extreme has culminated with their demands that the Church officially give Mary the title of "Co-Mediatrix" and "Co-Redemptrix." The opposite faction, that of the *minimalists,* feels that Mary should have no honor except that of being the Mother of Jesus. The two sides nearly came to blows at the Second Vatican Council in the early 1960s. The Church has officially said that neither side is right. Three of the most pro-Marian popes in history have publicly warned that our "exuberance to exaggerate" the role of Mary in our salvation must be curtailed; they also said that minimalizing Mary to a mere vessel for the birth of the human Jesus is also a mistake and an affront to the Blessed Virgin.

All this hoopla has fueled the Protestants' mistaken belief that *any* devotion to Mary is *praying to* Mary, an ordinary creature; they correctly say that scripture expressly tells us this is forbidden. In

Revelation 22:9, Saint John falls down and worships an angel. The angel firmly tells him, "Don't fall before me...worship only God. I am but a fellow servant and brother." Another point of contention is the role that Mary plays in our petitions as mediator and intercessor. Some extreme Mariologists have exaggerated and distorted Mary's exact role of intercessor for our prayers; they purport that Mary, as the Mother of Jesus, is able to change the mind of God. This exaggeration of Mary's power somewhat parallels the manipulation commonly seen in family dynamics: if we ask Dad and he says no, we can ask Mom and she'll get him to give us what we want. This notion is wrong; whatever Mary's role as mediator and intercessor is, she cannot change the will of God. Her role as mediator and intercessor is quite mysterious, as we'll see, and has nothing to do with manipulating the Lord.

We must be very careful with the title of "mediator," because scripture plainly tells us there is only one mediator between man and God, and that is Jesus Christ. We read from the apostle Paul: "For there is one God, and one mediator also between God and the human race, Himself human, who gave Himself as ransom for all" (1 Timothy 2:5–6).

We defenders of Mary soften the conflict by avoiding the term "mediator." Rather, we refer to the Virgin Mary as our "advocate" and "intercessor." Mary, a sinless human and perfect spokesperson for humanity, intercedes for our wants and needs between us—imperfect humans—and the only other perfect human, her Son Jesus, over Whom she has human, motherly influence. This is exactly the scenario in John 2:3 when Mary mentions to Jesus that the wine has run out at the wedding feast at Cana. To honor His mother's wish, Jesus miraculously changes water into wine. In this instance, Mary does not override divine will; she fulfills it. She is a human mother asking her human Son for help; the human Jesus hesitates because He fears the timing is wrong, but the divine Jesus knows it is time to start

His ministry. He uses His divine power—in full agreement with the Father—and changes water into wine, the miracle that begins His journey to Calvary and the glory that follows.

Yet Mary's role as intercessor for us humans goes much further. Our petitions are placed on an existential and personal plane, having everything to do with us, the individuals. Mary does not change God's mind in her intercession—she changes *ours*. As we've said, effective petitions in our prayers to God must be for the right thing, at the right time, in the right way, and with the right attitude. Mary's intercession in our prayers to God purifies, fine-tunes, and adjusts our petitions so that they fit these four qualities of prayer; in the process, we are changed in our petitioning stance—we literally see our petitions God's way, in the light of His plan to get us home. Whatever the outcome, we walk away feeling like the right thing has been done; if we are humble enough, we see this as Mary doing her job most effectively.

We must not let these arguments—maximalist versus minimalist, Catholic versus Protestant—divide us as believers. As the apostle Paul says in Romans 14:1–12, we all face judgment from the same God, and we must respect one another's opinions as long as they are held in good conscience. The important thing is that we pray, and pray daily. Prayer and meditation are the bonds that create and strengthen our connection to God, a connection that will be most critical in the afterlife. It must be a daily routine, not a matter of convenience or whim, or worse, an action put on a shelf until something terrible happens.

A Victim of All These Arguments Has Been the Rosary
The Rosary as a powerful prayer has suffered because of these arguments. It has been avoided by the faithful for a variety of reasons, all

of them wrong. The Rosary is literally the perfect prayer of recitation, meditation, and contemplation, and it is a prayer to God and about God. The substance of its meditation is the life of Jesus Christ, and it is entirely scriptural. Mary is present in some mysteries because Mary is ever present in Jesus's life, and if we let her be present in our lives, she can be an integral part of our sanctification. The honor we give to Mary in the background Ave Marias is well deserved, but Mary's wish is not for honor—she is too humble for that. Her only desire is that we grow closer to our Almighty Lord.

Prayer and Meditation: The Path to True Inner Peace
Meditations on the mysteries of the Rosary, then, show us in vivid detail how to deal with the world and its deceptions and pain. In this sense, our meditations fuel spiritual growth that gives us true inner peace here on earth. Something equally important occurs. We begin to understand the dynamics of heaven; we are literally infused with a picture of heavenly life that reinforces the notion that heaven will indeed be the end of our longing. We see with less and less doubt that the very things and people we yearn for most earnestly await us after our last heartbeats.

Prayer and meditation assuage not just the world's pain but also suffering arising from *within* ourselves. Through effective meditation, we begin to understand how these internal conflicts may be taking us down the wrong paths to true inner peace. I am speaking particularly of the uncomfortable, disjointed, or downright painful memories from the early years of our lives—especially childhood, adolescence, and early adulthood—that we have buried deep in our unconscious minds and which are therefore unknown to us in our daily conscious thoughts. These unresolved conflicts cry out from the hidden depths of our minds to be somehow fixed, and the need to fix such things drives us to think, feel, and act in sometimes destructive ways later in life—entirely without our conscious knowledge or control.

These conflicts and the need to fix them are common to all of us, but if they get out of control and begin to affect our decision-making process, we become victims of our *neuroses*. Without the strength of spirituality, these conflicts begin to pop up into our conscious minds and cause anxiety and depression. Our sense of worth becomes distorted into being less than it should be, and we begin the hopeless task of fixing our lives, trying desperately to accept ourselves. We waste our energy and constructive talents trying to replay our lives with different characters and different decisions, hoping the plot of our play will have a happy and conflict-free ending. Fixing our early conflicts by chasing after the corrupt values of the immanent world is a lesson in futility and pain. As Nick Carraway tells Jay Gatsby, we cannot go back and replay the past.

And yet, we push on, like Fitzgerald's Gatsby, rowboats against the current—contorting and manipulating our lives, trying to replay our individual plots of pain with new characters and situations. In our desperation and repeated failures at love and success, we damage the lives of others beyond sanity. For the people we love who are dragged into this neurotic fantasy of *la dolce vita*, life can be a living hell. We destroy ourselves too, by sapping our own energy necessary to live our lives away from the deceit of immanence and toward the truth of heaven. We will never experience true inner peace and fulfillment until we stop chasing rainbows and let the past die. Yet we must realize that the rainbows we chase on earth may very well be waiting for us in heaven—if we have the right, heavenly mind-set and if God wills it.

Meditations on the mysteries of the Rosary completely derail such a runaway train of suffering. When we superimpose our pain from wasted wandering through life, looking for happiness in others or worldly treasures only to be terribly disappointed, onto the mysteries of the Gospels and the lives of Christ and His mother, Mary, we are supernaturally reprogrammed onto a path of reality that leads to true earthly happiness. The septic tanks of our unconscious minds, filled with whatever gunk we may have accumulated in early life, are sealed forever. The lives of Jesus and Mary are meant to mirror ours exactly and show us life as it really is and should be—joy from the transcendent (spiritual) and suffering from the immanent (worldly). Daily prayer and meditation give us true reality and the strength to face life head on. We can, at last, feel real peace, knowing our odyssey is heading in the right direction—homeward to everlasting joy in the afterlife.

XI

The Catholic Rosary: Powerhouse at Lepanto

Give me an army saying the Rosary, and I will conquer the world.

—Blessed Pope Pius IX

The Rosary is a perfect canvas for our meditations.

—Pope Saint John Paul II

We've mentioned that the meditations on the twenty mysteries of the Catholic Rosary are the crux of this effective prayer, but the repetitive background prayers have their importance as well. As we said previously, the meditative portion of the Rosary consists of twenty events in Jesus's life taken from the New Testament; many involve Mary and her role in her Son's life. These events are called mysteries; the twenty mysteries are divided into four groups of five mysteries each: the Joyful, Sorrowful, Luminous, and Glorious Mysteries. Each day of the week has a different group of mysteries; these mysteries that we'll explore in some detail are the foundation upon which we meditate. In effect, we are praying one-fourth of a complete Rosary each day, since there are four groups of mysteries.

The mechanics of the complete Rosary, familiar to most Catholics—recitation of formed prayers while meditating on the mysteries—can be challenging to master correctly, much like learning to play the piano, where one hand does something entirely different than the other. We'll see in a bit that there is an easy way to overcome this challenge. Some people mistakenly believe that the entire substance of the Rosary is *only* the recitation of the background prayers, neglecting the impact of the meditations. It is no wonder, then, that some complain that the prayer is repetitious and tedious.

The background prayers consist of the words of Jesus Himself when asked by His disciples how to pray in Luke 11:1–4; this is, of course, the Lord's Prayer or the Our Father. The words *about* His mother, Mary, and *from* the angel Gabriel, Mary's cousin Elizabeth, and others *spoken to* Mary form the Ave Maria or Hail Mary. The third prayer is the Lesser Doxology, or, as we Catholics call it, the Glory Be. The recitation of these formed prayers create a background—a canvas, so to speak—upon which we can paint our thoughts on the mysteries: how we can understand the importance of these events as Jesus meant them to be understood, and how we can juxtapose our own lives—our joys, sorrows, and hopes—next to God's plan to get us home. As Saint Therese of Lisieux said, "The prayers of the Holy Rosary are not the essence of it, but a bed of rose petals upon which we can lay our petitions at the feet of Jesus."

The words of these formed prayers that we repeat throughout the Rosary have importance on their own, with hidden meanings that often align with our own personal meditations. The Catechism of the Catholic Church is nearly a thousand pages long; no fewer than a hundred of these pages are devoted to how prayer is critical to our salvation process. Of the hundred pages, nearly fifty are specific interpretations—from both the Old and the New Testaments—of the Lord's Prayer and the Hail Mary. It is an important read for Catholics whether or not the Rosary is their prayer of choice.

History and Beginning of the Rosary

It will cause good works to flourish; it will obtain for souls the abundant mercy of God; it will withdraw the hearts of men from the love of the world and its vanities, and will lift them to the desire for Eternal Things.

—MARY, THE MOTHER OF JESUS, IN CONTEMPLATIVE PRAYER TO BLESSED ALANUS OF THE ROCK IN THE FIFTEENTH CENTURY

The precise origin of the Rosary is somewhat cloudy. Sometime before the twelfth century, pious tradition tells us that the faithful used to recite the psalms—all 150 of them. Every ten psalms, they would stop and pray the Lord's Prayer. To keep track of this monumental prayer session, they used small pebbles carried in a pouch. They would take out ten at a time and drop one with the recitation of each psalm. For obvious reasons, this became quite cumbersome, so beads were strung in groups of ten with a larger bead between them for the Lord's Prayer.

Sometime in the twelfth century, the psalms were replaced with Ave Marias. Tradition tells us that the concept of the Rosary was given to Saint Dominic in an apparition of the Blessed Mother in the church of Prouille in the year 1214. There is no official historical evidence linking Saint Dominic with the modern Rosary, but it is well accepted that the Dominican Order as a whole is responsible for the development of this devotion. The important practice of meditation on the Gospels was started by Dominic of Prussia, a Carthusian monk, sometime in the fourteenth century. In the fifteenth century, the Rosary was promoted by Blessed Alan of the Rock, a Dominican priest and theologian, who, in a vision, was given Mary's fifteen promises to those who pray the Rosary faithfully. In 1569, the Dominican Pope Pius V made the Rosary an official part of Catholic prayer. It was in the sixteenth century also that meditation became a solid part of the prayer; Gutenberg's printing press made it easy for "picture texts" of the Gospel mysteries to be circulated among the faithful as aids to meditation.

In the last four hundred years, popes and saints have extolled the virtues of the Rosary, and more people are devoted to the Rosary than most Catholics realize. The twentieth-century Capuchin friar and mystic, Saint Pio of Pietrelcina ("Padre Pio"), the sometimes-controversial priest who was a confessor to popes and allegedly suffered the stigmata of Christ, emphasized that the Rosary was the perfect means to find God here on earth.

The Power of the Prayer

There are dozens of stories about the power of this unique devotion, and one of the most notable is the origin of a title given to Mary: Our Lady of Victory. In 1571, ships from the Ottoman Empire were threatening to invade Europe, and Pope Saint Pius V organized a small coalition of naval forces to meet the enemy at the Battle of Lepanto. The hopelessly outnumbered Christians were doomed to certain defeat, but the pope called for all Christendom to pray the Rosary during a procession in Rome. The Ottoman fleet was miraculously destroyed and was never able to recover.* A feast day was proclaimed for Our Lady of Victory; this label was later changed to

---

* Herbert Thurston, "Feast of the Holy Rosary," *The Catholic Encyclopedia*, vol. 13 (New York: Robert Appleton Company, 1912).

Our Lady of the Rosary, the title Mary used when speaking to the children of Fatima during their apparition in contemplative prayer.

Courage for the human spirit in times of despair comes to life in the story of Saint Maximilian Kolbe, a priest with great devotion to the Rosary who was imprisoned at Auschwitz during World War II. This is a tale of bravery and heroism that transcends anything we could imagine in these modern times. In the camp, Fr. Kolbe was well-known to the SS guards as a troublemaker; he was harassed and beaten because he continued his work ministering to his fellow prisoners. In the heat of summer, there was an escape attempt, and the SS decided to deter future attempts by picking ten prisoners to die a horrible death—they were to be deprived of all food and water while locked in a tiny, sealed cell until they died. One of the men chosen had a family and wept because he knew he would never see them again. Kolbe had compassion on him, left the ranks of prisoners, and brazenly walked up to the SS guard and offered himself to die instead. The guard was astonished that a prisoner would break ranks and confront him face-to-face. Normally, Kolbe and the other prisoner would have been shot on the spot for such arrogance, but the SS officer simply and unbelievably agreed. Kolbe and nine others were locked up; each day, Fr. Kolbe calmly led the men in saying the Rosary aloud. There was no wailing or screaming, only the sound of the prayers. One by one, the men died of thirst and hunger; Fr. Kolbe was the last to die. He hung on too long for the guards' liking and was finally killed by an injection of carbolic acid. I'm sure these men did not pray to be spared their fate but asked for courage and a strengthened faith to calmly surrender to their sufferings and deaths. "*Ora pro nobis peccatoribus, nunc et in hora mortis nostrae.*"*

---

* "Pray for us sinners, now and at the hour of our death": the last petition in the Hail Mary.

Learning to Pray the Rosary

The rosary is basically a circle of beads that begins and ends with a medal; this is usually a Miraculous Medal depicting Mary from an apparition to Saint Catherine Labouré or a medal with the image and symbols of Jesus on them. In the circle, there are fifty small beads in groups of ten called *decades*; these are separated by four large beads. The small beads keep track of the fifty Hail Marys, while the large beads and connecting medal are for the Our Father and other small prayers—the Lesser Doxology (the Glory Be), the Fatima Prayer, and the pronouncement of each mystery's title.

The Rosary begins with a short stem consisting of a crucifix and five beads. On the crucifix, we pray the Apostles' Creed, a prayer that goes back to the second century. There are ecumenical versions prayed by many Christian sects; the Catholic version was modified in 2011:

> I believe in God, the Father Almighty, Creator of heaven and earth. I believe in Jesus Christ, His only Son, Our Lord. He was conceived by the power of the Holy Spirit and born of the Virgin Mary. Under Pontius Pilate, He was crucified, died, and was buried. He descended to the dead. On the third day he rose again. He ascended into heaven and is seated at the right hand of the Father. He will come again to judge the living and the dead. I believe in the Holy Spirit, the holy Catholic Church, the communion of saints, the forgiveness of sins, the resurrection of the body, and life everlasting, amen.

The first large bead is for the Our Father, and the next three beads are for three Hail Marys, where we ask Mary to pray for us to receive the gifts of faith, hope, and charity. The fifth bead is for the Lesser Doxology, the Glory Be. The first mystery for that day's Rosary is

begun on the medal at the intersection of the short stem and the circuitous string of beads.

The Our Father—the Lord's Prayer—is recited at the beginning
of the decade for each mystery. We do not meditate on the mystery
during the Lord's Prayer—the only meditation during the Lord's
Prayer is the actual prayer itself. Jesus commanded the apostles to
pray this way for a reason: every verse in the Lord's Prayer has deep
and complex meaning (see Catechism 2,765 to 2,865): "Our Father,
Who art in heaven, hallowed be Thy name. Thy kingdom come, Thy
will be done, on earth as it is in heaven. Give us this day our daily
bread, and forgive us our trespasses as we forgive those who trespass
against us. And lead us not into temptation, but deliver us from evil,
amen."

Then ten Hail Marys are recited carefully, as a background for
our meditation on that particular mystery: "Hail Mary, full of grace,
the Lord is with thee. Blessed art thou amongst women, and blessed
is the fruit of thy womb, Jesus. Holy Mary, Mother of God, pray for
us sinners, now and at the hour of our death, amen."

At the end of each decade, the Lesser Doxology is said. Catholics
call this prayer the Glory Be: "Glory be to the Father and to the Son
and to the Holy Spirit; as it was in the beginning, is now, and ever
shall be, world without end, amen."

At the end of this Lesser Doxology, a short verse called the Fatima
Prayer is usually said at the end of the Glory Be before the next decade
is pronounced: "O my Jesus, forgive us our sins; save us from the fires
of Hell. Lead all souls to heaven, especially those in most need of thy
mercy."

Then the next mystery is pronounced and is started with the Our
Father again.

Meditation of the first group generally occurs on Mondays and
Saturdays, and its five mysteries focus on Jesus's conception, birth,

and early life. These are called the Joyful Mysteries. The events of the Joyful Mysteries are chronicled in the first and second chapters of Saint Luke's Gospel. The five Joyful Mysteries are the Annunciation, the Visitation, the Nativity of Jesus, the Presentation of the Infant Jesus in the Temple, and the Finding of Jesus in the Temple at age twelve. There are numerous events within each of these mysteries that provide the matrix for our meditation; we should be reading chapters 1 and 2 of Luke's Gospel as we pray this mystery.

On Tuesdays and Fridays, the Sorrowful Mysteries are said and meditated upon. These mysteries contain the events of Jesus's Passion and death, and they form a solid foundation upon which we can meditate, not only about Jesus's suffering, but on how our short-comings and sins are the reason for it all. We can also lay our own troubles and sufferings next to those of Christ; as we'll see, such med-itation will give us some insight into meaning about our pain. The Sorrowful Mysteries are the Agony in the Garden of Gethsemane, the Scourging at the Pillar of Antonia, the Crowning with Thorns, the Carrying of the Cross, and the Crucifixion and Death of Jesus.

On Thursdays, the Luminous Mysteries are recited. These mys-teries were added to the traditional rosary in 2002 by Pope Saint John Paul II and reflect some high points in Jesus's ministry and teaching. They are the Baptism of Jesus in the Jordan, the Wedding at Cana, the Proclamation of the Kingdom, the Transfiguration, and the Establishment of the Eucharist. Meditation on these mysteries again provides a learning matrix with which we can understand Christ's teaching as well as compare the course of our own lives with God's plan for us.

On Wednesdays and Sundays, we pray and meditate on the Glorious Mysteries. These mysteries are the culmination of Christ's earthly life and the role Mary plays in caring for the world after His departure. They are the Resurrection, the Ascension into Heaven, the

Descent of the Holy Spirit at Pentecost, the Assumption of Mary into Heaven, and the Coronation of Mary as Queen of Heaven and Earth.

At the conclusion of the fifty Hail Marys and intervening prayers, the Salve Regina ("Hail Holy Queen") is said. This prayer proclaims and affirms the queenship of Mary; it was composed by a German monk in the eleventh century:

> Hail, holy Queen, Mother of Mercy, Hail, our life, our sweetness and our hope. To thee do we cry, poor banished children of Eve; to thee do we send forth our sighs, mourning and weeping in this valley of tears. Turn then, most gracious Advocate, thine eyes of mercy toward us; and after this our exile, show unto us the blessed fruit of thy womb, Jesus. O clement, O loving, O sweet Virgin Mary.
>
> Pray for us, O holy Mother of God, that we may be made worthy of the promises of Christ.
>
> Let us pray. O God, whose only begotten Son, by His life, death and resurrection, has purchased for us the rewards of eternal life, grant, we beseech Thee, that in meditating on these mysteries of the most holy Rosary of the Blessed Virgin Mary, we may imitate what they contain, and obtain what they promise, through the same Christ our Lord. Amen.

Recognizing that meditations are the core of the Rosary prayer, many people find it difficult, even impossible to meditate while saying the background prayers of the Our Fathers and Hail Marys. This is a universal problem—we cannot think of two things at once; either the formed prayers suffer, or the meditations fade out. It's frustrating and probably why so many people neglect this powerful prayer. Both aspects of the Rosary are important, but the meditations are the backbone of the prayer experience; to solve this dilemma, it has become common practice to let someone else say the background prayers. This can be accomplished if we pray in groups, as in a Rosary after Mass, or, if we're alone, we use any one of the hundreds of media Rosary recitations on the radio, TV, or Internet.

This is not cheating; our minds still follow the words, and if there is a lull in our meditative thought, we become fully cognizant of the words prayed. The interesting thing is that the background words of the Lord's Prayer and the Hail Mary have their own mysteries to ponder—the meanings of each phrase are critical points in our salvation. After a while, we can see that these meanings often mix well and fit right in with our personal meditations on the particular mystery at hand.

Media sources of Rosary recitation are everywhere now, and they have an interesting history. The pioneer of using multimedia for the Rosary prayer is undoubtedly Father Patrick Peyton, an Irish Catholic priest known appropriately as "The Rosary Priest" who began his ministry on radio. Father Peyton concentrated on the Rosary as a group prayer, particularly the family Rosary.* His well-known phrases

---

* Father Peyton's strong endorsement of the family Rosary endeared him to our Catholic grade-school teachers, the Sisters of Saint Joseph. The nuns loved Fr. Peyton. My fourth-grade teacher, Sister Mary Grace, made us stand up each day and state in front of the class whether our family had indeed prayed the Rosary together the previous night. One did not disappoint Sr. Mary Grace; these stand-and-face-the-class sessions were terrifying for me. There was no way I could tell the truth; it was a matter of survival. I lied like a red-faced preacher caught in a liquor store. My father was a practicing Catholic but by no means devout. My mother was devout and prayed her Rosary at the Novenas I was forced to attend, and like so many before Vatican II, at Mass, and probably in the bathroom with the door locked. My father's devotions were plumbing and golf; we had no more chance of saying a family Rosary than of Jesus Himself teeing off on the first hole at 8:00 a.m. on Sunday. Even though I felt my lies were a matter of survival, I felt guilty and confessed them anyway. Every now and then, I'm sure I heard the monsignor sigh on the other side of that little screen in the dark confessional—apparently, I wasn't the only liar in my class.

were "The family that prays together stays together" and "A world at prayer is a world at peace." His Family Theater Production Company produced hundreds of radio and television broadcasts centering on group prayer of the Rosary, and he was admired by many celebrities on the Los Angeles media scene.

Current sources of the Rosary in the media are the many versions of the prayer in video form on sites like YouTube as well as on Catholic television—EWTN, the Eternal Word Television Network. There are dozens of presentations of the Rosary on YouTube from varying sources; they are tremendous helps in praying an effective Rosary. The audio portion of these productions consists of the formed prayers of the rosary, and the videos often show vivid reenactments of the mysteries—some from movies about the life of Christ and Mary. These are much like the "picture texts" from five hundred years previous, only a *lot* better. The prayers are said carefully and devoutly, and the images make meditation so much easier. The tempo of the presentation is a matter of personal choice. Some find that if the tempo is too slow, the prayers become tedious and interfere with effective meditation; a tempo that is too fast may lack serious devotion. A too-speedy Rosary reinforces the notion that the prayer is a mindless, dull repetition.

Our meditative thoughts should be ordered, concise, sincere, and laid out in our minds with absolute humility. A copy of the New Testament or personal notes can be very helpful. As we become familiar with our meditations through repetition, we can add our daily trials, joys, and woes to our meditations each day. We will be able to see the progress in overcoming our roadblocks to true happiness. It gets easier—a lot easier—with each day.

Exciting things begin to happen—we realize this prayer has *power*, power to overcome our most painful challenges in daily life. We realize that the lives of Christ and His mother, Mary—a creature just like us—mirror our lives, giving us partners in our sufferings and joys. Whatever Jesus and Mary see, hear, feel, and do become guideposts for our lives; the ordinary humanity of both gives us a consoling hug and vividly tells us we are not alone in this "valley of tears."

XII

The Joyful Mysteries: Discovering Who We Are and Why We're Here

I was sent to speak to you and to announce to you this good news. But now you will be speechless and unable to talk until the day these things take place, because you did not believe my words, which will be fulfilled in their proper time.

—THE ANGEL GABRIEL, RESPONDING TO
ZECHARIAH'S DOUBT ABOUT GOD'S PLAN

You live in a deranged age—more deranged than usual, because despite great scientific and technological advances, man has not the faintest idea of who he is or what he is doing.

—WALKER PERCY, *LOST IN THE COSMOS*

If we are to fill our "empty selves" by discovering just who we are and why we're here, we need someone to tell us the truth—and God does just that. The Self, in order to be complete, needs to have a purpose; this purpose must have transcendent meaning, a reason to exist that is consistent with the divine plan, not merely immanent or worldly. Our purpose—our fulfillment of Self—is inherent in God's wishes for us.

The First Joyful Mystery

Hail, favored one! The Lord is with you.

—LUKE 1:28

The theme upon which we will focus in the first Joyful Mystery, the Annunciation (Luke 1:26–38), is that God has a plan for the salvation of mankind as well as for each one of us and that He will always tell us or announce it to us in some way. The angel Gabriel suddenly appears to a startled Mary, a barely fourteen-year-old virgin living in the village of Nazareth in Galilee, a territory of lesser importance in the north of Palestine. The angel reassures her to not be afraid and that she has found favor with God; we must remember that Jews considered the name of God to be sacred—a faithful Jew was not allowed to even utter the name of God aloud. So Mary must have known this imposing figure was a being who had a Friend in the highest of places. The angel greeted her with the title "favored one," and Mary fully realized the importance of such a title; it was a really, really big deal. She then realized that what the angel had to say was from the mouth of God Himself. She listened with the utmost care.

Gabriel told her all the details she needed to follow God's plan—nothing more, nothing less. What he told this young teenage nobody living in a nowhere town must have been like a bombshell: the Holy Spirit was to overshadow her, and she would conceive a child that would be called the Son of the Most High. From the lineage of kingship that Gabriel gave for Jesus, Mary knew this child would be the Messiah—the Savior for which the Jews had waited three thousand years. She listened ever so carefully. She listened...and she *obeyed.*

"Behold the handmaid of the Lord. Be it done unto me according to thy word."

—LUKE 1:38

There are many variations on this statement of surrender, but the essence is that "I am a slave to God's wishes, and let it happen in spite of the risks and sufferings." And the risks and social ostracism for a pregnant, unmarried fourteen-year-old would have been a great deal worse in the small, gossip-heavy town of Nazareth than in today's world. She faced certain social and possible physical harm as well as rejection from her family and friends. Who would have believed such a story? Her betrothed (betrothal was as binding as marriage), Joseph, certainly didn't believe her and decided that the merciful thing to do was to "put her away" secretly, probably to prevent her being stoned to death. An angel appeared to him in a dream, explained the truth, and warned him not to divorce her. It was a dream that Joseph obeyed and probably never forgot.

Someone who did not listen and obey the news of God's plan was Zechariah, the father of John the Baptist. When the angel Gabriel appeared to Zechariah and announced the good news of God's plan for a son—Zechariah's wife, Elizabeth, had been barren and was well past child-bearing age, so this was truly a miracle—Zechariah doubted and wanted more details, a request that insulted the very truth from God Himself. For this, Zechariah was struck speechless until the birth of his son. It is important to listen and not doubt when God tells us His plan for us.

When Gabriel told Mary of this miracle for her cousin Elizabeth, the angel added, "For nothing is impossible with God." The message here for us is that no matter how difficult it seems to follow God's plan, we must believe the messenger and forge ahead with the absolute confidence that God can overcome any obstacle. The messenger leading us to God's way will probably not be Gabriel but may be people, events, and changes in our lives that show us, in no uncertain terms, the reason that we have been put on this earth. Our empty, vacuous Selves will be empty no more.

—◆◆◆—

As we said, the meditations on these mysteries should center around the fact that God has a very detailed plan for our odyssey into heaven, and, just as important, He always tells us exactly what we need to know about the direction our lives should take. He sends messengers to convey what we are to do—these may be people, events, life-changing joys, or tragedies; we must *recognize*—through the power of grace obtained through daily prayer—that the messages are indeed from God; we must *listen*, we must *believe*, and we must *obey* the sometimes difficult changes in our lives. If we fail to listen and insist on doing things our way, we must recognize that our failures will far outnumber our successes, and we will soon dread the dawn of each new day. This futile and misdirected path through life—waiting for the ship to come in that never does—is an allegory of Zechariah being struck dumb by the angel Gabriel. If we persist in chasing immanent wealth and celebrity instead of obeying God's message, we too will be struck dumb—our words and influences on the world will not be heard or be fruitful. If God's plan seems like a brick wall reinforced by adversity, we must remember, "nothing shall be impossible with God."

Recognizing, Listening, Believing, Obeying, and Facing Adversity with Confidence and Trust

In clinical psychiatry, many patients who seek treatment for emotional or psychosomatic problems seem to have similar patterns in their lives. The first is that they feel *powerless*. They have a hazy view of what they want and don't want from life, but they seem to run into one obstacle after another in recognizing and achieving real happiness. The second is that they have trust issues—they are *faithless*. They dismiss or ignore any substantive direction about how to live a well-lived life that comes from a source outside their own distorted value systems. Thirdly, they totally lack the ability to *delay gratification*. They want what they want now; their demands are rife with stubbornness and inappropriate pride—they always look for the easy way. Last, and most importantly, they lack any meaningful *sense of spirituality* in their approach to life. They may give lip service to a belief in God, but their participation in religious services and meaningful prayer-dialogue is thin or nonexistent.

All of us—if we are human—have some degree of these foibles in our lives that hinder not only a successful odyssey into the afterlife but also our happiness here and now. In order to change the course of our lives and grow away from these obstacles, we should first focus our meditation on this first Joyful Mystery by reviewing the events in Luke 1:18–38: Zechariah's doubt, Gabriel's words to Mary, the angel's reassurance about God's limitless power, and finally, Mary's surrender to God's will. Then, we should think about episodes in our daily lives when we feel powerless, lack faith and trust, are unwilling to delay gratification, and finally, when we question God and His limitless power and lack the trust to surrender with the same obedience and trust of Mary.

The Mystery of the Annunciation Is a Wake-Up Call for Us
The first few words of the angel Gabriel to Mary—"Hail, full of grace"—are not a mere greeting but are both a title of respect for Mary and, more important, a call for our own sainthood. Sainthood is not necessarily being sinless, but repenting of our shortcomings—going back and changing our attitudes toward what is right and wrong. This, in one sense, allows us to proceed in the right moral frame of mind to follow God's plan for us and to surrender, as Mary did. Any fears she may have had about the sacrifice and risks of her surrender to the Incarnation are washed away by Gabriel's words, "Do not be afraid, Mary; for you have found favor with God" and "For nothing shall be impossible with God." The angel reassures her that God is now a partner in her life—"the Lord is with thee"—and with the conception of Jesus, God is to be physically united with her, exactly replayed in Jesus's Eucharistic promise to us in John 6:56: "He who eats My flesh and drinks My blood abides in Me and I in him."

The Second Joyful Mystery

Most blessed are you among women, and blessed is the fruit of your womb.

—LUKE 1:42

In the second Joyful Mystery, the Visitation of Mary (to her cousin Elizabeth), two themes stand out upon which we can center our meditations. In this mystery, the newly pregnant Mary travels some fifty miles to visit her cousin Elizabeth, who is six months pregnant herself with Zechariah's son, John the Baptist. The Gospel of Luke tells us that the baby in Elizabeth's womb "leaped" upon hearing Mary's voice and greeting, and at that moment, Elizabeth was "*filled with the Holy Spirit.*" The first theme that we should personalize to our daily lives is that when we interact with or meet others ("visit"), the most important thing they should notice is that we are, through the presence and power of the Holy Spirit, carrying the Word of God within our beings—we are messengers of, witnesses to, and active participants in God's plan for us, for them, and for the entire world (Acts 1:8). Exactly how we project this is a matter of our personalities and levels of spirituality. What's *not* important for others to notice is our physical beauty, our wealth, our status, or any other immanent (worldly) trait; what *is* important to show others is our transcendent wealth within our souls that reflects our obedience and surrender to God's way.

The second theme is *humility*. Elizabeth recognizes the importance of Mary and the Child she is carrying: "Most blessed are you among women, and blessed is the fruit of your womb." Elizabeth expresses her own humble state by asking, "And how does this happen to me, that the mother of my Lord should come to me?" (Luke 1:42–43). Both Mary and Elizabeth know that the Child in Mary's womb is, indeed, the Son of God; the word "Lord" used by Elizabeth is one of seven sacred names for God in Judaism. She acknowledges that Mary is also a believer: "Blessed are you who believed that what was spoken to you by the Lord would be fulfilled." Scholars believe that Mary's response to such praise was her psalm of humility to God, the Magnificat: "For He has had regard for His handmaid's lowliness…For the Mighty One has done great things for me…He has scattered the arrogant and proud of heart…And has exalted those who were humble" (Luke 1:46–55).

We are shown attitudes and behaviors that are very different from those in our modern way of life. The phrase in the Magnificat of particular interest is "For He has done great things *for* me." It is the ultimate expression of Mary's humility. She acknowledges that all the blessings and triumphs in her life come from God and His goodness. Our premodern ancestors also did not hesitate to give credit to the Lord when the harvest was plentiful, the hunt was successful, and the family was healthy and safe. Today, things are very different—the security of our survival is attributed to the new gods: science and man's ingenuity. The only time we turn to the Lord is to blame Him when bad things happen—famines, droughts, epidemics of hideously strange diseases, mass murders, and war with the deaths of innocents. We cry out, "How can a good and loving God let this happen?" when such evil is the result of man's own sin of pride. It is indeed pride that engenders greed for wealth, power, and status.

It seems that humility is a lost virtue for modern mankind, yet it is humility that can turn this world around. Perfect humility is something for which we should always pray; our meditations on this mystery should focus on God as the source of all our blessings and successes in life. To continue to think otherwise leaves us mired in the muck of violence and hatred in which we now exist. Our pride will ultimately destroy us.

He has scattered the arrogant and proud of heart…And
has exalted those who were humble.

—LUKE 1:51–52

The Third Joyful Mystery

For today in the city of David a Savior has been born
for you who is Messiah and Lord.

—LUKE 2:11

The third Joyful Mystery is the Nativity of Our Lord. The birth story of Jesus is a human portrayal of God Himself—in the form of Jesus, the Second Person of the Trinity, emptying Himself of the glory of heaven to become man so that we might live. God, the possessor and purveyor of all wealth, becomes poor that we might become rich. The theme of this mystery is that we must keep our desires for immanent treasures and worldly wealth in their proper perspective. The greatest gift ever given—eternal life—was bestowed in abject poverty: it had no price tag; neither did it earn any money. The irony of the juxtaposition of our spending habits during the Christmas season and the overshadowing aura of poverty around this mystery is remarkable.

Everything about the first Christmas—the arrival of the ultimate transcendence of heaven into the ultimate nontranscendence of this material world—was surrounded by reminders of poverty. I am quite sure that the unfortunate circumstance of "no room at the inn" encountered by Joseph and Mary (Luke 2:7)—in the midst of her childbearing labor—wasn't so much due to the crowding of people obeying the census edict as Joseph not having enough money to grease the innkeeper's palm. Tradition says that Jesus was thus born in a cave, but biblical scholars think that the women in the inn took pity on Mary—she was, after all, only a very young teenager—and helped her with the birth in a basement-like area where the animals of the paying guests were kept. The King of Kings, the Transcendent Word Made Flesh, descending from the glory of heaven, arrived in a cellar, amid the stench of pack animals and their excrement. Our Lord and Savior spent His first hours sleeping in a dry, straw-filled drinking trough fit only to slake the thirst of common beasts.

These images of Christ's arrival on this money-driven modern world should form the backdrop of our meditations about our own attitudes toward wealth. In light of the Savior's poverty-ridden entrance into this world, the comical excess of colorful holiday catalogs from high-end stores becomes ironically tragic, yet we should not relegate our meditations on this mystery to criticism of any holiday generosity—giving to others to express love is *always* a good thing. Rather, we should examine our worldly goals for wealth and status and ensure that these are not interfering with God's plan for us. Indeed, God's plan may call for us to be wealthy and powerful; being poor does not guarantee sainthood. The wealthy company owner who is generous to his employees and his community may be in his position of power for a reason known only to God. The penniless burglar or robber who steals to feed a dissolute lifestyle of drug use is clearly not on the right team. A person who finds himself or herself wealthy by honest means should never feel guilty about being a "have" in the midst of "have-nots" but should meditate carefully on this mystery and make sure that the power of such wealth mirrors the humility of the Christ Child and the generosity of the suffering Christ on Calvary.

The Fourth Joyful Mystery

Nunc dimittis servum tuum Domine, in pace secundum verbum tuum.

—LUKE 2:29

The fourth Joyful Mystery of the Rosary is the Presentation of Jesus in the Temple. The Catholic feast of this event is celebrated on February 2, and this feast day has also been called Candlemas and the Purification of Mary. This mystery of the Rosary is confusing to many of us because it has a complex history full of different meanings and different messages. The Jewish tradition of presenting a newborn in the Temple in Jerusalem is based on several laws from the Old Testament, and how these laws were applied to Jesus, Mary, and Joseph is a topic of extensive debate and controversy among Catholic, Protestant, and Jewish scholars. It is best if we greatly simplify to the basics and avoid jumping into the fray.

At the simplest level, we must realize that Joseph and Mary were devout Jews who obeyed the laws of their faith, even in the face of great inconvenience and expense. After the birth, circumcision, and naming of a firstborn male child, the mother was required to do two things: the first was to be cleansed from the religious impurity of childbirth—her *tahara*—by certain rituals and offerings, and the second was to travel to Jerusalem in order to present the child to the Lord in the presence of a Levite priest in the Temple. The circumcision and naming of the newborn took place eight days after birth, in accordance with Leviticus 12:3. The mother was considered "unclean"—unable to touch anything sacred or enter the Temple—for forty days after giving birth; after this span of days had passed, Joseph took Mary and Jesus to Jerusalem for the rites of completing Mary's purification and for Jesus's presentation to the Lord.

Mary's purification was completed with certain prayers, a ritual bath in a pool with no flowing water called a *mikveh*, and an offering of a lamb for her cleansing and for her sin, in accordance with Leviticus 12:4–6. Mary and Joseph were too poor to afford a lamb, so the law allowed the offering to be two young pigeons. Mary, because of the Immaculate Conception, was free of any stain of sin in order to be the Mother of Jesus and did not need these rituals, but she obeyed the law as a devout Jew. Her *obedience* and *faithfulness* to her religious tradition are the first notions of this mystery upon which we can meditate.

Mary and Joseph were paragons of obedience to the laws of their religion. They traveled some sixty miles with a one-month-old infant, probably on a donkey, from Nazareth to Jerusalem to obey the Judaic laws of presenting the child to God and purifying His mother, even though it was theologically unnecessary. When we meditate on this sacrifice of the Holy Family, can we say the same thing about our own loyalty to our religious beliefs? Do we participate in the Eucharistic Liturgy or attend services in our church regularly as expected, or do we only pray when trouble strikes? Putting ourselves in the pew with others for social worship requires discipline; more important than that, it requires humility.

After completing Mary's purification, Joseph and Mary brought the Child Jesus into the Temple to present Him to the Lord in a ceremony called *pidyon ha'ben* that is still practiced today. The term literally means "redeeming the son." The child was considered to be the property of the Lord (Exodus 13:2), and thirty to forty days after being born, the child was brought to the Temple in Jerusalem to be literally "bought back" from God. The price of redemption was five shekels—about two ounces of silver; the parents were asked by the priest if they would rather have the coins or their child, and they, of course, answered that they would like their child. As the end of this presentation and redemption, the child was blessed, and the parents gave thanks and prayed for the child's life to be dedicated to the Lord's will. The Gospel of Luke makes no mention of Joseph paying this ransom, but the point is that all living things belong to the Lord. This is the second notion of this mystery upon which we can meditate.

Have we really given our lives to God? Our meditations on this point become very personal and require a lot of deep introspection. Can we visualize and understand the connection between our jobs, domestic duties, and schoolwork and God's plan for us with clarity and meaning? Trudging off to jobs we dread to support our families, facing mounds of thankless housework and rebellious kids to provide a decent home life, or putting our best effort into schoolwork to better understand the workings of the world around us may seem like immanent and worldly efforts; in reality, doing our best in our daily responsibilities may have outcomes that are *very* transcendent. No one finds happiness and fulfillment in this life or the next by chasing rainbows.

The third notion in this mystery is that there may be suffering associated with surrendering to God's will. During the Presentation in the Temple, a holy priest named Simeon prophesied about Mary's suffering: "And you yourself a sword will pierce" (Luke 2:35). The Church venerates this suffering as the Seven Dolors (pains) of Mary and bestows upon her the title Our Lady of Sorrows. These seven incidents in the life of Mary and Jesus are by no means complete but are only highlights of the many difficulties and sufferings in her obedience to God's will: the prophesy of Simeon, the flight into Egypt, the loss of Jesus in the Temple at age twelve, Mary's meeting of Jesus on His way to Calvary, Jesus's death on the cross, the piercing of His side by a soldier's lance, and His burial. Do we understand and accept that doing things God's way may sometimes involve suffering?

The fourth and most important notion of this mystery is that this event is the first public presence of Jesus as "light of the world." The priest Simeon was a righteous and holy man and had been promised by the Holy Spirit that he would not die until he had beheld the redemption and salvation of Israel. As he held the Child Jesus in his arms, he realized that God had kept the promise; he offered a prayer of thanksgiving in his canticle, the *Nunc Dimittis*. From the fourth century, the Canticle of Simeon has been sung or prayed during evening vespers and has been part of the divine office of Catholic clergy: "*Nunc dimittis servum tuum Domine, in pace secundum verbum tuum*" ("Now dismiss, [let die] O Lord, your servant in peace, according to Thy word; For my eyes have seen Thy salvation, Which Thou hast prepared in the presence of all peoples, A *light* of revelation to the Gentiles, And the glory of Thy people Israel").

The phrase "a light of revelation" identifies Christ as a light in a dark world, and this is reiterated in numerous New Testament passages. For this reason, the feast became known as "Candlemas," the light from candles being a symbol for the presence of the Light of Christ: "The people who were sitting in darkness saw a Great Light, and to those who were sitting in the land and shadow of death, upon them a Light shone" (Matthew 4:16). In some cultures, lit blessed candles are placed in the hands of the dying so that the presence of Jesus may accompany them on their odyssey into heaven. What does the light tell us?

The light tells us we must steadily put our desires for worldly gain, whether it is money, power, celebrity, or physical beauty, into proper perspective. Like Simeon, Catholics and other Christians who have "seen the light" of Christ ("a light of revelation to the Gentiles") and have lived life accordingly should die in peace. But the death in Simeon's prayer for us is an allegory: we must die first and then see the light. It is not death in the physical sense as it was for Simeon, but *death to the world*. Once we have seen the light, God calls us to let go of our attachments to worldly treasures—or, as scripture says, dying to the wants of the Self and dying to the world. There are numerous verses in the Gospels and Paul's letters that call for us to "die to the world," but one of the clearest comes from Jesus Himself in Matthew 16:24–26, where He boldly states that transcendent glory comes only after extinguishing the desire for immanent wealth: "Whoever wishes to come after me [into heaven] must deny himself, take up his cross [a symbol of death], and follow Me. For whoever wishes to save his life [worldly gain] will lose it [eternal life], but whoever loses his life [gives up the world] for My sake will find it [heaven]. What profit would there be for one to gain the whole world and forfeit his soul [eternal life]?"

This idea that we should begin this journey of giving up our love of the world so we may see the light begins with Simeon's prayer and is fulfilled in the above Gospel passage. It is an excellent source of meditations on our own lives as we pray this mystery. The need for the light of such spirituality to guide us toward a transcendent heaven and away from an immanence-ridden world is proclaimed repeatedly in art, music, literature, and the media. There is a sixties folk song written by Hoyt Axton and made famous by Arlo Guthrie that describes the blindness we suffer in worshipping worldly treasures. The song is "Somebody Turned on the Light."*

The Fifth Joyful Mystery

Son, why have you done this to us?

—LUKE 2:48

The fifth and last Joyful Mystery is the Finding of Jesus in the Temple. This mystery portrays both the pain and joy of Mary in following God's plan for raising the Christ Child. According to Jewish law, boys at age thirteen or girls at age twelve become responsible for their own actions, relieving their parents of that burdensome task. In a ceremony, usually in the Temple, the child is declared "a son or daughter of the commandments"—he or she is now a full member of the Jewish community and fully responsible under the law. The

---

* "Women, wine and fast red cars, / And I couldn't see to read the signs. / Somebody said, 'Whose life is this?'/ And I said that it can't be mine. / And I never saw the sun till '71, / But I never gave up the fight. / Sure was glad when I saw the dawn. / Somebody, somebody turned on the light."

ceremony is now known as a "bar mitzvah" for boys and "bat mitzvah" for girls, although the Hebrew to Aramaic translations refer to the child and not the ceremony.

In Jesus's time, a boy was brought to the Temple at age twelve in order to prepare for this important event; nowadays, the preparation is much longer, beginning at age five. Mary and Joseph obeyed the law and customs, bringing Jesus at age twelve to the Temple during the Passover Feast. For safety reasons, people traveled in caravans; the trek from Nazareth to Jerusalem was a perilous sixty miles and probably required a three-day journey each way. When Passover was finished, Mary and Joseph left Jerusalem for home, assuming that Jesus was in the caravan, visiting with relatives. In an apparent *Home Alone* movie scenario, the Boy Jesus stayed behind and lost track of time while discussing complex theological issues with the elders and teachers in the Temple: "All who heard Him were astounded at His understanding and His answers" (Luke 2:47).

After a full day's journey out, Mary and Joseph realized that Jesus had been left behind and began another day's journey back to Jerusalem to look for Him. Luke tells us that when they found Him, they were "astonished." A more accurate translation from the Greek would be "flabbergasted"—a mixture of relief, joy, anger, disappointment, and total incredulity. It would certainly be a case for a divine spanking. But Mary only asked, "Son, why have You done this to us?" Jesus answered, as if it were no big deal, "Why were you looking for Me? Did you not know that I must be about my Father's work?" Biblical scholars interpret this as Jesus matter-of-factly stating that obedience to God's will takes precedence over family ties. The entire story is in Luke 2:41–52.

Connecting the lessons of this story to our personal lives can go much deeper than the actual text, depending on the tragedies and joys we have experienced. A tragedy that comes to mind is the all-too-common personal horror of parents experiencing the loss of a child's joy, either through physical disruption such as disease, disappearance, or death, or emotional loss such as estrangement, mental illness, rebellion, or drug abuse. In mirroring our sufferings, Mary goes through at least three such events of loss of her Son, Jesus.

The first is the incident of this mystery. Some of us have lived through it, but the rest of us can only imagine the horror that Mary and Joseph felt, walking quickly back to Jerusalem to look for the lost Child. In panic mode, they walked some twenty miles, probably in the dark, facing great danger from getting lost or from encountering highway thieves. The second event is Mary watching her Son die on the cross and, later, cradling His dead body before its burial. Michelangelo tried to depict her grief in his sculpture *The Pietà*, but we can be sure such a representation falls far short of her real pain. The third incident is one we normally associate with joy and hope—the Ascension of Jesus into heaven; it is, in fact the Second Glorious Mystery of the rosary. After the horror of the Cross, the Resurrection gave Mary her Son back—Luke tells us that Jesus stayed on earth for forty days—but she again endured His loss as He was taken into heaven on the Mount of Olives. In spite of her faith and the events that cemented it, she still had to live out her years on earth without her Son. Scripture makes no mention of her presence on the Mount of Olives that day, but I'm sure she was there, feeling terrible loss once more. The Ascension of Jesus, His departure from His mother and all who followed Him, is not part of Mary's Seven Dolors—the episode has been deemed a time of joy and hope for our benefit. But the pain of a parent realizing her life will have to continue without a child mirrors the horrors felt by so many of us who have lost a child to heaven.

"Son, why have You done this to us?"

There is no greater pain on earth than what a parent, especially a mother, feels at the death of a child. The age of the child is no matter; the pain is still there, be it for the loss of a baby or an adult child. The very soul of the parent is torn apart, and life without the child is often intolerable; relief only comes with a peaceful death of the parent, who dies with the hope that he or she will at last be one with the lost child again. And it is the grieving mother whose soul is torn the worst.

People surrounding the grieving mother do their best to assuage the pain, but as any mother going through such agony attests, nothing that anyone says can plug such a hole in the heart and stop the bleeding from the soul. It is an inconsolable hurt that may or may not fade a bit, but it *never* goes away. Well-intentioned words and time do not make it better. The pain of a lost child is a lifelong cross on the shoulders of a grief-stricken parent.

What grieving parents do *not* need is time to heal, meaning in their suffering, or reassurance that such a tragedy makes sense—they need their child back. But the child is not coming back to this *Purgatorio* called earth, and this is the greatest test of faith anyone can endure. So the natural question to ask in such despair is, "God, why have You done this to us?" It is not a question put to God in anger but in total confusion. Becoming close to others who have to ask the same question eases the horror just a bit, often enough to go on one more day, but the torn soul never heals.

In meditating on this fifth mystery, we find that Mary may be just such a suffering friend with whom we can ask such a question of God. Jesus may have been only twelve years old, but He still was consubstantial with the Father—He was God. So when Mary asked the Child Jesus to explain His behavior, she was, in essence, asking the very same question as a grieving mother: "God, why have you done this to us?"

It is a very legitimate question in the light of such tragedy, but it is one steeped in mystery—one that requires great faith to go without an answer. Such faith tells us unequivocally that we will be with our children again and that God, through Mary, feels our pain as well. By bringing ourselves closer to Mary—a fellow creature and mother—through our meditation, we absorb her faith and feel a measure of comfort in our grief.

The confusion we feel in asking God, "Why?" is mirrored in Luke 2:50: "But they did not understand the words that He said to them." The Gospel is not saying so much that the death of a child is part of God's plan, but rather that the reason for God allowing such pain is beyond our understanding. It is the ultimate test of faith. It is the great faith of Mary throughout her life. It is a time when pious fideism must come to our rescue; yet it is often a time when even saintly faith fails to assuage the daily torture of life without a beloved child. Time, as we've said, does not make it better. Only the end of our odyssey—heaven—erases the pain with a joyous reunion. We can be absolutely sure of this.

XIII

The Luminous Mysteries: The Perfect Self-Help Book

The people who sit in darkness have seen a great light,
on those dwelling in a land overshadowed by death, light
has arisen.

—MATTHEW 4:16

The Luminous Mysteries or the Mysteries of Light were added to the meditations of the Rosary in October of 2002 by Pope Saint John Paul II in his pastoral letter *Rosarium Virginis Mariae*. The intent was to include specific teachings of Jesus in the meditations in order to help us change our lives—lives often imbued with disappointment, disillusionment, and dissatisfaction—into meaningful odysseys filled with hope and true fulfillment. The mysteries tell us how to live our lives here on earth as perfect shadows of how life will be in heaven. They do this by highlighting the actions, events, and teachings in Jesus's life and clearly demonstrate that He is, indeed, the Light of the world. When we successfully connect the meanings of these mysteries to the stresses and disappointments of our daily lives, we are shown a lighted path to a meaningful existence, a complete sense of Self, and the experience of real joy—it is better than any self-help book.

While easing our emotional angst of daily life is important, the Luminous Mysteries also give us a reminder about what is necessary for change in our lives—a reiteration that our spiritual well-being is critical to our earthly physical and psychological well-being. They do this by showing us that transcendent (heavenly) values can overcome immanent (worldly) disappointment, sometimes in miraculous ways. They are, in this sense, a perfect preparation for heaven—they connect our worldly existence with the hidden transcendence of heaven.

The First Luminous Mystery

This is My Beloved Son, in Whom I am well pleased.

—God's voice at Jesus's baptism, Matthew 3:17

The First Luminous Mystery is the Baptism of Jesus in the Jordan River by His cousin, Saint John the Baptist. Baptism is a sign—a sign that we accept passively, but we acknowledge actively that we are indeed unworthy of the joys of heaven but promise to repent, to go back. We accept a commitment to go back and start over, to completely change our attitudes and actions about what is right and wrong and about what we have done and what we have not done. Our commitment also demands a choice: the values of the immanent world—wealth, power, and physical beauty—or the values of heaven. Acknowledging that we need repentance is akin to buying a ticket for heavenly admittance. The Eternal Show hasn't started yet—we aren't even in our seats—but we know it's only a matter of time until the lights begin to dim.

Another analogy that may help in understanding the theological and existential nature of baptism is the image of two mountains side by side. The first mountain is the immanent Mountain of Worldliness. It is where everyone exists upon being born. This mountain is steep and difficult; the paths are full of sharp rocks that cause pain and suffering. But this mountain also gives fleeting pleasures: those on this mountain constantly seek out new pleasures as their interest in the old ones wanes. And this mountain has a visible summit; most strive for it, but few make it. To those few, the yearning to go higher is there, but the only path left is down. No matter where one is on this mountain, there is unfulfilled longing for something unseen.

The other mountain is the Mountain of Transcendence; it is a much better place to be, but it cannot be seen from anywhere on the Worldly Mountain because of a dense fog. People say it is so much better, but only some believe—those whose faith is strong. This Mountain of Transcendence has no visible summit—it climbs far above the clouds—and is much less steep; the ascent up the mountain is easy and pleasurable; the stones are smooth and supportive. Those lucky enough to be on this mountain know that life above the clouds is filled with pure bliss; their faith lets them almost see and hear the joy of those who have completed the ascent. The pain from the dissatisfaction of unfulfilled longings on the Worldly Mountain is assuaged here on the Transcendent Mountain; the smooth stones make the journey up the mountain easy: "For my yoke is easy and my burden light" (Matthew 11:30).

The denizens of the Mountain of Worldliness are curious about the Mountain of Transcendence, but the fleeting pleasures of their mountain distract them from trying to cross over, much like the seeds sown among thorns in the Parable of the Sower (Matthew 13:7, 22). Travel from the Worldly Mountain onto the Transcendent Mountain is not easy. The two mountains are only connected by a bridge that is sometimes invisible in the fog. The decision to step onto the bridge to begin the journey across is perilous at best—it requires a firm commitment and a leap of faith.*

Baptism is such a decision. Crossing the bridge is a frightening and uncomfortable journey; once the first step is taken, the fleeting and unsatisfying pleasures of the past are left behind. The actual crossing of the bridge is the act of repentance, the complete abandonment of putting worldly values ahead of God's plan. This journey across the bridge can be very quick, as in the good thief's repentance on Calvary (Luke 23:40–42), or it can take years, often suffered in brokenness. After crossing the bridge, life on the new Mountain of Transcendence is very different. In addition to the smooth stones underfoot and the gentle slope of the ascent, the air on this mountain is filled with *hope*. There are no false longings that can never be sated, and there is no top to cause despair. After passing through the clouds—our death—the odyssey is over, and life becomes eternally joyful.

We are all sinners in need of repentance, and the decision to step onto the bridge is the first step in our salvation. Jesus was not a sinner, but He chose to make the decision "to fulfill all righteousness" (Matthew 3:15). In order for God's plan for our salvation to take place—to fulfill all righteousness—Jesus had to mirror our lives exactly. He had to be human. He knelt down and took on the role of sinner and made the decision to repent, albeit unnecessarily. As such, He faced the same temptations and struggles that we face every day. The irony of His being innocent and yet admitting guilt certainly

---

* This entire allegory is played out in the movie *Indiana Jones and the Last Crusade*, a sequel to *Raiders of the Lost Ark*. In it, Jones is trying to cross from one steep mountain to another over a deep chasm in order to reach a chamber that holds the Holy Grail. His instructions tell him that the crossing will require a "leap of faith" since the bridge is invisible. He believes and steps into what appears to be empty space and a sure death. But the rickety bridge suddenly appears, and he is successful in his quest: the Holy Grail and its miraculous powers save his father from a certain death.

ablates any pride we may have in denying our need for repentance. It is also this irony that evoked the Father's blessing in Matthew 3:17: "This is My beloved Son, in Whom I am well pleased."

Our meditations on this mystery should center about our decision to repent, to take the first step of faith onto that rickety bridge. We may very well have been baptized in a church, but we need to look deep within ourselves to see if we've been baptized in the heart. Have we really made the decision to turn our backs on the world and its veneer of beauty and pleasure, a veneer that covers inevitable suffering? The roses are so beautiful but fade so quickly and are covered by such sharp thorns.

When we struggle with temptations to think or act in ways contrary to God's plan for us, and we look back at the safe Mountain of Worldliness behind us; when we hesitate to take that first step of commitment and faith, we need to meditate on the innocent Christ kneeling in the muddy Jordan River. He took on the role of earthly sinner and subjected Himself to the very same temptation we face every day: the temptation to seek out the top of the wrong mountain, thinking life there will never end but will be filled with endless wealth and power. These are, indeed, the very same temptations put to Jesus by Satan in Matthew 4:1–11: "Command that these stones become loaves of bread...If you are the Son of God, throw yourself down...He will command His angels...lest you dash your foot against a stone...the devil showed him all the kingdoms of the world in their magnificence...all these I shall give to you if you... worship me."

This mystery gives us strength to turn our backs on the world and to have the faith to step onto the bridge that puts our odyssey on a corrected ascent into paradise. If Jesus truly mirrors our humanity, then our kneeling in baptismal waters and acknowledging our need for repentance will most definitely bring the same praise as from God the Father to His Son. During this meditation, our ears and mind will resonate with His words, this time directed at us: "This is my beloved child in whom I am well pleased."

The Second Luminous Mystery

They have no wine.

—MARY TO JESUS AT THE CANA WEDDING, JOHN 2:3

The Second Luminous Mystery is the Wedding at Cana. The event is not mentioned in the synoptic Gospels and is told only in John 2:1–11. Mary, the Mother of Jesus, is invited to a wedding feast in Cana, a village about ten miles north of Nazareth; Jesus and His disciples are also invited. Weddings in first-century culture were usually huge, week-long affairs with large numbers of people invited. Wine was the beverage served, and it was the responsibility of the bridegroom to supply the large amount required for such a feast. When the wine gave out at Cana—for whatever reason, financial or otherwise—Mary approached her Son and said what may be the four most important words of this scenario: "They have no wine." Jesus, after some apparent grumbling, miraculously created 120 to 150 gallons of premium wine out of plain water by His mere presence—no puff of smoke, no abracadabra, no fanfare. The headwaiter extolled the quality of the new wine and nodded praise to the bridegroom because he had craftily saved the good stuff for last, when most others served better wine first.

The eleven verses covering the wedding feast at Cana have been interpreted in literally dozens of different ways by numerous biblical scholars. It is important for us to understand how this mystery is one of the Blessed Mother's shining hours in the scope of our salvation; deeper meanings of the events at this wedding feast give strong justification for Marian devotion. Yet many non-Catholic Christian writers disagree with this, and their interpretations of the Cana wedding downplay the importance of Mary. Some even suggest that Mary was a hindrance to Jesus's true mission and that Jesus's response to her statement about the wine running out was a well-deserved rebuke (John 2:4). In spite of all appearances in the English translation from ancient Greek, this is really not true. Any analysis of ancient texts must always keep in mind that people in the first century said and did things quite differently than now, and any interpretation—even in the simplest way—must take the temporal mores of that society into account.

In looking for theological interpretations of this mystery upon which we can meditate, most agree that the Wedding at Cana is not merely about people drinking wine at a wedding.* As is common in Saint John's writings, mysticism and Old Testament images underlie his simple but carefully crafted texts. As we dissect this passage, we will see that it is not the bride and groom who are seated at the head table of this wedding; it is Jesus and His mother, Mary, sitting together at the table of mankind's salvation.

A good starting point for interpreting this event involves the symbols used to portray the roles Jesus and Mary play in our redemption and transformation from worldly beings unworthy of heaven to children of God infused with the holiness necessary to attain eternal life. Our redemption and this holy transformation occur through the presence of Christ in our lives and through obedience to His

---

* Most scholars, Catholic and non-Catholic alike, agree that the events at Cana have nothing at all to do with the morality of serving alcohol to guests, the alcoholic content of wine, public drunkenness, a clueless Mary telling God what to do, Jesus being some kind of cosmic bootlegger, or, especially, Jesus sassing His mother with a harsh rebuke.

commands. At this wedding feast, it is Mary who brings Christ to us and our struggles to become worthy of heaven. Cana is not about wine as a celebratory beverage, but it is about wine as a symbol for the Divine and water as a symbol for the human—the transcendent and the immanent, the heavenly and the worldly—and, as we'll see, the Old Testament and the New. It is about the beginning of the public ministry of the New Eve—the role of Mary in our salvation as she erases the mistake of the old Eve.

What about water and wine as symbols? In the Roman Catholic Mass—at the start of the Eucharistic Liturgy—the Offertory is begun by the priest pouring wine into the chalice and adding just one drop of water. The wine in this mixture is to become the Precious Blood of Christ at the Consecration. The wine is thus a symbol of divinity; the tiny drop of water symbolizes our insignificant humanity. It is the mingling of the two that forms the basis for our petition to God in the Offertory Prayer: *Per huius aquae et vini mysterium, eius efficiamur divinitatis consortes, qui humanitatis nostrae fieri dignatus est particeps.**

The miracle at Cana is a perfect archetype for this prayer. Wine in ancient times was usually diluted with water—the mixture increased the amount of wine on hand and kept the guests relatively sober. The wedding feast represents a stage upon which symbols for divinity and humanity come together in order to bring joy to the guests and admiration for the bride and groom. When the wine runs out, the guests are analogous to this immanent world and those in this life who need a divine infusion—symbolized by wine—in order to experience the joy of the eternal feast of heaven.

---

* "By the mystery of this water and wine, may we come to share in the divinity of Christ, who humbled Himself to share in our humanity."

In one sense, filling the six jars to the brim with water is a symbol for calling together those in need of repentance into a place where God resides, as in a place of worship. Mary's directive to "do whatever He tells you" has a twofold meaning: one is to make sure that we get into the water jar in Christ's presence, and the other is to simply obey His commandments. It is by fulfilling both of these meanings that we are infused with the divine power to become worthy of heaven. Mary's utterance of those four words, "They have no wine," is an archetype of her intercession on our behalf to Jesus—whenever we of the world stray from God's plan (run out of wine), Mary goes before the throne of the Almighty and tells her Son that we need His help to be saved from death (symbolized by an early and embarrassing end to the wedding feast).

There are many writings that interpret John 2:4—Jesus's statement to His mother after she told Him the wine had run out—as a sharp rebuke. Careful study of the Greek words used and equally careful consideration of the customs of the day show this to be incorrect. In spite of the obvious inference in the translation, Mary was not trying to change Jesus's mind, she was not trying to goad Him into doing something he didn't want to do, He was not being disrespectful to His mother, and, most importantly, Jesus was not objecting to performing this miracle. The suggestion that Mary was a clueless kvetch who only wanted Jesus to show His power in order to start a political rebellion against the Romans—as many of the disciples did early on—is nonsense. Mary had been overshadowed by the Holy Spirit in the Annunciation and knew exactly what Jesus's mission was. In the mystical sense—the way John wrote—Mary's words "They have no wine" have nothing to do with wine but rather the need of the world to be sanctified by the presence and teachings of Jesus. Jesus's response in John 2:4 was not a challenge to His mother, but an agreement.

The last part of this mystery is in John 2:10, where the headwaiter praises the bridegroom for saving the "good" wine for last. There are numerous interpretations of this scenario, including the notion that Jesus represents the good wine and the prophets of the Old Testament represent the wine of lesser quality. There is a simpler idea: the wine is a symbol for perceived fulfillment of the Self—satisfaction with life, happiness, contentment. Good wine makes people happy to varying degrees and bad wine less so. Guests at other weddings who feel happy (from what they think is the better wine) at the beginning of the festivities (life on earth) will have a poorer experience in the transcendence of heaven. The guests at Cana, however, are analogous to those who put earthly fulfillment in its proper place, far behind a future in heaven. They drink the wine of lesser quality in this life but get to enjoy the good wine of transcendence in the next life. And it is the miracle of Jesus's presence that makes this possible.

Our meditations on this mystery should center on Mary and her intercession on our behalf to her Son. It is Mary who tells Jesus that we have no wine and need His help. Another interpretation of this mystery uses typology—going back into the Old Testament and finding patterns that are mirrored in the interplay between Jesus and His mother—to reinforce the importance of Mary at Cana. Universal customs involving ancient kings and their mothers vividly show us the importance of Marian devotion, and understanding the typology of these relationships helps us to realize why Rosary meditation is such a powerful prayer. We turn to Dr. Scott Hahn's book *Hail Holy Queen*, which beautifully expands on the reality of this typology, in order to see Mary in her role as the mother of the True King.

Throughout ancient times, the mother of the king held special influence in royal decisions, and there are many instances in the Old Testament that show this. Three such scenarios that reinforce this idea are also striking archetypes of Jesus and Mary at the Cana wedding. The first starts in Genesis 1:27–28: "And God created man [implying mankind] in His own image…male and female He created them. And rule over…every living thing that moves on the earth." This simply and clearly states that man and woman were given equal dominion over the world, Eve being the first queen and Adam the first king. In the first sin of mankind (Genesis 3:1–6), it is the queen, Eve, who is first tempted, and it is this first queen who tells the first king, Adam, to taste the forbidden fruit—the act that dooms mankind. At Cana, it is the second Eve, Mary, who undoes the mistake of the first by telling the ultimate King, Jesus, to restore the salvation of mankind by changing the water in the jars (immanent, sinful man) to wine (redeemed, transcendent man).

Earlier, we alluded to the second scenario that demonstrates the power of an ancient queen; it is found in 1Kings 2:13–22. Solomon, the son of David, is the king by a direct order from God, and his mother is Bathsheba. His half brother, Adenijah, is trying to steal the throne from Solomon by marrying into David's harem. To do so, he needs permission from the king; knowing Solomon would never grant him such a request, Adenijah approaches the queen, Bathsheba. Throughout these verses, it is clear that the mother of the king has a strong influence over her son.

> Then Adenijah said to Bathsheba, "Please speak to Solomon the king, **for he will not refuse you**"…And Bathsheba said, "Very well; I will speak to the king for you"…So Bathsheba went to King Solomon to speak to him for Adenijah. And the king rose to meet her, **bowed before her**, and sat on his throne; then he had a throne set for the king's mother, and **she sat on his right.** Then she said, "I am making one small request of you; do not refuse me." And the king said to her, "Ask, my mother, **for I will not refuse you.**"

Granting his mother's wish would be the end of Solomon's reign as king, but he could not refuse her. Displaying the true wisdom of Solomon, he solved the dilemma by having Adenijah killed for the attempted treachery.

The third scenario is in 2 Kings 4:1–7, and the scene eerily mirrors the Wedding at Cana. In this verse, a widow in the family of prophets cries out to Elisha—the successor to Elijah, one of the most influential prophets of Israel and who later appears in the New Testament as John the Baptist—that she is hopelessly poor, with her creditors threatening to sell her sons into slavery for repayment. Elisha asks her, "What shall I do for you?" The only thing of value she has is a single jar of oil, and Elisha miraculously fills as many containers as she can find. Elisha is referred to as the "man of God" and tells her to sell the oil and repay her debt so that she and her sons can be free and live out their years on the value of the remaining oil.

The woman is an archetype of Mary, and Elisha is an archetype for Jesus—"a man of God." Interestingly, it is Elijah who introduces Elisha as a prophet of God, and it is Elijah's reincarnation, John the Baptist, who introduces Jesus to the world: *"Ecce Agnus Dei"* ("Behold the Lamb of God") are John's words at Jesus's baptism in the Jordan. The jars collected by the woman represent the six stone jars of water at Cana—empty of transcendence at first, but then filled with wine, a symbol of divine redemption. Both the oil and the wine signify liquids of great value—gifts from God. In this sense, both could also signify the saving Blood of Christ, which is "poured out" freely for our salvation.*

We have given a lot of consideration to this mystery because there are so many underlying meanings that shed light on important

---

* The phrase "poured out" is used verbatim in the Old Testament story; the phrase is implied in the New Testament story of Cana when Jesus tells the servants, *"Draw some out now* and take it to the headwaiter…"

theological principles, and because it is this mystery that really demonstrates the role of Mary in our prayers to God. It is this mystery that vividly explains why the Rosary is such a powerful prayer.

The Third Luminous Mystery

Repent, for the Kingdom of Heaven is at hand.

—MATTHEW 4:17

The Third Luminous Mystery is the Proclamation of the Kingdom. After John the Baptist was taken prisoner, Jesus began His ministry in Galilee by proclaiming over and over to the crowds, "Repent! The Kingdom of God is at hand" (Matthew 4:17). The best interpretation of this is that the Person of Jesus Himself *is* the Kingdom—the directive simply means, "God and His plan for your salvation are now here on earth; it is time to change your ways about what you believe is good and evil, right and wrong, and pleasing and displeasing to God." In a broader, more literal sense, the Kingdom of God is the way things are done in heaven, infusing and ultimately replacing the way things are done on earth. As we'll see in five of the Beatitudes (Matthew 5:1–11) and in all the teachings of Christ that follow, the way of heaven is radically different—even an exact opposite—from the way of earth. The eternal, immortal transcendent is here now to replace the temporal, mortal immanent.

If we want to live after we die here on earth, we must embrace this with all our beings.

There are dozens of things that Jesus said in His teachings after His call to repentance, things that describe heavenly life as well as things we must do to make heaven heavenly. All of them demand that

Odyssey

we turn our backs to the world and its values and embrace a totally
different way of thinking and acting. While our meditations on this
mystery of light can include all of Jesus's teachings after Matthew
4:17, three of the most pointed directives in the teaching of Christ
stand out and have strong relevance to our daily lives. The first two
directives concern giving up our obsession with acquiring wealth,
power, and status:

> Do not store up for yourselves treasures on earth where moth
> and rust destroy, and where thieves break in and steal…But
> store up for yourselves treasures in heaven…for where your
> treasure is, there will your heart be also. (Matthew 6:19–21)
> But seek ye first His kingdom and His righteousness; and
> all these things shall be added unto you. (Matthew 6:33)

The third group of directives is the Beatitudes. These are not as
much commands as they are descriptions of what kingdom life is
like. These are the nine verses in Matthew 5:1–11 that begin with the
word "blessed." *Blessed* here means "happy" or "fortunate"; those following these directives on earth will be blessed with heavenly experience right now—a foreshadowing of what life will be like after our
earthly departure in death. Surprisingly, we will see that the values
and traits we extol and encourage in this modern, competitive society almost exactly contradict the ways things are in the Kingdom of
God. In four of the Beatitudes, heaven is the exact opposite of what
we consider acceptable, even admirable, in these modern times.

The first of four such Beatitudes is the most quoted and often
the most misunderstood: "Blessed are the poor in spirit, for theirs
is the kingdom of heaven." This beautiful set of words has nothing
to do with being strapped for cash, living beyond our means, being
depressed, being a doormat, or getting an earthly, royal inheritance.

The term "poor" in Old Testament writings refers to someone who gives up his or her power of choice to a greater individual; it is a synonym for obedience or cooperation with a master plan that will later bear fruit. It is precisely the same thing Mary said in her Magnificat prayer of humility: "For He has had regard for the lowly state of His handmaid." As brought out in Fr. Robert Spitzer's book *The Five Pillars of the Spiritual Life,* it is "contributorship"—giving up our own choices in life in order to contribute to God's plan for our salvation. The opposite is *comparing* ourselves—especially in the areas of wealth and status—to others and competing for dominance.

To suggest that our modern society is competitive is a gross understatement. For many of us, our daily lives are imbued with the ominous caveat that "to compete is to survive." Jesus is telling us to trust God for our daily needs and follow the divine plan that guarantees life after death ("Seek ye first the Kingdom of God."). The words "in spirit" in the first Beatitude were added by the Gospel writers to reinforce the message that such an attitude of surrender must be alive in our hearts. Living in the Kingdom of Heaven here on earth with such surrender is crossing over to the Mountain of Transcendence, where the path to eternal joy is gentle and paved with smooth stones.

The next Beatitude that directs us to a behavior that our modern society views as counterintuitive is the third: "Blessed are the meek, for they shall inherit the earth." It is well accepted that the word "meek" does not mean timidity or cowardice; it is better translated as "gentle." Jesus said, "Learn of Me, for I am gentle and humble of heart" (Matthew 11:29). Aquinas tells us that meekness assuages the passion of anger and quenches the desire for revenge. "See that none of you repays evil for evil, but always seek to do good to one another and to all" (I Thessalonians 5:15). When we seek revenge to satisfy our thirst for justice, we are not being meek or gentle; judgment and condemnation are best left to the Almighty and merciful Lord.

The fifth Beatitude, "Blessed are the merciful, for they shall receive mercy," seems to be the greatest challenge for us, the fallen children of Eve. Mercy is not only forgiveness but also tolerance. Mercy and tolerance are the hallmarks of divine values, and possessing and living these values bring us closer to God; they are an absolute necessity in our sanctification process. Simply put, one who does not forgive is not forgiven, and one who is intolerant is not tolerated. As a society, we dislike—even hate—anything that is different from ourselves. It may be a survival mechanism imbued in our evolutionary ancestry before we had immortal souls and before we were anointed by the Holy Spirit to become children of God. But intolerance and lack of mercy glare out of us, especially in social media, where hatred looms like a putrid boil. We must remember that one second after we die, we will all exist without gender, race, wealth, intelligence, political views, or religious beliefs. We will only exist as souls, and the value and quality of each soul will depend on how well we nurtured and developed that soul during our lifetime. Hatred and intolerance of others will follow us into the afterlife, perhaps with dire consequences. As we meditate on this mystery, we must cleanse ourselves of any hatred, intolerance, and lack of mercy, and embrace the words of Christ: "And you will be sons of the Most High; for He Himself is kind to ungrateful and evil men. Be merciful, just as your Father is merciful…do not condemn, and you will not be condemned; pardon, and you will be pardoned" (Luke 6:35–37).

The sixth Beatitude is "Blessed are the clean of heart, for they shall see God." This Beatitude is not only misunderstood but is greatly underestimated. As children, we were taught that this Beatitude warned us that "naughty thoughts" would keep us from ever being in heaven and seeing God face-to-face. Undoubtedly, this arises from the word "clean" that is often translated as "pure." Actually, the word "clean" in this Beatitude is better understood as "honest." The

Beatitude tells us that we must be honest down to the core of our beings about what is right or wrong. It is a statement against today's tendency to rationalize our sinful ideas as being socially necessary; we literally make our own rules about what is good or evil, even if our decisions are contrary to God's wishes. In a word, this Beatitude is a divine statement against moral relativism.

At baptism, the Holy Spirit begins to dwell within us and guide our consciences to make moral decisions that agree with what God wants for us. Making our own rules that are in direct conflict with God's wishes is truly "quenching the Spirit" (1 Thessalonians 5:19).* Moral relativism is a sin of modern times; like a cancerous growth, it is destroying us from within. Any moral decision that is based on comfort, convenience, or social wants is a death sentence for our souls; making such decisions trumps the will of God and makes our earthly lives most unheavenly.

The Fourth Luminous Mystery

His face shone like the sun, and His garments became white as light.

—MATTHEW 17:2

The Fourth Luminous Mystery is the Transfiguration; understanding the subtleties of this mystery can help us with our quest to visualize what heaven might be like; we discussed in an earlier chapter how the Transfiguration could be a peek at the reality of heaven. Our

---

* The apostle Paul used the phrase in a broader sense to include any action by an individual or by a church that went against the teachings of the Holy Spirit.

meditations on this mystery during the rosary can open a floodgate of grace to fill our minds with wondrous images of the coming glorified state.

Jesus took his closest apostles—the so-called "inner circle" of Peter, James, and John—to a high mountain, the most agreed-upon site being Mount Tabor, about seven miles southeast of Nazareth and ten miles southwest of the Sea of Galilee. There, the physical presence of Jesus was transformed or transfigured into an indescribable but perfectly recognizable glorified person. This paradox of logic—someone being recognizable but indescribable—is a conundrum we must deal with when trying to visualize the transcendent realm using immanent language. In Matthew 17:1–7, Jesus's glorified state is described with similes: "His face shone **like the sun,** and His garments became **white as light**." Two long-dead, important figures of the Old Testament, Moses and Elijah, appeared and were speaking with Jesus about His upcoming suffering and death.

The three apostles were awestruck; Peter could only babble an incoherent and inappropriate suggestion to set up tents for the glorified Jesus and Moses and Elijah—as if they needed a place to stay. In the midst of this confusion, God spoke through an overshadowing cloud and gave a direct and ominous command to the three disciples: "This is My beloved Son, in Whom I am well pleased; **listen to Him**" (Matthew 17:5). These are the same words from God at Jesus's baptism in the Jordan, with the added command "listen to Him."

Our meditations on this mystery require a backstory and an understanding of the significance of the mountain, the choice of the three apostles, and the two Old Testament figures. The backstory of the Transfiguration begins in the sixteenth chapter of Matthew, immediately before the Gospel writer's account of this event. Jesus and His disciples have just come into the territory of Caesarea Philippi after leaving the shores of the Sea of Galilee, where Jesus had miracu-lously fed five thousand people (not counting women and children). In Caesarea Philippi, Jesus must have felt the awe and wonder of His disciples after they witnessed such a miracle. He asked His disciples, "Who do people say that I am?" The disciples answered that some said He was John the Baptist and that others said He was one of the prophets of the Old Testament; they mentioned Jeremiah by name, but, more importantly, they mentioned Elijah.

To the disciples, first-century Jews, Elijah was a cultural hero, a religious leader who had restored worship to Yahweh from the pagan Baal. With Peter's confession in Matthew 16:16—"Thou art the Christ (Messiah), Son of the Living God"—the disciples clearly saw Jesus as the culmination of the restoration of the Kingdom of Israel—both religious and political. In the face of such a miracle of feeding so many from a few loaves and fish, the disciples were sure it was Jesus who could defeat the occupying pagan Romans and restore Jewish royalty to Israel with Jesus as King; they, of course, would possess positions of power in the kingdom with all the perks associ-ated with being Jesus's chosen ones. The disciples were dreaming of immanent (worldly) wealth, power, and status; they did not, in any way, shape, or form, see the transcendent plan for Jesus to be a sacrifi-cial lamb for the world's salvation. And they certainly did not foresee themselves as martyrs for anything but an open war with the Romans. Jesus knew this and realized it was time to reset the disciples' goals from achieving worldly success to following the will of God—the disciples needed to leave the immanent behind and seek the transcen-dent, even if it meant death: "From that time Jesus began to show His disciples that He must…suffer many things from the elders and chief priests and scribes, and be killed…Peter took Him aside and began to rebuke Him, saying, 'God forbid it, Lord! This shall never happen to you.' But He turned and said to Peter, 'Get behind Me Satan…you are a stumbling block to Me; for you are not setting your mind on God's interests, but man's'" (Matthew 16:21–23).

The disciples must have been stunned by Jesus's words to Peter. We can be sure that Jesus took the time to explain exactly what He meant, and He followed up His teaching with a vivid demonstration on Mount Tabor. Caesarea Philippi is about thirty-five miles as the crow flies from Mount Tabor, and the journey took six days. We can only imagine the conversations between Jesus and His disciples on that journey. He must have driven home the message that what is really crucial in this life is getting to the next life—where life does not end. Again, the message and meditation for us is that we must put the treasures of this life behind, contributing to the plan of God to get us to the next life of heaven. Some of Jesus's teachings on this directive are found in the discourse in Matthew 16:24–28: "If anyone wishes to come after Me, let him deny himself…for whoever wishes to save his life shall lose it…for what will it profit a man to gain the whole world, and lose his soul…Truly I say to you, there are some of those standing here who shall not taste death until they see the Son of Man coming in his Kingdom."

The last phrase of this discourse refers to Peter, James, and John, who are about to see with their own eyes exactly what Jesus is talking about. In the Transfiguration of Jesus, three immanent, physically real creatures come face-to-face with the transcendent—heaven. Aquinas tells us that the mountain is a focal point where the natural meets the supernatural; it is where the temporal comes into physical contact with the eternal. Christ is exposed in physical reality as the bridge between heaven and earth. This event is not merely a spiritual vision; two such visions are described in other places in the New Testament: Paul's vision of heaven in 2 Corinthians 12:2–4 and John's vision of his entry into the throne room of heaven in Revelation 4:1–2. The Transfiguration occurred in the physical realm, smack into the faces of three completely awestruck men. Peter was ready to provide shelter for the figures he saw; we have to wonder if he didn't also offer to cook supper for them. Our meditations on this mystery should center about this fact: what the three apostles saw was not a vision—it was physical reality, the very thing empiricists and cynics demand in order to prove the existence of heaven. If we are suffering, if we have lost loved ones, if we are abandoned, rejected, depressed, lonely, or facing despair, then this event concretizes our hope for eternal relief in the form of a real, physical reunion with loved ones and a real, physical cure for our sadness.

Two of the figures, Moses and Elijah, had been dead for several hundred years, and yet, here they were, conversing with Jesus, exactly as they appeared in life.* Both Moses and Elijah are very alive in this scenario—God Himself reiterates this in Matthew 22:32: "I am the God not of the dead, but of the living." We may wonder why these two figures of the Old Testament were chosen by God to be present at this crucial event. Along with Jesus, these two figures vividly demonstrate exactly what Jesus was teaching them on the long trek to Mount Tabor: that Jesus was indeed here to restore Israel, but not by defeating a political force. Jesus was not just a bridge between the Old Kingdom (Covenant) and a new Kingdom that the disciples hoped for, but the absolute presence of God coming here on earth to create a New Kingdom (Covenant) in His blood. This New Kingdom was not temporal and worldly as the Old Kingdom was, but eternal and transcendent. The Transfiguration showed the three disciples that what they yearned for now really existed in the afterlife of heaven.

---

* No mention is made in Matthew's passage that Moses and Elijah were also in a glorified state. This makes sense chronologically, since Jesus had not yet died and redeemed mankind; freeing the souls occurred while Jesus was in the tomb before He rose on the first Easter morning: "He descended to the dead, and on the third day, He rose again" (from the Apostles' Creed). There is controversy in the form of insistence that Moses and Elijah should not have been there at all, since they too were in the "netherworld." We'll discuss this later with the idea that the Transfiguration may have taken place *after* the Resurrection.

Man, the creature of mysterious longing, finally saw fulfillment and satisfaction of his earthly desires.

The theological significance of Moses and Elijah being at the Transfiguration is found in Old Testament history. Moses, a revered figure of first-century Jews, was the absolute symbol of the Old Covenant. He was the *first* "bridge" between God and man on Sinai when he brought down the Ten Commandments. He also was the *first* religious leader to give the children of Israel national identity by leading them out of Egypt into the Promised Land. He was also the author of the *first* five books of the Old Testament, the Torah. Moses represented the kingdom that the disciples and all Jews wanted restored. Elijah was the *first* harbinger of the coming of the Lord—the Messiah for which the Jews so patiently waited. In Malachi 4:5–6, God sent Elijah to proclaim to the people that "the day of the Lord" was soon to come. This proclamation occurs again in the New Testament with the new Elijah, John the Baptist, who, at Jesus's baptism in the Jordan, proclaims to the crowds, "Behold the Lamb of God, who takes away the sin of the world" (John 1:29).* God's sending John the Baptist as the New Covenant Elijah to proclaim the arrival of Jesus is clearly detailed in Luke 1:17, where the angel Gabriel tells Zechariah, "He will go before Him in the spirit and power of Elijah, to turn...the disobedient to the understanding of the righteous, to prepare a people for the Lord."

In meditating on this mystery, we must put ourselves into the group of three disciples and witness for ourselves the miracle of the transcendent realm, where we can see in physical reality that all that we yearn for in this life is alive and well in heaven. Putting ourselves in this group of Peter, James, and John has a price: we must accept the

---

* In the Latin Mass, this is the beginning of a prayer before communion at the exposition of the Sacred Host: *"Ecce Agnus Dei, ecce qui tollit peccata mundi."*

suffering associated with our salvation by praying the words of Christ in Gethsemane: "Not my will, but Thine be done." It was Peter, James, and John whom Jesus called close to Him in that dark garden: "And He took with Him Peter and the two sons of Zebedee...My soul is deeply grieved...remain here and keep watch with Me" (Matthew 26:37–38). The three never heard Jesus's prayer of acceptance and obedience to His Father's will; they were asleep. We must never be so weak.

The Fifth Luminous Mystery

And the bread also which I shall give for the life of the world is My flesh.

—JOHN 6:51

The Fifth Luminous Mystery is the Institution of the Eucharist by Jesus at the Last Supper. The accounts of this major event are pretty much the same in the three synoptic Gospels of Matthew, Mark, and Luke. At the end of the supper, Jesus took ordinary unleavened bread, blessed it, broke it, and gave it to the disciples, saying, "Take and eat; This is My Body." He then took a cup of ordinary wine from dinner and again blessing it, gave it to the disciples and said, "Drink from it all of you, for This is My Blood of the Covenant, which will be shed on behalf of many for the forgiveness of sins" (Matthew 26:26–28). Some question why the account is not in the Gospel of John.

John the evangelist was certainly at the Last Supper; he described himself as the disciple whom Jesus loved,* and he is frequently depicted

---

* The root for the word *love* here is from *agape*, not *eros*, signifying divine love, not sexual love.

as leaning on Jesus during the meal. The Gospel of John as we know it today was written some thirty years after the last synoptic Gospel, probably by at least one other author in addition to John, and all who contributed to this Gospel knew very well the content of the earlier Gospels. By the time John's Gospel was written somewhere in the AD nineties, believers were well aware of what had occurred at the Last Supper, and the doctrine of the Real Presence—Christ's physical presence in the consecrated bread and wine—was well accepted and not disputed. In keeping with John's theme of *Christology*, he simply felt that retelling the happenings at the Last Supper was not necessary.* Instead, he focused on Christ's Eucharistic discourse in the sixth chapter—Jesus spent considerable time explaining what the Eucharist meant in terms of His ultimate sacrifice and mankind's redemption from death.

Even though John's Gospel concentrated on the divinity of Christ as well as clearing up and filling in gaps in the earlier synoptic Gospels, all four Gospels have the central theme that Jesus was an innocent sacrifice sent by God to save mankind. To manifest His image as an innocent lamb whose blood on the Cross saves the lives of mankind, Jesus chose to endure His passion and death just before the Jewish feast of Passover, and the typology behind Jesus's mission and the Jewish customs of this feast is extraordinary.

Passover commemorates the sparing of Jewish children from the wrath of God's avenging angel sent to slay Egyptian firstborns as part of the ten plagues put upon the pharaoh for keeping the Israelites in captivity. The Jews were instructed to slay the Paschal

---

* Interestingly, the account of Jesus's Transfiguration on Mount Tabor is also absent in John's Gospel, even though John was one of the three disciples present. Scholars explain that John's entire Gospel—with its theme of Christology—is a reiteration of the Transfiguration. In addition, the event, like the Last Supper, was well-known and accepted by the time John's Gospel came out in the nineties.

lamb and smear its blood on the doorposts of their houses (Exodus 12:13) in order for the Angel of Death to "pass over" those children. The wooden doorposts are archetypes for the Cross of Calvary; the Paschal lambs were slain the day before the start of Passover—the Day of Preparation or Nisan 14; at the time of Jesus, this is Good Friday. On the day of preparation, the last lamb must be slain by 3:00 p.m., as Passover begins at sundown. This corresponds to the time of Jesus's death on the Cross: "It was now about noon and darkness came over the whole land until three in the afternoon...He breathed His last" (Luke 23:44–46). After slaying the last lamb in preparation for the Passover feast, the Rabbis utter the Hebrew word "*Kalah*" or "It is finished." The last word uttered by Jesus on the Cross before He died was "*Kalah*" (John 19:30).

The notion behind the Eucharist is the climax of this typology of Jesus as the sacrificial lamb. Jews are required to eat the sacrificial lamb by divine command in order to live and prosper: "And they shall eat the flesh that same night...with unleavened bread" (Exodus 12:8). Christ repeats the divine order to eat His own flesh in the Eucharist form of unleavened bread: "Truly, I say to you, unless you eat the flesh of the Son of Man and drink His blood, you have no life in yourselves" (John 6:53). The parallels between Christ and the saving sacrificial lamb of Passover cannot be any clearer.

Inherent in this mystery of the Rosary on the Eucharist is the doctrine of the Real Presence. This doctrine affirms that ordinary unleavened bread in the form of a host and ordinary wine—containing alcohol from fermented grapes—are changed by the power of Jesus's word and the Holy Spirit, in the presence of an ordained priest, into the Body and Blood, Soul and Divinity of Jesus Christ. This is called *transubstantiation*. This is a decidedly Catholic doctrine and belief and is sacrosanct to every Catholic, but sadly, a quarter of Catholics attending weekly Mass do not grasp the full meaning of this miracle. Even sadder, about half of baptized Catholics don't believe it to be true. Before Constantine made Christianity the official religion of the Roman Empire in AD 325, many believers were martyred defending this doctrine. Three church fathers come to mind: Saint Ignatius of Antioch was torn apart by lions, and Saints Justin and Cyprian of Carthage were beheaded for holding fast to this belief in the face of pagan rulers.

Arguments against the Real Presence are everywhere outside the Catholic Church, and every Catholic should have at least some inkling about how to respond to these arguments. Excellent and succinct apologetic essays have been posted on the Internet domain of Catholic Answers (www.catholic.com), a wonderful and scholarly apostolate started in 1979 by an attorney, Karl Keating. Any Catholic with questions about this topic should read these writings. I recommend two: the essay on the Mass and the one on the Eucharist. A firm knowledge of the importance of the Eucharist is essential in order to benefit from the graces bestowed by meditating on this Luminous Mystery.

Our meditations on this mystery should center on three notions: what the Eucharist is, what the purpose of it is, and how a deeper understanding of it can show us an image of what heaven and the afterlife might be like. To illustrate our first notion, what the Eucharist is, we'll go to the sixth chapter of John's Gospel, where this mysterious Bread of Eternal Life is not merely described but *defined* in the clearest way possible. For our second notion, the purpose of the Eucharist, we'll turn to the Catholic Catechism as well as shuffle through some of the verses in John's sixth chapter but also reiterate a very concise image of the Eucharist from the *Sancrosanctum Concilium* 47 of Vatican II; there, the purpose of the Institution of the Eucharist is crystal clear. To discuss the third notion, a picture of the afterlife in heaven, we will use the Catechism, the writings of

Aristotle and Aquinas, and sacred scripture to present a novel way of thinking about what the Eucharist shows us concerning life in heaven.

In defining the Eucharist, we look at the events in Jesus's ministry described in John's sixth chapter. The crowds following Jesus, especially His close disciples, must have been awestruck by what had happened in the space of two days. Jesus had just miraculously fed five thousand people with only a few loaves and fish and then had gone off to pray alone. That night at 3:00 a.m., they saw Him walking on the surface of the lake; to the amazement of everyone, He appeared on the other side of the lake by Himself ahead of the crowds, as if to transcend time. If that wasn't enough to rattle everyone's nerves, what He said in John 6:26–59 dropped a proverbial bombshell. It was Jesus's discourse on the Bread of Life.

Jesus began this shocking discourse by answering a challenge from some in the crowd who asked for a miraculous sign that would prove Jesus was really the One sent by God. This must have truly been a "tough crowd"—they demanded proof *after* Jesus had just miraculously fed five thousand people. Skeptics in the crowd showed their cynicism by pointing out that Moses had done the same thing with the manna from heaven. The totality of Jesus's answer is in John 6:26–59; Jesus starts by pointing out the shortcomings of the manna from heaven: "Your ancestors ate the manna in the desert, but they died" (John 6:49).* The rest of the discourse on the Bread of Life defines, in the clearest manner, exactly what the Eucharist is. The entire discourse—John 6:26–59—is a beautiful example of clear

---

* They died spiritually as well as physically, since Jesus had not yet died on the cross and redeemed the world. They remained in a mysterious netherworld until Jesus "descended to the dead" immediately after his burial, before He rose on that first Easter morning. We pray in the Apostle's Creed, "He was crucified, died, and was buried. He descended to the dead, rose again, and ascended into heaven."

and direct verbiage: Jesus means exactly what He says. Here are some highlighted verses particularly pertinent to our notion of defining the Eucharist *cum veritas* and *sine dubio:* "For the Bread of God is that which comes down from heaven and gives life to the world...I am the Bread of Life; whoever comes to Me will never hunger, and whoever believes in Me will never thirst...I am the Living Bread that came down from heaven; **whoever eats this bread will live forever; and the bread that I will give for the life of the world is My flesh**" (John 6:51).

Those who deny the doctrine of Transubstantiation attempt to twist semantics in the Aramaic and Greek translations; the language, however, in Aramaic, Greek, and English is clear and precise. At the Last Supper, when Jesus instituted the Eucharist by taking bread and saying the words "This is my Body"—"*Touton estin to soma mou*" in Greek—controversy exists around the word "is." Fundamentalists who reject the Real Presence claim that the Greek word *estin* is ambiguous and can be translated as "is" or "is figuratively." In accepted Greek grammar of the day, however, *estin* is nearly always translated literally as "is," meaning that the subject and the object of the sentence are exactly the same thing. If Jesus had wanted to say that the bread was merely a symbol of His body, He would have said so; it is highly doubtful that the perfect God would slip up and allow ambiguity for such an important statement.

The words of Jesus about actually eating His flesh also caused a stir, back then as well as now. In John 6:52 and 6:60, the crowds said it aloud: "How can this man give us his flesh to eat?" and, "This saying is hard; who can accept it?" Jesus understood their disbelief but told them that if they rejected His words, they rejected Him, and many "left Him and returned to their former way of life." No doubt the idea of eating His flesh and drinking His blood were very difficult notions for the marginal believers to accept, but the Greek translations for "body" and "eating" are very clear and eerily stark. The Greek word for "body" when Jesus said, "This My Body," is *sarx* and translates as "flesh" or "meat." When Jesus said, "Unless you eat the flesh of the Son of Man," the Greek word here for "eat" is *trogon*; it translates literally as "gnaw" or "chew." Clearly, the Lord was not using metaphorical prose.

The second notion about this mystery upon which we should meditate—the purpose of the Eucharist—begins at the Last Supper, the night before Jesus died. After Jesus gave the apostles the first Eucharist—His Body and Blood from ordinary bread and wine—He added the words "Do this in memory of Me." The older version of this command is a bit longer: "As often as you shall do these things, in memory of Me shall you do them."* In both cases, the Lord is not merely asking us to remember His sacrifice for mankind's salvation but to reenact it during the Eucharistic Liturgy of the Mass. It is a unique reenactment; it is more than some kind of instant replay, but rather a replay of the death of Jesus on the Cross—one where the Victim is physically present but does not die again. The Eucharistic Liturgy is more than a memorial service for the dead; it is a living sacrifice where we are able to offer ourselves with Christ in order to plead to the Father for the merits of the Cross. The Greek term for "remembrance" is *anamnesis*, and it is always used in the context of a sacrifice. In the tradition of Jewish blood sacrifices, we are able to consume our sacrifice in the Eucharist, thus assimilating Jesus into our physical and spiritual beings; this is a perfect analogy to the Passover celebrants eating the flesh of the Paschal lamb that saved them from death.

The third notion about the Eucharist—an idea upon which we can meditate—is what the Real Presence of Christ on the altar can

---

* In the Latin Mass, the longer version is used: *Haec quotiescumque feceritis, in mei memoriam facietis.*

tell us about heavenly life. Foremost, the Eucharist gives us a straight-forward promise of life after death. Ordinary perishable bread from the earth becomes heavenly and incorruptible after "God's blessing has been evoked upon it...it is no longer bread but the Eucharist" (Catechism 1000). Our bodies, at first perishable, become incorrupt-ible with hope of the resurrection after we partake of the Eucharistic meal. In discourse on the Bread of Life in the sixth chapter of John's Gospel, Jesus says it several times in no uncertain terms:

> He who eats My flesh and drinks My blood abides in Me, and I in him. (John 6:56)
>
> I say to you, whoever believes has eternal life. I am the bread of life...this is the bread that comes down from heaven so that one may eat it and not die. I am the living bread that came down from heaven; whoever eats this bread will live for-ever. (John 6:47–51)
>
> Unlike your ancestors who ate and still died, whoever eats this bread will live forever. (John 6:58)

Again, the verbiage in these verses reassures us that Jesus is saying exactly what He means. The existence of a life after death is here, plain and simple. Any doubt we have about the existence of heaven should be completely erased by these words; to hold lingering doubt is tantamount to calling the Lord a liar. Such disbelief is a source of universal existential angst: as Albert Camus wrote, "I would rather live my life as if there is a God and die to find out there isn't, than live as if there isn't and to die to find out that there is."

Thus, the Eucharist tells us there is a heaven, but does this immanent-to-transcendent miracle tell us anything about what heaven is like? The answer is yes, and the proofs for our assertions go back to ancient Greece. As we have seen, the doctrine of the Real

Presence can be a tough sell, even for devout believers; placed side by side, ordinary bread and wine and the Eucharist look, smell, taste, and feel identical. Yet one, we believe, is the ordinary product of the earth, the work of human hands, and the other is the body and blood, the soul and divinity of Jesus Christ. There is no scientific way of distinguishing them; if such immanent methods fail, we must look to transcendent thinking (going beyond science). Two experts in such metaphysics are Aristotle—considered to be the best thinker of all time—and Saint Thomas Aquinas. Aristotle said that everything had two parts to it: a substance and an "accident." The accident was that part of something that could be empirically proven—seen, smelled, heard, tasted, and felt; the substance was the unseen, metaphysical part. Together, these two parts made up the entirety—something could not exist without both parts. Aquinas changed the term *accident* to the term *form*. So, *substance* and *form* are the components of everything in nature, including the bread and wine of the Eucharist as well as man himself.

In this immanent realm—the human world—man is thus made up of a substance (the soul) and a form (the body). A soul by itself is a ghost, not a man; it is the soul of a man. Likewise, the body alone is a cadaver, not a man; it is the body of a man. The worldly realm of Satan gives the body power over the soul through free will, and this perishable body is fixed in its form while on earth as a recognizable, physical thing. In the divine realm, the realm of heaven, the soul is made supreme by the presence of the Trinity, and the soul determines what form the new, imperishable body will have.

The divine Person of Jesus allowed Him to determine the form of His existence. In scripture, we see Him in four different forms: His regular, earthly form like us, from His birth to His death on Calvary; His post-Resurrection form or body, where he had supernatural powers but still ate, drank, and socialized; His glorified heavenly body of the Transfiguration on Mount Tabor, where He was recognizable but not describable—different from His post-Resurrection form; and in the Eucharist, where He held bread and wine in front of the apostles and said, "This is My body." All four forms were part of the complete Jesus—a divine soul and His body.

It seems that the soul, under divine influence, can change the form of the body to fit whatever the situation demands. Immediately after the Resurrection, Jesus made His glorified body earthlike—wounds and all—to avoid frightening the disciples and, more importantly, to reassure them that their post-Resurrection bodies would be the "same as those they now bore" (Catechism 645, 999): "But they were startled and frightened and thought that they were seeing a ghost. And He said to them, 'Why are you troubled and why do doubts arise in your hearts? See My hands and feet, that it is I myself; touch Me and see, for a spirit does not have flesh and bones as you see that I have...Have you anything to eat?'" (Luke 24:37–41).

At the Ascension into heaven, Jesus's body was in the post-Resurrection form; He had just finished preaching and reassuring the disciples about the Kingdom of Israel as well as giving them specific instructions on being His witnesses. During His Second Coming, the Rapture, He will again have the post-Resurrection form—nail wounds and all, but still being able to eat and speak. This we are told by the angels at His Ascension: "Men of Galilee, why are you standing, there looking at the sky? This Jesus who has been taken up from you into heaven **will return in the same way** as you have seen Him going into heaven" (Acts 1:12).

His post-Resurrection form is no doubt a completely different form than the heavenly glorified state He exhibited on Mount Tabor. Jesus's heavenly glorified body "was veiled in earthly form"—the post-Resurrection body in which Jesus ate, drank, and preached in front of hundreds of disciples after His death and raising (Catechism

645, 659; Acts 1:3 and Acts 10:41). Jesus thus had the power to change His form into whatever was necessary to instill belief into His followers. The Eucharist is simply another, different form for the body and blood, the soul and divinity of Christ.

Will we inherit this power of "transformation" of form by our souls in heaven? As we explained in our earlier chapter on heaven, yes. That is a perfectly logical assertion. Since Jesus could change His earthly form to whatever the will of God deemed necessary—everything from becoming completely invisible from fellow travelers on the road to Emmaus to appearing as an earthly cemetery gardener, a living itinerant preacher, and a fully glorified being—*we can assume the same powers with an earthlike, imperishable body in heaven.* Since Jesus mirrored our lives exactly, including being born, living as a normal human, suffering as a human, and dying as a human, His Resurrection and ability to change form would also be ours.

We do not have the power to change our bodily forms on earth as Jesus did, because we have not completed the process of transformation of our souls known as *theosis.* John 1:12—"He gave the power to become children of God"—tells us we can loosen our earthly grips on our souls and begin to become empowered by the will of God through sanctifying grace. The process of *theosis,* begun here on earth, is completed in heaven by the Beatific Vision and union with the Trinity. So, our souls powered by the Beatific Vision in heaven will have the ability to take on any form (body) we want—again, only if such a choice is consistent with God's will—just as Jesus did with His four known forms.

Our souls (substance) in heaven, powered by the presence of God, will be able to combine with any type of body (form) deemed appropriate by the will of God just as Christ did on earth. Our free will from earth—the one that is capable of sin—will no longer exist; our long-sought-after goal of union with the Trinity makes God's will our only desire and choice, and this union is what gives our souls the power to determine our heavenly forms.

This has tremendous implications for our picture of what heaven will be like. What form (or body) will we have in heaven? What will we look like there? What age will we be? What will we be able to do in heaven? The answer is, anything we want, if it is consistent with God's will. Those who have lost a child or other loved one and are wondering if they will recognize him or her at the first heavenly reunion should take particular note of this; the lost child may choose to be a child at the first joyous reunion, and a lost loved one may choose to look exactly as we expect. This power of sanctified, heavenly souls to take on any form necessary mirrors Christ's heavenly soul taking on the form of ordinary bread and wine in the Eucharistic miracle.

There are, however, two snags in this joyful scenario: the first is that every soul might not have equal powers or the same experience in heaven—those souls in a greater state of *theosis* (souls that have grown closer to God through earthly sanctification by prayer and repentance) will have a greater experience with the Beatific Vision. The work of such souls on earth to know the unknowable God will come to complete fruition upon seeing God face-to-face; the earthly grown familiarity with God will impart the infinite power of the Trinity to those who turned their backs on the world's treasures. Souls that neglected spiritual growth on earth and derailed their transcendent purpose by being obsessed with worldly treasures will experience the same Beatific Vision, but their distance from God on earth will follow them into heaven—they will literally have a back-row seat to eternity's greatest show. Their power over form in heaven may very well be diminished.

If there are heavenly golf courses, we need to make sure we're not stuck in the caddyshack.

The second unpleasant thing we must accept in order to perfectly mirror Christ's earthly life and achieve the power of substance over form in heaven is suffering. Suffering is a worldly thing, and to question or reject our suffering is to question or reject Christ's suffering—the very tragedy that gives us a key to the afterlife of heaven. As we said in a previous chapter, suffering is what makes the soul strong and transcendent directed. It is what allows us to absorb the power of the Trinity and make heaven…well, heavenly.

The acceptance of suffering is reflected in our divine mirror—the Passion and death of Jesus Christ vividly portrayed in the five Sorrowful Mysteries of the Rosary.

XIV

The Sorrowful Mysteries: Our Connection to the Suffering Christ

The Son of Man must suffer many things...and be killed.

—LUKE 9:22

When earthly life—prayerfully called the "valley of tears"—hands us suffering, it is the Sorrowful Mysteries of the Rosary that are the strongest opiates for our pain. They show us, in a very graphic way, that suffering, along with its natural endpoint, death, is most definitely a human thing. Meditating on the sufferings and death of Christ reminds us of the humanity of this God-Person, a humanity that was absolutely necessary for the redemption of mankind to be valid. In another sense, our meditations on Jesus's sufferings give us a measure of ease for our own human condition; the near despair of the horrors in the Sorrowful Mysteries plant seeds of hope—a hope that is unequivocally revealed in the Glorious Mystery of the Resurrection. The transcendent power of God reassures us that indeed "death shall have no dominion," in the famous words of Welsh poet Dylan Thomas, based on Saint Paul's message to the Romans in Romans 6:9.

In taking a closer look at these mysteries, we will, of course, be reflecting on Christ's suffering, reminding ourselves that it was very real and that the pain and sacrifice of God Himself were for *us*. In addition, we are going to dissect the meanings held within the mysteries and find pieces of ourselves and our own suffering in this life. Our daily personal connections to these mysteries will sometimes seem endless in the face of all our woes, but we can add these to our meditations every time we pray. The troubles we face run the gamut of suffering in this modern world: anxiety, depression, dread, fear, loneliness, wrongful accusations, abuse of power, the humiliation of suffering, chronic illness, loss of any kind, and the fear of death itself.

The First Sorrowful Mystery

My soul is deeply grieved, to the point of death.

—MATTHEW 26:38

My Father, if it is possible, let this cup pass from Me; yet, not as I will, but as Thou wilt.

—MATTHEW 26:39

So, you men could not keep watch with Me for one hour?

—MATTHEW 26:40

The First Sorrowful Mystery is Jesus's Agony in the Garden of Gethsemane. The first notion we can extract from this mystery is that true love is never selfish—there is no *I* in love. In Matthew's Gospel, we read of the scene where Jesus and the Twelve have finished their one-day-early Passover meal, the Last Supper, in the upper room and are walking along the Kidron Valley to the Mount of Olives and Gethsemane—a distance of about a mile. During this walk, Jesus tells the apostles that He is about to be arrested and killed and that they will be forced to flee for their lives: "This night all of you will have your faith in Me shaken, for it is written: 'I will strike down the shepherd, and the sheep of the flock shall be scattered'...But Peter answered and said to Him, even though all may fall away because of You, I will never fall away" (Matthew 26:31–34). It is then that Jesus foretells of Peter's three denials.

Peter's arrogance is lost amid Jesus's startling words, but it is there and should remind us of our own boasting when we profess to love someone. Peter is, in essence, saying that his love is better than the love of the others and that the Lord should somehow be comforted because Peter loves Him more than the others do. The folly of Peter's selfish pride is manifested in all the Gospel accounts of his three denials, culminating in the crowing cock—truly God's way of humbling Peter with an "I told you so" moment. There is a shrine on the eastern slope of Mount Zion called Saint Peter in Gallacantu that commemorates this event.[*]

Peter's implied boast that he loved the Lord more than the others is replayed exactly at the end of the Gospel of John. Seven of the apostles have just witnessed the risen Jesus's miracle of the 153 large fish in their nets; Jesus is about to serve them breakfast of bread and fish, but Peter is about to be fed back his boastful words from the night of the Last Supper. There is a charcoal fire set, as there was in the courtyard where Peter's faith failed. Jesus replays the denials, asking Peter three times, "Do you love me more than these?"—meaning more than the

---

[*] *Gallicantu* is translated as "crowing cock."

other disciples. Jesus asks Peter each time if he loves Him enough to die for Him, denoted in Greek as *agape*. Peter's faith fails again: he answers three times that his love for the Lord is of the lesser degree of love—that of a friend—denoted in the Greek as *philea*. It is not until Pentecost and the descent of the Holy Spirit that Peter can experience agape love, the love that God expects from all of us who have received the Holy Spirit in baptism. Peter's love did not fail after his baptism by the Holy Spirit at Pentecost; can we say the same about our decisions and ways of life since we too have been so baptized?

The apostle Paul tells us about real love, both for God and for others, in 1 Corinthians 13:4–7: "Love is patient, love is kind, and is not jealous; love does not brag and is not arrogant." In our love relationships, there is no more toxic word than "I." Genuine love is all about giving, sacrifice, and selflessness toward the other, the objects of our love, and yet, Kierkegaard tells us, the human condition has perverted this into some kind of glorification of the self: "Love has become the reward of the one who loves, not of the one who is loved. Those who think they can love only the people they prefer do not love at all."

A boastful Self makes us act as if our love somehow transcends the love of other potential lovers. It makes us feel important, secure, and somehow noble, as if we are giving a gift. This type of self-aggrandizement is the hallmark of a needy, insecure, and potentially controlling individual, and such an attitude objectifies and debases those we purport to love. There is great danger in hearing "I love you" too soon or too often; it is a sure sign of pathological neediness and dependency. The most overused and misused words of all time have to be those three—words that we all long to hear but soon realize are a lie more often than a truth. Someone we love doesn't want to hear those words as much as they want to *feel* them and *see* them in action. Boastful and hollow expressions of love only require hot air, but "walking the walk" of love requires sincere effort and sometimes tears. Our meditations on this mystery of the Rosary should take a good hard look at how we love one another.

The second notion of this mystery of Jesus's Agony in the Garden centers about some of the most quoted words from scripture: "Father, if Thou art willing, take this cup from Me; yet, not My will, but Thine be done" (Luke 22:42). We have talked extensively about surrendering to God's will, but in this, we have most often referred to a passive surrender such as we might experience in a loss—loss of a loved one, our own health, a job, our status, and so on. But here, Jesus is surrendering by *actively* doing something: He is giving Himself up for torture and execution. He does not have to do this; He only has to say the word—appeal to His Father—and the entire angry mob in the garden would be reduced to dust, or worse: "Do you think that I cannot appeal to My Father, and He will at once put at My disposal twelve legions of angels?" (Matthew 26:53).

What about active surrender to God's wishes in our own lives? When asked about it, we undoubtedly can talk the talk, but do we actively follow His plan and walk the walk? The "cup" of suffering Jesus asks His Father to remove translates for us into all the things in life that we may not want to do. Active acceptance of God's will is manifested in two words: obedience and responsibility. Do we get up each day and perhaps go to a job we really don't like—our cup—so that we can support our families, pay our taxes and bills, and give security to those we love? Do we take our love relationships, especially marriage, seriously by being honest, faithful, and constructive and doing our best to preserve the union? Do we love our children and parents in positive, selfless ways that give guidance and discipline to the children and support and encouragement to our parents? Do we try our best to remove feelings of vengeance and hatred from our daily lives? Do we think first, restrain ourselves, and perhaps try to understand others' misfortunes *before* we post guile-filled messages on social media?

God's will in our lives is sometimes difficult; nearly every one of the twenty mysteries of the rosary—an overview of God's plan in our lives—remind us there can be pain associated with obedience to God's wishes. Our prayers to the Father should mirror those of Christ in Gethsemane. We can legitimately tell God that His plan for us hurts sometimes but that we actively accept it. Life is not to be our way, but His way: "Thy will be done."

The third notion for meditation on this mystery is a common group of maladies most of us suffer through every day of our lives: stress, worry, anxiety, depression, dread, and sometimes, loneliness and abandonment. Some of these words cross over in meaning, but one or more may fit our own personal fears of something bad that has happened, is happening, or is about to happen, and we may have to face these things alone and abandoned. Jesus mirrors these feelings perfectly.

He said to His three closest disciples, "My soul is deeply grieved to the point of death; stay here and keep watch with Me" (Matthew 26:38–39). Jesus was afraid...very afraid. He was afraid of what was *imminent* (about to happen) and of what was *immanent* (worldly suffering by torture and death). What most of us forget is that Jesus's greatest fear—and by far His greatest suffering—was something that was to about to happen in the transcendent realm: He was about to be separated from the Father by taking on all the sins of mankind. It was this fear of separation from the Father that caused the outpouring of sweat, likened to falling drops of blood to fall. In this drama, we get a clue about what heaven will be like for us: our union with God in the afterlife will be a momentous and spectacular event, enough to make a human sweat blood at the very thought of losing it. He asked Peter, James, and John to stay close to Him, no doubt for emotional support but also to watch for the mob that was going to take Jesus away; the Lord was about to be arrested as a criminal. He had plenty of reasons to feel anxiety and dread.

When we find ourselves in the emotional turmoil of fear and dread, whether the causes are real or imagined, we can, in our meditation on this mystery, fall down next to Jesus in Gethsemane, see His drops of blood fall to the ground, *and be afraid with Him at our sides.* In an almost eerie emotional moment, we will be overcome with an overwhelming sense of peace and calm. The many reasons that this epiphany of peace happens are for speculation; we should only know that it happens every time we kneel next to Christ in the darkness of the garden. It is a most remarkable experience; it's as if Jesus leans over and whispers in our ears: "My peace I leave with you; My peace I give to you...let not your heart be troubled or nor let it be afraid" (John 14:27).

The fourth notion upon which we can meditate in this mystery of Christ's agony is that the world (the immanent, the flesh) tries and often succeeds in blinding us to the transcendent gift of salvation, made possible through the sufferings and sacrifices of Jesus. This notion is illustrated in the Gospel of Saint Mark: "And He came and found them sleeping, and said to Peter, 'Simon, are you asleep? Could you not keep watch for one hour? Keep watching and praying that you may not come into temptation; the spirit is willing, but the flesh is weak'" (Mark 14:37–41). This occurs three times, foreshadowing Peter's three denials that are about to take place in a few hours. Matthew also records three episodes but does not mention Peter by name. Luke mentions the sleeping only once and takes the liberty to soften the disciples' guilt by adding that they were sleeping "out of sorrow."

Once again, Peter's faith has failed the Lord. The needs of the flesh—his immanent body being tired, perhaps from too much wine at supper—have stained his soul with one more disappointment in the face of the suffering Christ. Peter's heart and soul were committed to God's plan ("the spirit is willing"), but the needs of his body were too much to overcome ("the flesh is weak"). He had an excuse—he had not yet been overshadowed by the Holy Spirit at Pentecost; we, however, do not have such a pass. Yet, despite our culpability from our weaknesses—running the gamut of the seven deadly sins of anger, pride, envy, greed, lust, gluttony, and sloth—Jesus understands and forgives our shortcomings. It is the very purpose of His suffering and death. "Are you still sleeping and taking your rest? It is enough; the hour has come" (Mark 14:41).

Are we sleeping when we should be awake? In our meditation on this mystery, we must recognize that the world and its treasures are constantly lulling us into a vacuous stupor, and the forces pulling us away from the transcendent are often too strong for us to overcome. We have been born "of the world" and, through the sacrifice of Christ, we have become "not of the world." Yet we still struggle to be "not of the world," to think and act as souls called to the transcendent realm. The world, the immanent realm, continues to make us sleepy, so we are oblivious to any backward slide away from God and heaven. We must be ever so aware: "Keep watching and praying that you may not enter into temptation" (Matthew 26:41).

Even Virgil said as much in the *Aeneid*: "*Facilis descensus Averno*" ("The descent into hell is easy").

The Second Sorrowful Mystery

> *Then he released Barabbas for them; after having Jesus scourged, he delivered Him to be crucified.*

> —MATTHEW 27:26

The Second Sorrowful Mystery is the Scourging at the Pillar. Jesus was scourged in the Fortress of Antonia by Roman torturers. And it was indeed torture: the Roman scourging of Jesus was not a simple whipping or caning; the instrument was a *flagrum*, a flogging whip made up of several leather strands into which bits of bone and metal were embedded. Repeated blows across the bare back of the victim literally ripped off the flesh. The idea was to cause as much pain as possible without killing the accused; death was reserved for the final punishment—crucifixion. The torture of scourging was used only on murderers, traitors, and noncitizens who were considered less than human.

The traditional writings about this mystery point to personal mortification—acts of extreme self-denial, even self-punishment—to overcome and control our immanent, inborn sexual urges. The act of self-flagellation, a voluntary self-scourging as an outward act of penance, crept into religious practices in the Middle Ages. In strict monastic orders, the practice was carried out to mirror the sufferings of Christ at the pillar and to purify the flesh of sinful urges. Yet we must look beyond sins of the flesh as targets of the Scourging at the Pillar. There are three notions that can help us connect with Christ's suffering at the pillar.

The first notion is that self-penance helps us to free ourselves from obsessive attachments to *all* the pleasures of the world. Material pleasures are "Satan's stumbling blocks" (Matthew 16:23) that we must "put behind" us in order to keep our final odyssey moving in the right direction. There is a direct and literal reference to Christ's scourging helping us to effect this change in our lives: "And by His scourging we are healed" (Isaiah 53:5). By meditating on this mystery, we strip away our desires for the world's treasures just as the torturers stripped away the flesh off the innocent Christ.

The second notion can help those of us living in chronic physical or emotional pain. For those of us living with unrelenting pain, our meditation on this mystery of Jesus's scourging places us next to the suffering Jesus, and this may give us just enough relief to make it through another day. Like the agony in Gethsemane, feeling the pain of Christ up close and personal may not only assuage our own suffering but also give it transcendent meaning.

The third notion concerns *false accusations* and *innocent suffering*. Scourging before crucifixion was reserved for the worst of the worst; Jesus was both completely innocent and falsely accused. If we look closely into our lives, we may see times when we have been wrongly accused and punished unfairly; for some, the wrongs may be worse than for others. Many of us know the pain of being blamed for something at work that was not our fault but the doing of a jealous coworker or the failing of an insecure supervisor. Some of us may be living with obsessively jealous spouses or partners who constantly accuse us of disloyalty when there is none. The meteoric rise of social media and public blogs has made libel and slander the new hobbies of haters everywhere.[*] More serious examples of false accusations and innocent suffering are the lives of children trapped in an abusive home; they suffer horrible punishments, both physical and verbal, and they see no end of their misery. In a different segment of society, there are many innocent people wasting away in prisons, wrongfully convicted of crimes they did not commit. Indeed, this is a world filled with injustice and suffering—it is, after all, the Evil One's domain.

The evil in the world is ubiquitous; Satan is doing an effective job of planting it in as many of us as possible, from the Roman torturers to jealous individuals to horribly deranged caretakers to unjust and ineffective officers of the court system. If we are victims of such treachery, meditation on the scourging of Jesus at the pillar may ease

---

[*] Libel is defamation of character in print or written word; slander is defamation by spoken word. In social media, both terms apply for trying to hurt someone with false statements.

our angst for just one more day—one day closer to hopefully being rescued or exonerated, all the while moving closer to our suffering God and the perfection of our odyssey.

There is the story of Anthony, a young, mentally ill man who was always smiling, always gentle, and always grateful for the help his family gave him to make it through a tough life. He had trouble with the simplest of the activities of daily living, and he was totally dependent on his loving and close family. He was arrested and taken from his home to jail for three brutal rapes he did not commit. By a horrible fluke of nature, he was an exact physical double of the real perpetrator and was convicted based only on victim identification. Nearly twenty-two years later, he was completely exonerated by DNA evidence.

The toll on his family, especially his mother, was horrific. Because of his physical similarity to the real perpetrator, no one believed his pleas of innocence except his family. His mother believed in him, and her faith in God was unimpeachable. Every morning for twenty-two years, she walked to morning Mass and then prayed the Rosary earnestly for Mary to ask God for the truth to come out. She never doubted that her prayers would be answered...and some eight thousand Rosaries later, they were. Such unwavering patience and trust in God is undoubtedly a sign for us to trust and believe in this powerful prayer.

The Third Sorrowful Mystery

The soldiers wove a crown of thorns and put it on His head.

—JOHN 19:2

The third Sorrowful Mystery is the Crowning with Thorns, and the notion upon which we should meditate is the *humiliation of the innocent*. Pilate was warned by his wife that Jesus was an innocent victim: "Have nothing to do with that righteous man; for last night I suffered greatly in a dream because of Him." Pilate knew this in his heart: "For he knew that it was because of envy they had delivered Him up" (Matthew 27:18–19). Pilate, however, was a weak, self-serving, and ineffective leader bent only on saving his own skin. His reputation for keeping the peace in these outlying districts was already in jeopardy in Rome. Pilate was both vicious and cunning: he thought if he tortured this troublemaker from Galilee nearly to death, it would satisfy the jealousy and greed of the chief priests and elders of the people.

So, once again, in true immanent fashion, weakness, jealousy, and greed engendered violence, as they have throughout the ages. Pilate turned Jesus over to the Roman guard, conscripted soldiers of fortune who despised the Jews and the desolate outpost of Judea. Pilate gave free rein to the torturers—they could do anything they wanted except kill Him. And they did, in a most gruesome way. These men were not society's best; they were crude, vulgar, half humans who considered sadistic cruelty mere entertainment. After scourging Jesus nearly to death, they "crowned" this rebellious Jew who claimed to be a king with a thistle-like vine common to this region called *nubka* in Arabic. The soldiers' intent was dual: humiliation and pain. The fake laurel-like crown was a mockery of the laurel wreaths worn by Gentile emperors and heroes of battle. This was done to humiliate the Jewish people; the vine itself was covered with hundreds of sharp, needlelike thorns that easily pierced the scalp.

The scalp is one of the most vascular and innervated parts of the body; thousands of blood vessels and nerves crisscross the head, guarding the bony enclosure for the brain. It is sensitive to pain and vulnerable to heavy bleeding. The massive blood loss from the puncture wounds of hundreds of thorns has rarely been accurately depicted in artwork; in movies depicting the Passion of Jesus, the actual blood loss is more accurately shown. Clearly, the hemorrhaging from the Scourging at the Pillar and the Crowning with Thorns was enough to put Jesus into near hypovolemic shock—complete organ shutdown from blood loss. The bleeding from the injuries inflicted by the Roman guard in these two mysteries of the Rosary was probably the beginning of the end for Jesus.

Yet the suffering we should take note of in meditating upon the mystery of the Crowning with Thorns is not only the pain and violence of the act itself but the humiliation of Christ by the soldiers. After He was "crowned," a reed was placed in His hands as a mock scepter of authority. Jesus was slapped, spat upon, and beaten on the head with the reed by the soldiers. Each of these three acts had significance in first-century Judea. Slapping someone with an open palm was an act of derision for slaves and noncitizens of Rome, both considered to be lower life forms. In Semitic culture, spitting on someone is the worst form of open derision, especially when carried out by a non-Semite on a Jew, and in ancient times, beating a king with his own scepter was mockery carried to the extreme. The irony of this is painful: here is the King of all Kings being debased as if He were nothing more than a common criminal. Such humiliation transcends anything we might experience today.

Transposing this degree of humiliation to our own lives is thus nearly impossible, but if in our meditations, we look carefully at our daily interactions with others, we can often see some type of character assault. Sometimes we give it, sometimes we get it. Is it ever justified?

Never. "Judge not, lest you yourself be judged. With what measure you judge, you shall be judged" (Matthew 7:1–2).

Many of us have been judged harshly, sometimes for things we haven't done, sometimes for things we have done. Mankind has always been a skilled predator; the technology of modern times has given us new and much more effective weapons to hurt one another. There are no more secrets, no closets to hide in, no more bedcovers to pull over our faces in abject terror; *they* will find us. The saddest thing about our human condition is that "they" are we ourselves. We literally can know everything about everybody: we just know too much for our own good. The damage to the human spirit by the weapons of modern interaction and social media is limitless.

None of us is perfect. We've all experienced humiliation from the world—some based on truth, but most based on Satan's forte of lies. The humiliation we've suffered is never justified, but it is an ugly fact of life in this *Purgatorio* in which we live, and the list of things we throw back in others' faces is endless. The most obvious are things about which we can do nothing: race, gender, gender orientation, and physical appearance—there is probably more hatred and derogatory venom in these four categories than all others on the list. The entertainment industry and the rise of social media are undoubtedly the worst offenders—debasing and mocking people based simply on who they are is big business. In our meditations on this mystery of the Crowning with Thorns, we need to ask ourselves if we have been guilty in any way. Have we crowned our fellow man with painful thorns from our words and attitudes?

Sometimes, society can be a cruel and unforgiving bedfellow. Those of us who've ever gone through the humiliation and pain of being physically imperfect or handicapped, getting arrested, being divorced, going bankrupt, losing a job, or having certain gender orientations and religious or political views know very well the pain our fellow man can inflict upon us. Even sillier things like our occupations, what we wear, what kind of cars we drive, and what streets we live on are often targets of derision and remind us of the potential for cruelty. Meditations on this mystery can soothe our angst; for as many of us already know too well, the thorns of this world never really go dull.

The Fourth Sorrowful Mystery

> *So they took Jesus, and carrying the cross himself, he went out to what is called the Place of the Skull, in Hebrew, Golgotha.*

—JOHN 19:17

The Fourth Sorrowful Mystery is the Carrying of the Cross. Forcing a condemned man to carry his own instrument of death was Rome's version of forcing a murder victim to dig his own grave. There is a great deal of debate about what the instrument of death was for Christ's crucifixion. Most evidence shows that the Romans used two types of crosses for executions: the *crux immissa*—shaped like a lower-case letter *t*, and the *crux commissa*, shaped like an upper-case *T*. Throughout the ages, nearly all art depicting Jesus carrying His cross has shown the crossbeam or *patibulum* being one piece with the longer upright stake, and currently, images and reenactments show Jesus dragging a complete *crux immissa* over one shoulder through the Via Dolorosa (Way of Pain or Grief). This does not seem possible, as such a cross would weigh nearly three hundred pounds.

Historians such as Josephus and archeological evidence suggest that the Cross of Jesus was a Latin cross in two separate pieces: the stipes or vertical stakes that were permanently in place at the execution site, connected by a frame-like structure (to accommodate multiple crucifixions), and a crossbeam that was lashed to the outstretched arms of each condemned. The victim was forced to carry this *patibulum* across the shoulders, naked or nearly naked, through the streets to the crucifixion site in order to be further humiliated by the crowds. To feel the pain of Christ, we need to imagine ourselves on such a forced march. The Carrying of the Cross would have been a very difficult trek for Jesus—He was already weak and near death from the blood loss of the scourging and crowning with thorns. The crossbeam on His back was the size and weight of a railroad tie sawed lengthwise in half: about three and a half inches thick by seven inches wide and about six feet in length. It must have weighed somewhere between sixty and a hundred pounds. This would explain His three falls—a fact not recorded in scripture but depicted in the Stations of the Cross on the current-day Via Dolorosa in Jerusalem.

Once at Calvary, the victim was thrown down on his back, and his hands were nailed to the crossbeam with seven-inch iron nails that pierced the wrists through the carpal tunnel. The victim and the crossbeam were raised via pulleys up the stipes, and the crossbeam was affixed to a vertical part of the frame with a mortise-and-tenon joint. Above this, a plaque was hung, displaying the crime of the condemned. The feet were nailed to the stipes either through the tops of the feet (piercing the metatarsal bones) onto the front of the stipes, or through the heels to the sides of the upright stake.* Death by crucifixion was meant to be a horribly painful, protracted, and humiliating spectacle for all to see.

Jesus died on the Cross, but His actual cause of death probably occurred during the Carrying of the Cross. Jesus was nearly in shock when the crossbeam was strapped across his shoulders. He had to carry this heavy beam on uneven ground some fifteen hundred

---

* The footrest seen beneath Jesus's feet is probably an addition by medieval artists; there is no evidence to suggest its presence on the Cross. The Romans were only concerned with prolonging death, not providing comfort.

feet—about five football fields; the strain on his heart must have been tremendous. He fell three times; He could not break His fall with outstretched hands as we normally could, so He landed on His face and chest. Happening once, this would be a potentially fatal fall because the heart sits just beneath the sternum of the chest, but He fell three times, so a *cardiac contusion* (bruise) surely occurred. Each fall accelerated the bleeding into the *pericardial sac* (lining around the heart), causing a compression of the heart called *cardiac tamponade*. His heart was literally squeezed into stopping by His own blood. This would explain His death after only three to six hours on the Cross—crucifixion was designed to keep the victim alive for several days. His diminished capacity allowed Him to utter only three or four short phrases before dying: His reassurance to the good thief, His words to His mother, His cries of despair, and His final words to His Father.

Once Jesus began His walk on the Via Dolorosa to Calvary, there was no going back—every step brought Him closer to death. Our meditations on this mystery can center about this notion that Jesus knew His earthly life and mission were drawing to a close. There would be no more joy of seeing His mother's smile, His disciples' loyalty and eagerness to hear the Word, the looks of gratitude and awe in the faces of those He cured, or the way people's lives and hopes changed simply by His presence. He would never again laugh with His friends or enjoy the festivities of happy events like the wedding at Cana. His life was over.

Did Jesus know with absolute certainty what was coming after His death on the Cross? It is a matter of great debate. If Jesus had a clear and certain picture of His Resurrection and reunion with the Father in heaven after His death, His dread and fear of the impending horrors of His Passion would be lessened. This would not be consistent with Jesus's wish to experience the complete suffering by the Son of Man necessary for mankind's redemption; this wish for total surrender to the Father's will was played out on the Cross when He refused the pain-deadening wine mixed with myrrh (Matthew 27:34). We must then surmise that Jesus's knowledge about His mission and fate after death must have come through His unwavering faith and intense prayer sessions with His Father. As such, Jesus mirrors exactly what we must do in order to endure our own sufferings and deaths. We must rely on faith to quiet our fears of death, faith that can be strengthened through prayer and meditation; the Rosary is a perfect vehicle.

It is only with such quieted fear that we are able to finally face our own mortality—the irrefutable fact that all earthly (immanent) life comes to an end. The Father sees victory in Jesus's death—mankind is redeemed at last. Jesus sees victory in His death because the Father's will has been fulfilled. We see victory in Christ's death because we have been saved from our own deaths. But before the victory of death, we must carry our own crosses: the difficult, painful, and sometimes lonely journey when we know all that we have enjoyed on earth—our immanent joys—are behind us.

For some of us, letting go of life is more difficult and sad than for others. Those of us who are older and feel a growing sadness because our life's joys and achievements are behind us need to meditate carefully on this mystery. We may be sad and not even realize it; watching younger people carry on with all that we once achieved and enjoyed is a double-edged sword. We're glad the world is renewed in the younger, but we can't help but feel a bit nostalgic and maybe a little jealous. These feelings are more obvious when we've lost something we will never get back, such as health, love, or perhaps money and status. This mystery of the Carrying of the Cross shows us that Jesus—now sitting on the Throne of Thrones—felt *exactly* the same things.

If we wish to assuage our sadness of growing old, we need to redirect our desires for joy into the transcendent realm. We may have lost our money, status, power, love, and health, but at the end, so did Jesus. This mystery tells us just that. We may be crippled and sick, lonely, and perhaps poor, but, through Jesus, a new life is closer than ever, a life with no tears or pain and a life sharing the status and power of God through a miraculous union with Him forever. The portal to this new life is death; if we pray and meditate, it is not a sad end but a victory of the greatest dimension.

The Fifth Sorrowful Mystery

Father, into thy hands I commend my spirit.

—MATTHEW 23:46

The Fifth Sorrowful Mystery is the Crucifixion and Death of Jesus. Throughout the ages, there have been heresies and disputes about whether Jesus really died a physical death at Calvary. All these fabrications can be dismissed as self-serving attempts to discredit Christianity; facts from eyewitnesses clearly show no human could survive the injuries endured by Christ in His Passion. The death of Jesus was a blood sacrifice to God in order for God's wrath to "pass over" believers. It was mankind's redemption from death. If Jesus did not physically die, there would be no redemption and no forgiveness of sins. As we said, it is no coincidence that Jesus died on Friday before sundown—the beginning of the Jewish feast of Passover—the day the lambs were slaughtered for the feast.

We have discussed in some detail the awful mechanics of Jesus's suffering and death. To guide our meditations, we need to look at some of the theological implications of an innocent God-Man sacrificing Himself in order for a sinful mankind to share in the glory of victory over death—the Resurrection. The first notion is that death is a human thing. It is the end of all immanent existence and the portal into the transcendent realm. It is truly a victory and not a defeat. The second notion is that Jesus is innocent and we are not; we deserve our fate in this *Purgatorio,* and it is through His death that we can escape and share in His victory of the Resurrection. At last, we *can* be immortal—the ultimate fantasy of mankind. The third notion is that Jesus did not leave us alone in our odyssey; He left us a caretaker and overseer of our salvation process, a human creature in the person of His mother, Mary.*

The first notion, that death is truly a human event, reassures us that there is no death or end of consciousness in the transcendent realm of heaven. In this sense, death is both an end and a beginning. Our faith tells us that heaven is so much better than this life—a place of no tears, where the lion lies down with the lamb. Death truly becomes a victory. Our meditations on this mystery of sorrow should first center about the times in our lives when the lion did not lie with the lamb in peace, when there were tears we could not stem, when the pain did not subside, or when a joyless day crumbled into weeks of sadness and despair. When we resurrect these dark times while praying on this mystery, our bad times blend with the bad times of Christ's last days—both die in an instant on the Cross. Our earthly suffering ends with the Cross on Calvary, replaced with the joy of a new life and union with God forever.

---

* For Catholics and those accepting the doctrine of Transubstantiation, Jesus first and foremost left us His real and complete presence—body and blood, soul and divinity—in the Eucharist. The words of Jesus creating this "true gift" form the Fifth Luminous Mystery of the Rosary (Catechism 1373).

The second notion, that we should recognize the innocence of Christ along with our own sinfulness, is depicted in Luke 23:39–43: the good thief acknowledges the innocence of Jesus and contrasts his own sinful life. In the instant it takes him to utter the words "We justly are receiving what we deserve for our deeds; but this man has done nothing wrong," he has merited eternal life in heaven, in spite of a long life of mayhem and perhaps even murder. Jesus, with His dying breath, said to him, "Truly, today you shall be with Me in paradise." In meditating on this mystery, we should not so much connect our suffering with specific wrongs in our lives but rather concentrate on the innocence of Christ and the noninnocence of mankind.

It was His innocence that brought Jesus so much pain throughout the entire Passion. We need to meditate on the fact that, on the Cross in the moments before His death, Jesus assumed the weight and guilt for *all* the sins of mankind for *all* ages, and this guilt from all the sins of man drove a huge wedge between Jesus and the Father. It was this separation from the Father that caused Jesus to cry out in utter despair at the moment of His death: "Eli, Eli, *lama sabachthani*"—"My God, My God, why hast Thou forsaken Me?" (Matthew 27:46). Culpability for the pain of this separation and Jesus's despair falls squarely on our backs; the very least we can do is to recognize this fact in our prayer and meditation.

The third notion upon which to meditate is the fact that we have not been left alone to suffer out our time left on this earth. Jesus left us His body and blood in the Eucharist, an immanent form of transcendent reality. But He left us another immanent form of spiritual support: the presence of His mother, Mary, a creature like ourselves, to guide us, support and protect us, and show us the will of God through the meditation on the mysteries of the Rosary. She was given the mission in a directive from Jesus Himself as He was dying on the Cross. In John 19:26–27, Jesus said, "Woman, behold your son," and then to John He said, "Behold your mother." Mary was "taken into the household of John" and in the literal sense was given a place to live and be cared for after Jesus's death. It was an accepted custom in biblical times to take care of widows and orphans who generally had no means of support.

Yet this does not make complete sense and opens the possibility that there is a deeper theological significance to this directive by Jesus. We know that John's entire Gospel is written with symbolism, mysticism, and deeper meanings. Mary was a widow who must have been forty-seven to fifty years of age and on her own for at least the previous three years of Jesus's ministry, so it is somewhat unlikely that she was a weak and abandoned woman who needed the guardianship of John's household. As such, it was unlikely that Jesus would waste one of His last breaths worrying about the physical welfare of such a strong woman; He knew very well that she would be cared for by His disciples. A notion that lies beneath this scenario is that Jesus was conferring on Mary her queenship and motherhood of all mankind.

Saint John is a surrogate for us. He represents the children of the earth for all time; Mary is thus truly our mother—to nurture, guide, and protect us until we reach the end of our odyssey. It is precisely this mission of Mary that, in part, explains her bodily preservation in her Assumption into heaven. Her earthly but glorified body is the vehicle that allows her to be recognized and venerated in the dozen or so apparitions accepted by most Catholics. Mary is a true caretaker of us until Jesus returns as He promised, and praying and meditating on the Rosary is perfect praise for our heavenly mother and the very reason this is such a powerful prayer. It acknowledges and praises our dearest creature-friend in the transcendent realm—truly, the best friend we could have in the highest of places.

XV

The Glorious Mysteries: Victory at Last

He plunged me to victory beneath the cleansing blood.

—E. M. BARTLETT'S HYMN "VICTORY IN JESUS"

Winning isn't everything; it's the only thing.

—UCLA COACH RED SANDERS

Of all the mysteries of the Rosary, the Glorious Mysteries are...well, the happiest. There seems to be no other way to say it: they are the deepest fulfillment of everything we desire in this life. Yet it takes a deeper analysis of each mystery for most of us to see why this is true. Nearly all writings on the Glorious Mysteries present them as disjointed, separate events that are surely important but have little connection to one another or, worse, to us. Nothing could be further from the truth. In fact, each of the five mysteries represents an earthly introduction—a vivid preview—to the afterlife of heaven.

Traditionally, meditations on the Rosary center about "fruits" of the mystery, a one- or two-word notion that, in the simplest sense, sums up what the mystery means. For the Resurrection, the fruit of the mystery is "faith": we pray for a strengthened faith to believe that this crucial event occurred. For the Ascension, it is "hope," reassurance that we too will one day reach heaven. For the Descent of the Holy Spirit, the fruits are "zeal" and "wisdom": we pray for enthusiasm to know God. For the Assumption, it is the desire for a "happy death": we pray that we will die in a state of sanctifying grace, enabling us to be accepted into heaven. And for the Coronation of Mary, the fruit is "true devotion to Mary": we pray for trust in Mary's intercession on our behalf. These are certainly wonderful notions upon which to meditate, but as we look deeper into each mystery, we will also see meanings and wonders that truly make these mysteries "glorious." We will see heaven.

The First Glorious Mystery

Why do you seek the Living One among the dead?

—LUKE 24:5

The first mystery—and probably the most important of all twenty mysteries of the Rosary because it is the cornerstone of all Christian faith—is the Resurrection of Jesus from the dead. Faith in this mystery literally guarantees us immortality, the one thing that we crave most, both from our nature as living organisms and from our supernatural callings to be reunited with our Creator. If we believe this, we will rise from the dead in some unknown temporal frame and in some unknown place with physical properties.* Our faith can

---

* A physical, perishable body dies, and a physical, imperishable body rises from death. It was not merely Jesus's soul that walked out of that garden tomb; it was the complete Jesus, nail punctures and all.

be strengthened by simple logic. Rev. Charles Stanley, repeating an earlier assertion by Saint Thomas Aquinas, pointed out that Jesus mirrored our human lives exactly in order to fulfill the Redemption of man and it would make no sense if the Resurrection were not included in His imitation of our humanity (affirmed by Saint Paul in 1 Thessalonians 4:14). Given this joyous notion, we naturally want to know the details—*when, where* and *how?*

Unfortunately, these details are clouded in a fog, probably for the better. For two thousand years, they have been the subjects of inter-pretation and misinterpretation of scripture, vague and somewhat confusing definitions by the Catechism of the Catholic Church, and a lot of creative speculation and imagination by well-meaning biblical scholars. We don't know for sure either; we only know that after death, our disembodied souls will, at some time, in some place, and in some manner, be reunited with physical-like but imperishable bodies that can be identified as ours. This is a rather striking state-ment, given that all of us face *terra es, terram ibis*—"Thou art dust, and dust thou shall be."

If this challenges our faith and makes us cringe with dread, we must call to mind the words of the angel Gabriel in the First Joyful Mystery: "For nothing shall be impossible with God" (Luke 1:37). This miracle of recreating us from dust is prophesied in Ezekiel 37:1–14, in verse 6: "And I will put sinews on you, make flesh grow back on you, cover you with skin, and put breath in you that you may come alive; and you will know that I am the Lord."

Our meditations on Jesus's Resurrection can give us several hints about our own resurrection, easing our fear of the unknown. But, more important, we should remember that Jesus's Resurrection must come first—no Resurrection of Christ, no afterlife for us. Three notions on which to meditate come to mind; the first two reassure us that God really can raise us from the dead. The first notion is that the Resurrection of Christ really did take place; it was not a fabrication of the apostles as touted by the Jewish elders (Matthew 28:11–15). Second, and most important, the Resurrection of Jesus is the surest visible proof that the transcendent has absolute power over the immanent—even stronger proof than Jesus's miracles (some cynics contend that His miracles were trickery and illusions). These first two notions allow us to meditate on the third: scripture tells us a lot about our own resurrection, and if we look carefully enough, we'll see images of an eternal life in our own bodies—changed, improved, and closely related to the bodies we have now; we will not be floating ghosts.

Faith in the first notion, that Jesus did indeed rise from the dead, is the sine qua non of being a Christian; if our faith fails to convince us of this fact, we cannot be Christian. In reality, however, it is difficult *not* to believe in it. The New Testament references to eyewitness accounts of Jesus alive after dying on the cross are too numerous to mention. There are also dozens of references in both the Old and New Testaments predicting that the Resurrection would take place. All the teachings in the New Testament, especially in the Acts of the Apostles and the letters of Saint Paul, are based on the fact of Jesus's rising from the dead. The conspiracy of the chief priests and elders to debunk the reality of the Resurrection by bribing the guards into saying that Jesus's body was stolen by His disciples is exposed in Matthew 28:11–15. And the resurrected Jesus Himself confronted Doubting Thomas: "Reach here your finger and see My hands…be not unbelieving, but believing…Blessed are they who did not see, and yet believed" (John 20:27, 29).

The second notion, that the transcendent has absolute power over the immanent, is obvious since Jesus's worldly death was reversed by the power of God. The immanent is, of course, everything in the world, including us and everything that happens to us. When we pray, we are really asking that God's power (the embodiment of the transcendent) is showered upon us to not only guide and protect us but to bring us joy that never ends. At the end of the Angelus prayer, we ask "that we may, by the passion and cross, be brought to the glory of His Resurrection through the same Jesus Christ Our Lord."

The Resurrection is one of three key connections between God and man: the Incarnation—God is made man; the Resurrection—God overcomes man's greatest dread; and the Ascension—man, through the person of Jesus Christ, although not a creature, becomes the first human to enter heaven and be with God the Father. The notion that God's power can overcome man's greatest dread can be expanded to give us hope and relief in the time of pain, suffering, or loss: if we pray, the transcendent God can defeat any immanent, worldly tragedy: "Ask and it shall be given to you; seek, and you shall find; knock, and it shall be opened to you" (Matthew 7:7). Again, it will happen in His time and in His way, and His divine plan to bring us all home will always take precedence. So our prayers must be for the right things, at the right times, and with the right attitudes.

The starting point of our meditations on the third notion, the afterlife of heaven, is assurance that *our* resurrection will really occur. In John 5:28–29, we hear such assurance in Jesus's own words: "For an hour is coming in which all who are in the tombs shall hear His voice, and shall come forth; those who did the good deeds to a resurrection of life." In Romans 8:11, the apostle Paul also refers to God the Father giving us life after death. "But if the Spirit of Him who raised Jesus from the dead dwells in you, He who raised Christ Jesus from the dead will also give life to your mortal bodies through His Spirit who indwells you."

Once we have been assured that physical death is merely a passage to a glorified body—changed, imperishable, and improved over our bodies now—we ask the natural question of when this will occur.

The question of when is more vexing than the questions of how or where: *how* God resurrects a physical-like body from dust is His business; we shouldn't care. *Where* it happens also doesn't matter, as long as it is a physical-like place that is compatible with our new, glorified bodies. But the question of *when* evokes a curiosity that is sometimes disturbing. Will we be conscious of our surroundings after the moment of death, or will we be in for a really long slumber?

In numerous passages, scripture—including Jesus's own words—is vague on this question, probably because we cannot comprehend the answer with our limited, earthly intellects. Another big problem is that the question of when is based on our worldly construct of time, and Aquinas tells us that after the moment of death, there is no more dimension of time—the afterlife is eternal. This conundrum by itself puts the answer we seek out of the range of our minds, like our idea of a one-ended stick: it can exist mathematically, but we cannot imagine it in our minds.

Jesus frequently uses terms like "an hour is coming" and "on the last day" in describing the eschatology of the world and man. All the Gospels as well as the writings of Saint Paul and Revelation allude to a point in time when everything we know ends—a better phrase would be "comes to a climax." The "end of days" refers to four events: the Second Coming of Christ (Matthew 24:1–31); the Rapture—which most accept as occurring with Jesus's Second Coming—where tombs open up and the dead rise, and the living rise upward to meet Christ in the air (1 Thessalonians 4:13–18); the Final Judgment or Judgment Day (Revelation 20:11–15); and a resurrection that imparts glorified and imperishable bodies to us that are somehow changed and immortal (Romans 8:11 and the Catechism 989–990). Yet none of the scriptural writers is specific about precisely when the "end of days" occurs. Is the term allegorical or literal? Is it our end—death—or is it the literal final moments of the earth's existence?

Jesus answers this in a most literal and plain fashion. He is quoted in Matthew 24:36–39, but His most telling words are in verse 36: "But of that hour, no one knows, not even the angels of Heaven, **nor the Son, but the Father alone**." It's a sure bet that if Jesus Himself doesn't know when, we won't know either...nor should we know.

There is no doubt, however, that these four events will occur as written, but here, we are concerned with when we will have new bodies *and* conscious minds. Traditional religious beliefs, including Judaism and Christianity, believe there is some sort of "intermediate heaven" where souls go to float around in perfect calm and peace, waiting for the "end days." This notion is a necessary, speculative deduction from the many puzzles created in scriptural passages about the last days. Jesus says the "end" will be marked by the "sun being darkened, the moon not giving its light, and the stars falling from the sky" (Matthew 24:29). Basic science shows us that Jesus must be speaking in metaphors; if He were not, then we will be disembodied spirits wandering about in some unknown dimension for the five billion years the sun has left to shine. And since heaven has no time—waiting does not exist—who is keeping track of the calendar?

Peace and calm aside, no one wants to be a ghost for five billion years, stuck in some intermediate heaven and waiting for the good news or the bad news of Judgment. Judgment Day is a scary notion,* but God is a God of comfort and love, not terror, especially after we've just endured the trauma of death. Moreover, the soul has been a natural partner to the body since our creation, so to separate the two is unnatural. There must be an alternative.

---

* Judgment Day has always been depicted as a terrifying spectacle, especially in medieval paintings. Stefan Lochner's 1435 painting *Judgment Day* and Michelangelo's 1534 painting *The Last Judgment* on the altar wall of the Sistine Chapel depict an angry Jesus doling out eternal judgment to hordes of naked people, some happy, some very, very upset. Why everyone is naked is a point of pure conjecture.

The alternative also relies on speculation and deduction, but it is just as logical as the intermediate-heaven notion. Since there is no time in heaven, we must assume it all happens "in a moment, in the twinkling of an eye" (1 Corinthians 15:52), immediately after we die. Death, purgatory, judgment, resurrected body, and heaven, from our conscious perspective, will all occur instantly. Jesus's words to the good thief on Calvary ("**This very day**, you shall be with Me in paradise" [Luke 23:43]) and the Catholic Catechism (1021) affirm an instant Primary Judgment, where we learn our eternal fates at the moment of death. The Catechism goes further in easing our angst by stating that we all very well know our fates while still here on earth. The Final Judgment, the reading of names in the Lamb's Book of Life—these will still occur as written, but after five billion earth years in heaven, our fear will surely have faded.

Yet even if we have difficulty accepting these highly speculative notions about what happens after we die—what, when, where, and how—there is one solid fact about which we can be absolutely sure. Every shred of pain, sadness, disappointment, loss, longing and want, anxiety and fear, curiosity, and even our speculation will disappear the moment we die. Our new heavenly consciousness will be filled with unimaginable fulfillment and complete joy.

The Second Glorious Mystery

And after He had said these things, He was lifted up while they were looking on, and a cloud received Him out of their sight.

—ACTS 1:9

At the end of our earthly voyage, we naturally wonder about the accommodations in the afterlife. We loathe the idea of being floating ghosts, so there must be a place or a state that is "user-friendly" to our new, imperishable, and familiar glorified bodies. Jesus tells us with absolute sincerity in plain, straightforward language—no metaphors here—that "in My father's house, there are many dwelling places; if it were not so, I would have told you; for I go to prepare a place for you" (John 14:2). The preparation of our heavenly dwelling places is the work of Jesus—the first human to touch the face of God. This miracle is one of the cornerstones of the Second Glorious Mystery of the Rosary, the Ascension of Jesus into Heaven.

Like the other Glorious Mysteries, the Ascension of Jesus has enormous hidden significance, beyond it being the end of Jesus's earthly mission and His being lifted up into a cloud out of sight. The fruit of this mystery is hope—hope that we, as humans, will be admitted to the glory of heaven; the cloud is a symbol of the transcendent realm. Humanity disappears from earthly sight and passes into the invisible glory of the Father's house. Throughout scripture, we are told that no one can come to the Father except through the Son. We are told that Jesus is our bridge to the Father, our eternal priest who acts on our behalf with the Father; He is our mediator and key to getting into heaven, the Father's house (1 Timothy 2:5).

The Ascension marks the beginning of this eternal mediation—no human has hitherto come face-to-face with the Father. Once the redemption and sacrifice of Jesus have been accomplished, this reunion of Christ—both divine and human—with the Father allows us to enter heaven, and not a moment before. This is the substance behind Jesus's words in John 14:2: "For I go to prepare a place for you." Meditation on this mystery must center about this idea: no Ascension, no heaven for us.

There is the unresolved issue of Moses, Elijah, and Enoch from the Old Testament being assumed into heaven hundreds of years before Christ was born. The debate is tiresome and probably moot. At the Transfiguration, *only* Jesus was in a glorified state; the faces and clothes of Moses and Elijah did not "shine as the sun." As Christians, we must assume that the Old Testament accounts were allegories. If they were literal, the redemptive suffering of Jesus was unnecessary. The point of these allegories is still important, however; the images of the assumptions of these three Jewish heroes into heaven, body and soul, is an allegorical prophesy of the Assumption of Mary, the New Eve, into heaven.

We can meditate on one other reason that it was necessary for Jesus to ascend into heaven. Our sanctification—the journey to holiness that makes us worthy of heaven—completely relies on the indwelling of God within us, in our hearts, minds, and souls. An earthly Jesus was shackled by the limits of humanity: He could only be in one place at a time. To reach the hearts of all men, two things must happen. The first is that Jesus must be restored to a fully divine state, free of worldly limitations, so that He can dwell in all of us in the Person of the Holy Spirit. The second is that His message and commands must be spread to all of us so that we have the choice to believe or not believe. The choice to believe is the commitment we make at our baptisms, and this must occur before God comes to us. Spreading the message of Christ is the work of the Body of Christ on earth, the Church. The Church is made up of witnesses, believers who attest to the truth of Christ's words. These witnesses take over for Christ on earth, spreading His truths. The last words Jesus spoke to His disciples the moment before His Ascension into heaven plainly give this command: "And you shall be My witnesses both in Jerusalem, and in all Judea and Samaria, and even to the remotest parts of the earth" (Acts 1:8).

This transfer of evangelical responsibility allows Jesus to ascend to the Divine and fill mankind with His Spirit, not one heart at a time, but the hearts of the entire world. Jesus's commitment to fill the hearts of all believers with His presence, in the Person of the Holy Spirit, is begun at Pentecost. Peter stands before the crowds and reassures them of this by quoting the prophet Joel: "And it shall be in the last days, God says, that I will pour forth My Spirit upon all mankind" (Acts 2:17, Joel 2:28).

This outpouring of the Holy Spirit upon all mankind, bringing Jesus into the hearts of believers, begins with the official birthday of the Church, Pentecost. This important event is the Third Glorious Mystery of the Rosary: the Descent of the Holy Spirit on the Apostles and Mary.

The Third Glorious Mystery

And they all filled with the Holy Spirit and began to speak with other tongues, as the Spirit was giving them utterance.

—ACTS 2:4

In previous meditations, we have asked *when* our own resurrection from the dead and into glorified bodies will occur. Confusion over a precise time lay in the many possible meanings of the Gospel words "end of days." Meditation on the Third Glorious Mystery of the Rosary, the Descent of the Holy Spirit, gives us an answer...of sorts. It gives us the starting point for the "last days"; the end point, as we said above, is known to the Father alone. The starting point of the "last days" is that Pentecost when the disciples and Mary were overshadowed by the Holy Spirit in the forms of wind and tongues of fire.

Pentecost is the Jewish Feast of Booths that is celebrated fifty days after Passover to commemorate the Children of Israel escaping slavery and entering into a new age of spiritual birth. The number fifty in both Judaic and Christian mysticism signifies the eternal: the Old Covenant is fulfilled on the first Pentecost with God's eternal presence in the Promised Land. Fire and wind are Old Testament symbols for the presence of God. In Exodus 3, Moses stood before a burning bush—brambles that were aflame but did not burn up[*]— listening to God direct him to free the Children of Israel from slavery in Egypt. Later, in Exodus 20, the Old Covenant with God was affirmed with Moses receiving the Ten Commandments on Mount Sinai.

These symbols reappeared 1,400 years later in the Upper Room fifty days after Christ was crucified, when the Holy Spirit descended upon the disciples and Mary, signifying the affirmation and fulfillment of the New Covenant. On the Passover previous to this New Pentecost, the New Passover Lamb—Jesus—was slaughtered, His blood smeared on the wooden posts of the Cross, and mankind was saved from the Angel of Death. The fire of the burning bush, the fire that does not consume (God is eternal), reappears as the fire in the flaming tongues that settle over the disciples' heads—fire that does not consume but gives eternal life.

The tongues of fire gave the disciples the gift of speaking in a universal language of the Spirit that could be understood by all peoples of the known world. In Genesis 11:1–9, there is the story of some of Noah's descendants who disobeyed God's commands and built a tower that they thought would give them divine power (much like Satan's lie to Eve in the Garden of Eden). God's punishment for this

---

[*] In Latin, this phrase is *"Nec tamen consumebatur,"* the motto of the Church of Scotland.

Tower of Babel was for these people to be scattered throughout the earth and speak in many different languages unintelligible to others. The gift of tongues to the disciples was God's return of this universal language, a reward for obeying His divine will.

That first Pentecost of the New Covenant has greater significance, however. It represents the fulfillment of Christ's mission on earth and the birth of a new age of man's redemption, fortified and held together by the mystical presence of the Spirit of God. Pentecost is referred to as an "Apocalyptic Day," the day of final revelation to us, when God's written and spoken teachings are replaced by a never-ending flow of grace through His Spirit. This grace from the Holy Spirit gives us the fortitude, unity, and love to spread God's message "even unto the ends of the earth." That Pentecost in the Upper Room heralds the beginning of the new and final age, about which God declared, "In those last days, I will pour out My Spirit upon all flesh" (Joel 2:28).

For us and our meditation on this mystery, Pentecost represents the first step in our sanctification process and the beginning of our odyssey. Our own Pentecosts occurred at our baptisms, when we made a commitment to do things in life God's way, not ours. As we meditate, we acknowledge the priceless gift of God indwelling within us and the endless graces we receive if we open our hearts and minds to change—the change of crossing that bridge onto the Mountain of Transcendence, where the rocks of life are cool and smooth beneath our feet, and the climb is easy.

—m—

Note: The last two mysteries of the Rosary are about Mary, the Mother of Jesus. In the most obvious sense, these mysteries honor Mary, and rightly so, but in a more important sense, they acknowledge the relationships between Mary and Jesus, between Mary and the Trinity, and between Mary and us. The study of devotion to these relationships is called Mariology. Since its birth in the fourth century, some extreme notions in Mariology have engendered controversy both within and outside of the Catholic Church. Countless words have been wasted on tedious and often contentious polemics over the minimalist and maximalist extremes of some Marian devotion. The Church has handled the controversy with great delicacy, hoping not to offend anyone but officially favoring neither side, recommending appropriate honor to Mary. We agree and will walk the middle road of doctrinal propriety, embracing the official views of the Catholic Church. All Christians should agree that Mary, as the Mother of Jesus, is a substantive and precious help to our spiritual growth and, as such, she does not deserve the harsh words of silly doctrinal polemics.

The Fourth Glorious Mystery

*Do not be afraid, Mary; for you have found favor
with God.*

—LUKE 1:30

The Fourth Glorious Mystery of the Rosary is the Assumption of the Blessed Virgin Mary into heaven. Mary was free from original sin, a necessary condition if she was to be the Mother of Jesus, and so, she was spared the human sentence of death. Her freedom from sin is disputed by some outside the Catholic Church but is absolutely affirmed in the Church doctrine of the Immaculate Conception. As we said, dying is one result of Adam and Eve's sin in the Garden of Eden, and

Mary, at the end of her days, simply "fell asleep," which is called her dormition, or in Greek, her *koimesis*. This mystery of the Rosary is all about what happened next. God pulled or "assumed" Mary into heaven, body and soul. Her Assumption is dated somewhere between AD 50 and 60;* if Mary was fourteen when Jesus was born, she must have been sixty-five to seventy-five years old at the end of her earthly odyssey.

The Assumption of Mary is rejected outright by many non-Catholic Christians and is even doubted by many Catholics. The arguments are tedious and sometimes contentious, and they are really unnecessary, since our focus here is on Rosary meditations; those who reject the Assumption of Mary are unlikely to have any interest in this special prayer. So, it is best if we bypass the arguments for and against the Assumption and, as Catholics, simply accept the infallible teaching of the Church that declares the Assumption of Mary a real event. Skipping the apologetic fireworks allows us to jump into the substance of this mystery and, during our meditations, to marvel at what is really there.

The first notion about this mystery of the Rosary is the obvious: that Mary was, in the most basic way, rewarded by God for her sinless obedience in doing whatever she was asked in order to fulfill God's plan for us. *Sinless obedience* is something we all should emulate in our decisions about the courses of our lives. In the simplest sense, we should meditate about whether we are living our lives

---

* Mary was the source for details about her life found only in Luke's Gospel, written somewhere around AD 60; Mary's relating these events to Luke must have occurred prior to this date. The details about Mary make up the first two chapters of Luke: the Annunciation by the angel Gabriel, the visitation to her cousin Elizabeth that included the lengthy Magnificat prayer, the Nativity of Jesus, the presentation and purification in the Temple, and the finding of Jesus in the Temple when He was twelve years old.

by the way of God or the way of the world. Do we truly fight for transcendence—the things that are important in the afterlife—to dominate our earthly lives, or do we choose the immanent trends of these modern times, trends that pull us away from a proper preparation for heaven? If, in this life, we experience joy only from immanent (worldly) treasures, what will our experience be like after death when immanence takes a backseat to transcendence, or perhaps doesn't even exist in the afterlife? The trite expression "You can't take it with you" has a scriptural basis: "Do not lay up for yourselves treasures upon earth, where moth and rust destroy, and where thieves break in and steal. But lay up for yourselves treasures in heaven, where neither moth nor rust destroys...for where your treasure is, there will your heart be also" (Matthew 6:19–21).

The second notion about the Assumption of Mary is that it is more than a simple reward for her obedience; this mystery affirms that Mary is a crucial part of the history and salvation of mankind. We have already spoken about the typological images that are present throughout the Old Testament and that are fulfilled in the New Testament. The three most significant are the old and new Eves, the role of the mother of a king in the Old and New Covenants, and the Ark of the Covenant. It is the typology of the Ark of the Covenant that most vividly demonstrates the necessity of the Assumption of Mary into heaven.

We know there were several figures—people and items—from the Old Testament that were taken into heaven by God. The accounts involving people were probably allegorical yet still critically important. These people and items were so important to Israel's history that Old Testament authors, in several different verses, described these figures being physically assumed into heaven and thus protected from earthly decay by God and, in so doing, created perfect archetypes of Mary's Assumption. The stories of Moses, Elijah, and Enoch tell us via allegory that they were assumed into heaven—horses, chariots, and all—mainly because the ancients saw the natural process of bodily decay after death as a sign of God's disapproval. And, more important, the Ark of the Covenant was also taken into heaven in order to protect it from the destruction of earthly aging. The presence of the Ark of the Covenant in heaven is most likely not allegorical, but literal; the presence is noted in Revelation 11:19.

Apparently, the notion that the decay of the dead is a bad thing stuck in biblical writers' heads. In Acts 2:27, Peter, preaching on Pentecost about Jesus, quotes David in Psalm 16:10: "Because Thou wilt not abandon My soul to Hades, nor allow Thy Holy One to undergo decay." Even in modern times, the lack of bodily decay is considered praiseworthy in the canonization of saints. If any creature deserves to be spared of *terram ibis*, it should certainly be the Mother of Jesus, for her body is the Vessel of the Incarnation—the source of our salvation. No Mary, no Incarnation; no Incarnation, no Redemption; no Redemption, no heaven.

People noticed that decay began on the fourth day after interment, and this may be why Jesus was prophesied and reported (in the Old and New Testaments, respectively) to rise from the dead on the third day. The most notable prophesy of this three-day window is the story of Jonah, who disobeyed God's command to "go to Nineveh" and was swallowed by a whale, only to be vomited out after three days and given another chance. Jesus was the new Jonah, but One who obeyed God's will and was raised after three days into a state of glory. In John 11:1–44, we read the story of the illness, death, and raising of Lazarus—the beloved brother of Martha and Mary (Mary of Bethany, who anointed Jesus's feet, not the Blessed Mother or Mary Magdalene)—that tells of Jesus purposely letting Lazarus die and remain in the tomb beyond the critical three-day window. Lazarus's sister Martha protests, "Lord, there will be a stench, for he has been dead for four days" (John 11:39). Jesus explains to His disciples that the delay was purposeful in order to show the glory and power of God over death and to "glorify the Son of God" with a vivid and dramatic miracle.

"Father, I thank Thee that Thou heard Me. And I know that Thou always hears Me, but because of the people standing around I said it, that they may believe that Thou didst send Me" (John 11:41–42).

The piercing odor of the stench from bodily decay and the vision of Lazarus coming forth from the tomb still wrapped in his burial cloths transfixed the crowds and brought many to a state of belief in Jesus. Unfortunately, the frenzy around this dramatic miracle got back to the Pharisees, who feared Jesus's crowd appeal. Scholars consider this event to be the final impetus that convinced the Jewish elders that Jesus needed to die.

While protecting Mary's body from decay is one obvious result of the Assumption, we need to meditate on two very different reasons behind this mystery. One is the typology of the Old Testament Ark of the Covenant, which was, along with its contents, taken into heaven by God to preserve it from decay. The Ark of the Covenant is the sacred object upon which the Spirit of God—the *Shekinah*—descended, and connected the people of Israel to God Himself. Mary is the Ark of the New Covenant: we see the Holy Spirit descending upon her in Luke 1:35 when she conceives Jesus, and one of Jesus's roles is to connect all people to God.

It is Mary's body that is the Ark of the New Covenant, not just her soul, and her Assumption is the fulfillment of the Old Testament event. The Old Ark contained a jar of manna, the staff of Aaron, and the tablets of the Ten Commandments from Mount Sinai. The contents of the Old Ark are archetypes for Christ, who was *contained* within the body of Mary, the Ark of the New Covenant. Jesus is the New Manna ("I am the bread of life" [John 6:35, 48]). Jesus is the New Law of Moses, not replacing the old law but fulfilling it. Jesus on the Cross at Calvary is the New Staff of Aaron, a symbol of authority over the Israelites, but also a miraculous symbol of deliverance from death. The New Testament is the fulfillment of the Old; important people or images in the New Testament are always foreshadowed in the Old Testament. Without Mary's bodily Assumption into heaven, the Ark of the New Covenant would be lost, thereby lessening the prophetic power of the Old Testament. The Word of God makes no such mistakes.

Another potential reason for the Assumption is that it demonstrates the possibility and the importance of a creature's mortal body physically existing in the heavenly realm. If such possibility and importance exist, we have reassurance that our theory of an instant resurrection for all of us at the moment of death is credible. If we reject this, we are left with the idea that Jesus and His mother, Mary, are the only physical bodies in heaven, surrounded by a lot of floating spirits. But what can the presence of physical bodies in heaven tell us about our experience after death? Will I look like I do now? Will I be recognizable as me?

The answers have to do with the difference between an earthly form and a heavenly form for our bodies. Here we must digress from the Assumption of Mary and talk again about Jesus's bodily forms, as we did when discussing the Luminous Mystery of the Eucharist. We previously said that Jesus is to return to earth at the Rapture (1 Thessalonians 4:16–17), and His bodily form at that descent from heaven will be the same as His post-Resurrection form of the forty days before His Ascension into heaven on the Mount of Olives.* The angels

---

* The Power of God gives us four different forms of the physical Jesus: the normal body of a man during His thirty-three years of life; His post-Resurrection body, appearing normal but having some supernatural powers; His heavenly, glorified body at the Transfiguration on Mount Tabor; and His body and blood in the form of the bread and wine of the Eucharist.

who appeared to the disciples after Jesus ascended are very clear about this: "This Jesus, who has been taken up from you into heaven, will come **in just the same way** as you have watched Him go into heaven" (Acts 1:11).

And, as we said before while discussing the Transfiguration, Jesus's glorified image on Mount Tabor (Matthew 17:1–7) appeared quite different from His post-Resurrection form. He had no need for food, drink, or shelter, yet there was enough familiarity of the glorified Jesus and the yet-to-be-glorified Moses and Elijah to fool Peter into setting up tents for the heavenly trio. Jesus's form was changed into His true, heavenly, glorified form—the exact meaning of "transfigured"—and although different and indescribable, He was still recognizable. We can expect the same transfiguration after death.

It is not a stretch of the imagination to visualize Mount Tabor as a nexus between heaven and earth; the entire Transfiguration scene may very well have been heaven itself appearing on earth, and this may be why Jesus "lost" His earthly form in order to appear in heaven. As we discussed in detail previously with our notion of "polymorphism," *heaven, in all probability, requires a heavenly form, and earth requires an earthly form.* This would explain why Jesus looked normal in His glorified, post-Resurrection state where He ate, drank, and socialized with the disciples. The Catechism of the Catholic Church explains to us that Jesus's true heavenly glorified state was "veiled" with human form (659–660) during this period; this allowed Jesus to appear exactly as He did before His crucifixion. Such a veiling would reassure the disciples that Jesus really rose from the dead and was not a ghost (Luke 24:37–40). As we said, this "earth-friendly" form is how Jesus appeared at His Ascension (He was still on earth) and how He will appear at His Second Coming (His return to earth). It is as if Jesus needs to put on an "earthly cloak" when He leaves heaven and visits earth.

We need no such dual wardrobe; once we die and leave earth, we are not coming back. At death, our earthly "cloaks" disintegrate to dust—*terra es, terram ibis.* We will be changed into our heavenly cloaks, our glorified state, and we will be different but perfectly recognizable to others. Only one other person besides Jesus would potentially have use for an earthly cloak after entering heaven: that would be Mary. Her Assumption into heaven would preserve her earthly cloak.*

We'll see in a bit why Mary might need an earthly cloak, but a question about the Transfiguration remains: how could Moses and Elijah be in heaven (on Mount Tabor) if Jesus had not yet died and redeemed the world? The answer is intriguing and also clears up some of the confusion around Jesus being in human, veiled-glorified form and unveiled-glorified form. The answer to both paradoxes is that the Transfiguration may have taken place *after* the Resurrection. This notion is highly speculative.

The Transfiguration story is exclusive to the synoptic Gospels of Matthew, Mark, and Luke, but many of the details and stories in these three Gospels originated in Mark's Gospel, written ten years earlier than the other two: Mark was written in the AD fifties, and Matthew and Luke were written in the AD sixties. Based on the most reliable manuscripts available, scholars generally agree that the end of the original Mark's Gospel was lost somewhere before AD 60; reliable verses of Mark end abruptly at Mark 16:8 with the scene in the empty tomb where an angel tells the astonished women on that first Easter morning that Jesus has risen from the dead: "And they went out and fled from the tomb, for trembling and astonishment had gripped them; and they said nothing to anyone, for they were afraid."

---

* Our notion of polymorphism gives us this ability in our glorified state to change form as the milieu demands.

The rest of Mark's Gospel, verses 9–20, is considered unreliable and is probably made up of *glosses* added into later, medieval manuscript copies. So, all the events of Jesus's forty days of post-Resurrection activities are absent from the real Gospel of Mark. This opens the possibility that the Transfiguration occurred after Christ's Resurrection, not before. The earliest transcribers of Mark's Gospel—before AD 60 when Matthew and Luke got copies of it—must have felt that the Transfiguration was too important to leave out completely and simply stuck it in the middle of the Gospel, before Jesus suffered and died. Most of Jesus's post-Resurrection time was spent in Galilee, and Mount Tabor was right in the middle of this region. So, it makes perfect sense that the Transfiguration took place during the forty days after Jesus's Resurrection, when Moses and Elijah had been freed from the "netherworld of the dead" and were fully redeemed by Christ's death on the Cross. Also, when the Transfiguration account was "stuck" in the middle of the synoptic Gospels, Jesus and the disciples would have had to travel sixty miles from Caesarea Philippi to Mount Tabor; this makes little sense because the equally holy Mount Hermon was much closer to Caesarea Philippi. After the Resurrection when Jesus was in Galilee, Mount Tabor was right there, ten miles from Nazareth, at the crossroads of the two main Roman roads that traversed the region. Again, this is a very speculative thought.

But what about Mary's earthly cloak? Her body-and-soul Assumption tells us emphatically that she has retained her earthly cloak in heaven; she has neither died nor turned to dust. And she also has her heavenly cloak; her presence in heaven gives her a fully glorified form. Does this dual wardrobe mean that Mary is able to show up on earth again? One answer lies in the notion of Mary's earthly apparitions, something we all have heard about, but there are other less obvious possibilities that we will consider in our meditations on the last Glorious Mystery, the Coronation of Mary as Queen of Heaven and Earth.

The Fifth Glorious Mystery

> *And a great sign appeared in heaven: a woman clothed*
> *with the sun, and the moon under her feet, and on her*
> *head a crown of twelve stars.*

—REVELATION 12:1

> *Woman, behold your son.*

—JOHN 19:26

The fifth Glorious Mystery of the Rosary, the Coronation of Mary as Queen of Heaven and Earth, is perhaps the most mystical and enigmatic of all the mysteries of the Rosary. It is also one of the mysteries that generate the most acrimony among non-Catholics and others who reject the idea of Marian devotion. There are at least two reasons for this ill will against Mary's heaven-given title of queen. The first is a concern that veneration of Mary takes away from the glory of Jesus Christ. Dr. Scott Hahn notes that honor to Mary no more steals honor from Christ than the moon steals light from the sun; indeed, like the moon and sunlight, honor to Mary reflects the glory of the Lord. No, Catholics do not adore the Blessed Mother; neither do they pray *to* her. No, Mary as queen does not usurp the powers of the King; neither does she tell the King what to do. No, Mary cannot change the King's mind; neither does she sit on a throne next to the King. And, yes, there are numerous scriptural references to her title. Yet there are still naysayers who reject the stature of our heavenly mother and queen.

The heaven-given title of queen was from Jesus Himself on the Cross when He told His mother, "Woman, behold your son" in John

19:26. The reference of "son" was to the Beloved Disciple John, the very author of this Gospel. As we said before in discussing the Crucifixion, understanding the mystical and symbolic nature of all of Saint John's writings shows us unequivocally that the person of John is an archetype and symbol for all of mankind. Mary's stature as queen does not arise from any rule over us but rather from her role as the mother of the King—one who softens and improves the relationship between errant subjects and the Throne. Mary thus fulfills the typology from the Old Testament that we previously discussed.

The second source of disdain for Mary as queen is our historical and secular image of someone we call "queen." Throughout history, the queen has been a woman of power and rule, of discipline and pardon, of regality deserving life in a castle, a jeweled crown, servants, absolute fealty, and conspicuous public appearances in ornate carriages accompanied by loud fanfare. Even the Catholic Church persists in using some of these stereotypes in depicting Mary—nearly all paintings of Mary from the Middle Ages onward show a regal, authoritative Mary often wearing a crown, sitting next to Jesus on the throne of heaven. In reality, there are no man-made images that can worthily depict Mary in her full heavenly glory; the immanent cannot describe the transcendent. The magnificent images of Mary we paint are certainly deserved and are well intentioned, but the real Mary, our queen, probably lived a very different earthly life.

The real, living Mary is meant to be a perfect paradigm for us, a sinless and obedient creature who sometimes has to suffer to fulfill God's will.

In earthly reality, our queen was dirt poor, living in an ancient hovel; her daily activities didn't include attending magnificent galas but probably sweeping animal dung off the earthen floor of a primitive and tiny shelter called home. When the meager family finances allowed, she ate the food of the poor: pickled fish and coarse bread.

She sat on no throne, and she held neither rod nor scepter in her hand; her only challenge for much of her life was caring for the Child Jesus, who undoubtedly was a real handful. She did not travel by ornate carriages with white horses, accompanied by fanfare, but rode on the back of a donkey—the common ass, a beast of burden of the poor.

She is a very different kind of queen, but a queen nonetheless. She is a queen who far transcends every image we have of the earthly word "queen." She is not judgmental or authoritatively cruel, but loving, nurturing, and protective of her subjects. Unlike the stereotypical image, she is always there to hear our smallest request, and she is quick to take those petitions to the ears of our merciful King. Likewise, she brings the wishes of our King to our ears, that we might please the True Ruler over us. She is the perfect mediator between her Son and us, softening our mistakes from the wrath of deserved judgment.* She is, as Jesus said from the Cross of Calvary, "our mother" (John 19:26–27).

A lot of folks support the validity of this mystery of Mary's queenship with the image in Revelation 12:1: "And a great sign appeared in

---

* I remember being thirteen and seeing my sixteen-year-old brother crying. My brother never cried. He had just gotten his license and was telling my mother that he just had an accident with the one and only family car. This news had to be broken to my father, a sweet, quiet man in the summer months when the golf course was open, but a sullen, unpredictable powder keg during the snowy winters of no golf. I was sure my brother was dead meat. Our mother calmly soothed my brother and told him she would take care of it. It was already dark when my father's truck hunkered into the driveway; my only thought was to hide. If I had been a smaller kid, I could have fit under the kitchen sink, but my mother prevented mayhem at the back door by meeting my father with a story later proved to be a fabrication. With a straight face, she told my old man that his golf crony had called saying a midwinter trip to Pinehurst was in the works, and by-the-way-Jackie-dented-the-car-no-biggie. It's what mothers do.

heaven: a woman clothed with the sun, and the moon under her feet, and on her head a crown of twelve stars." Yet there is controversy over what the image represents. Our meditations on this mystery of the Rosary should not center about the polemics of whether the crowned woman in Revelation 12:1 is Mary or the nation of Israel or the city of Jerusalem or the faithful of the Church. We should forget the arguments and accept that the woman with a crown of twelve stars is all of these. As we previously discussed, her queenship has been affirmed by the Old Testament archetypes and by Jesus's own words on Calvary. We should meditate about all these things and realize that they constitute a summary of her mission from God to be our heavenly mother—a powerful figure who deserves the honor given her and who looks after all of us until her Son Jesus returns. She is truly a friend in the highest of places.

Is Mary Coming Back to Earth?

She still has her earthly cloak, her body, so it could happen. Many say she already has, appearing in hundreds of apparitions around the globe, often to the simplest of folk. Believe in them or not, the apparitions have brought tens of millions of people back to a life of prayer and belief. In all likelihood, though, they have not been physical visits but rather the visions of contemplative prayer, that third stage of prayer we all crave. They were, however, very real to the people seeing her. Contemplative prayer is heaven talking back to us in the ecstasy of total separation from the world. If Mary's visits to us in these apparitions were truly physical, we would all be able to see and hear her, but that's a personal opinion. A physical visit from Mary would no doubt be earthshaking and would probably change the course of history. Such a visit from heaven affecting earth would be an interference with man's free will, and we know that unfettered free will is necessary for man's salvation. After the Ascension of Jesus, the next time heaven physically touches the earth is to be at the Second Coming and First Judgment; it is then that the ability to choose good or evil will end for believers. Until that time, daily devotion to prayer can lead all of us to a contemplative state at some point; if our devotion is to the Rosary, Mary may very well speak to us in our own, very real apparition. Like the visionaries, we should listen carefully.

We are told, in 1 Thessalonians 4:13–18, that Jesus, in His post-Resurrection body, will descend from the sky to meet the faithful, and it is no stretch of the imagination that there will be another physical presence behind Him—our earthly Mary. Hopefully, she will be whispering in His ear that those of us who have prayed throughout our lives should be included in the final odyssey.

Such a whisper might gently remind the Lord—like the scene at the Cana wedding—we truly have "no wine" and would be grateful for His good wine, saved until now. His blood shed at Calvary—the good wine—will quench our thirsts for final forgiveness. She will whisper in our King's ear that our shortcomings in this life are really…well, no biggie.

XVI

Conclusion: The End Is Just the Beginning

At first glance, it would seem that we've covered three topics in this book that are weakly connected: a self-help guide on how to live life well, a look at the afterlife, and a primer on how to pray and meditate effectively. The connections of the three, however, are quite solid; they all are harbingers of hope—hope for easing the pain in our daily lives. Yet, volumes have been written about how to discover the Self, how to love and suffer, and how to justify the bad times in the presence of a loving God. Many books too have been penned about the afterlife of heaven, often giving great detail about what we face, but most of these have been written from the perspective of near-death experiences. These are first-person accounts of actual voyages to heaven, but in spite of the compelling descriptions, they are yet to be proven as scientifically valid. And, needless to say, there are multitudes of books and pamphlets available that describe how to pray. So, how does our promise of hope offer anything new and useful?

This is really a book about healing.

It is a book about coming back from a life filled with brokenness from a misguided sense of self, coming back from a broken heart, surviving the overwhelming suffering of losing a child or other loved one, or regaining a grasp on life after facing serious disease or injury.

Hope for such healing arises from our lives here and now and from what really happens after our last breaths.

Healing from the pain of our lives here and now, of course, seems to be the more urgent matter; that is because our angst now is immanent—we can feel and touch it. The healing from immanent suffering demands that we strengthen our spirits, our souls, in order to reinforce our supernatural armor, the transcendent defenses that protect us from earthly pain. In a word, we must thicken the skin of our souls; this reinforcement of our souls through spiritual growth puts our pain into a heavenly perspective. Such a perspective gives our suffering meaning, and in some strange way, this meaning assuages our pain. Viktor Frankl says just this in his book *Man's Search for Meaning*: "In some way, suffering ceases to be suffering at the moment it finds a meaning."

Believers have an easy path to spiritual growth, and that is to forge a connection with the ultimate transcendent spirit of God Himself. The natural result of spiritual growth is sanctification, and sanctification is the existential transformation of the Self into a holier state; in one sense, we actually grow to be more like our Creator. This is exactly why we have been created, and interestingly, the promise to be like God is the very temptation laid before Eve by the Serpent in the Garden of Eden. Our path to sanctification, however, is legitimate but requires more effort than simply biting an apple.

Effective prayer and meditation is our "good" apple. A third of this book has dealt with what many consider the perfect and most powerful prayer: meditations on the twenty mysteries of the Catholic Rosary. Daily prayer and meditation on these hallmarks of the life of Jesus from the New Testament and on the life of Mary from Catholic dogma change us by strengthening our transcendent souls to grow toward heaven. Such growth forcefully puts our earthly lives into the shadows of our existence. While earthly life has moments of joy, it also has many times of suffering; it is truly a rose with very sharp thorns.

And so, it is spiritual growth through effective prayer and meditation that helps us to heal by strengthening our faith in the unknown. We enter this world needing this healing. Teilhard de Chardin tells us we are born with a *divine privation*, a missing part of us that dulls the thorns on our roses.

Healing can also blossom from using our strengthened faith to seriously consider what happens after we die. We've made a good case for the existence of heaven; clearly, our consciousness lives on after death. The rest may be educated speculation, but there is one indisputable fact upon which we can rely: one second after our last heartbeats, every single thing in our earthly lives that caused us pain, suffering, or worry disappears. This is the miraculous message of Christ's Resurrection; our greatest existential fear—death—is vaporized forever.

Trying to create a believable image of what the afterlife is really like is akin to building a house on sandy soil; sooner or later, whatever we construct sinks into oblivion. Yet, we have pressed onward and, in some ways, have succeeded in portraying some credible aspects of what we face, using our logic, reason, and other sources of transcendent knowledge. The image we desperately seek, however, is veiled in the notion of *Deus absconditus*; God and His heaven are hidden from us. We can only speculate as to why such joy is kept from our consciousness. The impetus behind our stubborn attempts to know the unknowable is our unquenchable desire for hope.

Hope is the foundation for healing a broken soul.

The most broken souls in need of healing surely belong to those of us in pain from the loss of a cherished love. The category of those of us suffering thusly is wide, but foremost is the parent who has lost a child to death. The soul of that parent is torn and rarely heals on its own. Comforting words, prayer, and even psychotherapy can ease the pain, but the suffering parent only wants to have his or her child back. The only notion for such a miracle is the hope of faith in an afterlife of joyful reunions with those we have lost. We know heaven exists; we only need to wait until our own lives play out. It is spiritual growth through effective prayer that gives us the patience we need to assuage the pain.

Of course, heaven is universal in its joy, and the loss of loved ones can run the gamut of deceased parents, friends, and even pets. Many of us suffer from the loss of love through abandonment, rejection, and separation beyond our control. Such pain too is healed the moment after we breathe our last. There are no broken hearts in heaven. None—it is a place of absolute joy.

We also worry about what we will be like in the afterlife; will we be glorified ghosts, or will we be completely earthlike, without the suffering? Heaven is a state of completeness; there are no fragments of existence in the afterlife. A soul without a body is a spirit; the body without a soul is a cadaver. Our existence in heaven is clearly a mysterious replay of our complete being on earth; at death, our immanence becomes transcendent.

The engine that drives this transformation at death is how familiar we manage to become with the transcendent; how forcefully we turn our backs on the immanent world and grow toward the transcendent values of heaven. We accomplish this through effective prayer and meditation; indeed, this entire book of healing is really a prayer book. A firm commitment to pray and meditate is the best way to engender the patience we need to wait out our exile on earth. It is really the only way.

—⚹—

Sitting quietly one evening, I smiled at the humor in this book, the humor about whether there was golf or beer in heaven. My mood turned serious, and I thought of my father and his love of the game. My father's true loves in life were undoubtedly golf, plumbing, good scotch whiskey, us kids, and my mother, probably in that order. So the golf thing, and really, the whole "Is heaven a physical place?" question began to burn uncomfortably in my mind.

So I asked my father again.

A response came in a most unusual way. The phone didn't ring; neither did the lights flash. But for five minutes, I smelled an unusual odor, something that was clearly out of place in a living room. It was the unmistakable smell of dewy grass and fertilizer. Anyone who has walked out onto the first tee at six thirty on a summer morn knows the smell perfectly well. Memories flooded my mind of being ten years old, wearing poorly fitting golf shoes, feeling the familiar first-tee jitters, and sauntering like a big shot up to the white markers of the first hole.

I had my answer.